"I am so excited about this cookbook! It's not just beautiful—the recipes are fresh and exciting. I want to cook everything in this book!"
—**Gina Homolka, *New York Times* bestselling author of the Skinnytaste cookbooks**

"Suzy Karadsheh's style of cooking reminds me much of my own. She grew up in Egypt in her mother's kitchen, and for her, the smells and flavors of Egyptian-Mediterranean cooking are memories steeped in her childhood. I visited Egypt for the first time with my daughter, and Suzy's recipes bring me right back. I am looking forward to cooking more from this cookbook and reliving those flavors. Her recipes are straightforward and simple but carry all the complex flavors, aromas, and colors of the Mediterranean. Brava, Suzy."
—**Lidia Matticchio Bastianich, bestselling author, Emmy Award-winning TV personality, and businesswoman**

"By sharing everything from time-honored family dishes to brilliant updates on the classics, Suzy Karadsheh shows us how versatile, delicious, and healthy Mediterranean cooking can be. These produce-forward, super-fresh, healthy recipes will become staples in your kitchen!"
—**Adeena Sussman, author of *Sababa: Fresh, Sunny Flavors from My Israeli Kitchen***

"Suzy Karadsheh packs her debut cookbook with dishes we all want to be eating right now: vibrant, bold, and unfussy recipes you can make any night of the week. Recipes like The Meanest Loaded Hummus Dip, Melty Sweet Potato Rounds with Honeyed Tahini, and Date Night Crab Spaghetti have already got me hooked. If you're a lover of herbs, tangy citrus, and spices, you'll no doubt be a fan of this book."
—**Andy Baraghani, chef and author of *The Cook You Want to Be***

THE
Mediterranean
DISH

SUZY KARADSHEH

WITH SUSAN PUCKETT

THE
Mediterranean
DISH

**120 Bold and Healthy Recipes
You'll Make on Repeat**

PHOTOGRAPHS BY CAITLIN BENSEL

CLARKSON POTTER / PUBLISHERS
NEW YORK

FOR MY LATE BABA,
   Nothing has given more purpose
   to my work than your words,
   "Make it your job to put a smile on
   someone's face."
   I hope this book does just that.
   P.S.: I miss you every day.

FOR SABA,
   In life and in work, I could not have
   prayed for a better partner.
   Your unwavering love and support
   make all the difference.

contents

introduction

Port Said: My Mediterranean Roots

My love for the big, bright flavors and intrinsically healthy ingredients of the Mediterranean was born long before I ever heard of this thing called "the Mediterranean Diet."

It began in my birthplace, the cosmopolitan city of Port Said, Egypt, a nineteen-mile stretch of Mediterranean coastline at the north entrance to the Suez Canal. Since its construction more than 150 years ago, the waterway connecting the Red Sea with the Mediterranean Sea—and offering a more direct route between the North Atlantic and northern Indian Oceans—has opened a world of trade, bringing in boatloads of goods and tourists from all over the world and influencing all aspects of the city's culture, from food to architecture and fashion. When I was growing up, the Suez Canal was only a fifteen-minute leisurely walk from my family's flat,

and we would often stroll along its boardwalk enjoying Italian gelato and roasted nuts while watching large white passenger ships, flying flags from Europe and elsewhere, go by. Our favorite pastime was cruising the canal with our church friends in small motorboats we'd rented for the day.

Like most Egyptians, we walked practically everywhere: to work, to the beach, or to a restaurant to meet up with friends. Public transportation was so crowded, and while we did have a car, we still preferred to walk whenever we could.

One of my earliest memories was tagging along with my dad, Baba, and walking to the open-air marketplace we called the souq. I must have only been five or six. Baba was in charge of picking up ingredients that my mother turned into simple but bountiful *azoomas* (feasts) for our family and frequent guests. These souq outings were not about quickly gathering groceries; for Baba, it was about connecting with people, and I loved being out with him for hours in the community. Baba was a well-loved pastor and a very busy man, who had friends from all walks of life and in all corners of Port Said, across Egypt, and in fact, around the world. He was friends with dignitaries and government officials, he conducted business with all sorts of people, and he was also a friend to many locals no matter their occupation. He never met a stranger and he took pride in knowing everyone by name. And many of the merchants at the souq knew his name.

On souq days, I remember vividly how his hand held tightly on to my tiny one as we navigated the busy, narrow streets lined with carts and merchants. All around us, the warm, salty air teemed with scents of fresh herbs, especially mint and dill, or the sweet fruit from the stands where fresh mangoes, bananas, and strawberries were being pressed into juice; just-caught fish were displayed in bins of ice or were broiling in the forn, our local clay oven, at the neighboring souq el samak (fish market).

Whenever a vendor called out to Baba, he always stopped, even if we had already bought what they were selling. I remember thinking, "But Baba, we just bought oranges," as he bought yet one more kilo of them from another vendor. And he would always be sure to buy those last few bunches of parsley from the older widowed women who sat on the ground, barefoot, wearing black garb from head to toe. He was keen on noticing those quieter, frail ones who were not waving large signs to advertise their goods, and whose voices were often drowned out by the shouts of other merchants—some with megaphones—competing for shoppers' attention. "Since we bought the last of her herbs, she can go home and rest. It's our job to care for the widows in our community," he explained.

My dad had a knack for picking the most perfect produce. He would hold up a tomato, feeling its skin, and giving it the gentlest squeeze, he would bring it a little closer to my face. "Smell it; it smells ripe, right?" Or he would pick up a watermelon and say, "This one is not too large, but it's heavy for its size. You know what this means?" I did—

it was a juicier watermelon. Then he'd bring it up closer to his ear and give it a tap as I stood there thinking, "What is he listening for? Is the watermelon speaking to him in some sort of code?" To this day, I cannot buy a watermelon without giving it a quick *thunk*. Does it really make a difference? I just do it. My favorite stop on those leisurely souq excursions was Mr. Bishay's falafel joint. Mr. Bishay and Baba were good friends, and while the two men caught up on life, I snacked on freshly fried falafels—so herby and fluffy.

Even decades later, when Baba and Mama visited us in America, we kept up some of these same souq rituals as we strolled together through the farmers' market of our Atlanta suburb. I was now the one to lift the heavy watermelon and give it a tap to blindly determine if it was sweet. Baba watched, smiling proudly. Like him, I too developed a knack for picking out the best produce.

By now he was in his early 70s, his hair had thinned and turned a silvery gray, and he had added a few pounds. But to me, he was still his handsome self: tanned skin, dark eyelashes and eyes—one brown and one black, which absolutely fascinated my girls—and chiseled cheekbones that we called pharaoh cheeks (which I like to think I inherited).

He loved the weather in Atlanta and the fact that the farmers' market carried gorgeous stone fruit that he thought were just like the ones you'd find at the Port Said market. In my kitchen, I often charred the fruit and finished them with a little honey and crushed pistachios (see page 258); or I made something like a Mid-Summer Tomato and Peach Panzanella (page 50) with toasted day-old bread to enjoy out on the back porch.

We'd come home with our spoils from the market plus a few organic lamb shanks from the local grocery store. Baba loved it when I braised them in a red wine sauce with cinnamon and rosemary (see page 244), which was one of the most popular recipes on my website, *The Mediterranean Dish*. He never understood exactly what I did and how millions of people could stumble upon an article I'd written or a recipe of mine on the internet, but he didn't care about the logistics. What excited Baba most was that his little girl was "breaking bread with the masses."

The last time I made my lamb shanks for Baba was Christmas of 2018. That was also the last time I ever saw him. One early morning in January I received a phone call informing me of his sudden passing. He had been well. He simply went to bed and did not wake up.

I was fortunate to attend his funeral with a couple thousand of his closest friends from all over Egypt and the world. It was my first time back to Port Said in fifteen long years, and I spent my days listening to story upon story about this man I called Baba, his legacy of love, and the profound impact he had both on individuals and on the city as a whole. The governor stood to share a few words at the post-funeral celebration. He said, "Today the city lost one of its greatest pillars, and I lost a dear friend." As I listened, I simply wished that I could hold Baba's hand to walk through the sunny souq one more time.

It took me a good month to return to the kitchen again, but I had to do it. So, I put on Baba's gray V-neck wool sweater, which I had brought back with me from Egypt—the last thing he wore. It was warm. It smelled like him—

spicy and sweet, but subtle. He was not a flashy guy.

Then I stepped into the kitchen and made lamb shanks.

Baba had a saying: "Make it your job to put a smile on someone's face." He made so many people smile—at the souq and everywhere else he went—and I have tried to live my life accordingly, no matter where I lived, be it the Mediterranean Basin, Canada, the American Midwest, or finally Atlanta, the hub of the American South. The best way I know to make

WEARING BABA'S OVERSIZED SWEATER AND HOLDING HIS FAVORITE LAMB SHANKS.

people smile is by sharing the hospitality, instilled in me as a child, that comes with a simple, nutritious home-cooked meal.

My Culinary Heritage

The Mediterranean Basin is a large, diverse part of the world that stretches from southern Europe to North Africa and the Middle East; and among these kitchens, there are unique differences that I very much respect.

ORANGE-CARDAMOM-OLIVE OIL CAKE, PAGE 268

There is also a certain interconnectedness—the great "middle sea" pulling us together in a shared love for the bright, evocative flavors of the sunny region. And because the people of this land—and their ingredients—have migrated and traveled across this area for centuries, culinary borders are sometimes blurred.

As a port city, my hometown Port Said's culinary influences span well beyond Middle Eastern and North African cooking to include Italian, Greek, French, English, and even Indian cuisines. So, when people ask me, "What's Egyptian food like?" my answer is a bit complicated.

Don't get me wrong, Egyptian culinary traditions extend back at least 5,000 years, since the time of the pharaohs. Wall paintings and carvings in tombs and temples show how much we loved and celebrated fruits, fish, and grains, including wheat and barley which were important in making bread and beer. There are some distinctly Egyptian dishes that have become popular throughout the Middle East and have even garnered some international buzz. Ful Mudammas (page 102), for example, is a cumin-spiked porridge of fava beans, often drizzled with tahini sauce, and is considered the national dish of Egypt. Along with falafel, which we call ta'amiya, ful mudammas is basically the people's daily grub, eaten for breakfast, lunch, or dinner. Freekeh, the ancient whole grain with a faintly smoky flavor and chewy texture that's been showing up on trendy menus lately, has long been mixed into Egyptian pilafs for stuffing game birds and added to broth to bulk up a soup base (see page 144).

We have other local foods, too, like hawawshi (see page 215), which are pita-like pies stuffed with a spicy meat mixture. And speaking of stuffed, there is Mahshi (page 230), a whole genre of vegetables filled with tantalizing herby rice (my favorites are stuffed bell peppers and zucchini), as well as braised or stewed vegetables we call tabiekh, which rely heavily on homemade tomato sauce, like Fasolia (page 142) stewed green beans, sweet peas, potatoes, or eggplant (with or without small chunks of meat). These stewed vegetables are often served along with a piece of warm, puffy pita bread that's been baked in an outdoor oven we call a forn. (By the way, to pronounce *tabiekh* with an Arabic accent, work the back of your throat to create a small funny, guttural sound like you're clearing your throat from an odd tickle—that's the sound you make at the end of the word!)

Yet, over the many centuries that Egyptian cuisine has been around, its people have also adapted the flavors and the cooking methods of our neighbors and those who have tramped across the land. This is especially true in Port Said, which has been a global city since its founding in the mid-nineteenth century. Tourists and traders of various nationalities and religions, from neighboring Mediterranean countries and otherwise, routinely visited the city and brought their culinary traditions.

While local restaurants serve traditional Egyptian fare, you'll also find variations on adapted dishes, from tapas to Italian pastas like cannelloni, several Greek-influenced fish dishes (the Greeks ran many restaurants in Alexandria), Levantine dishes including kibbeh and shish barak (lamb dumplings in warm yogurt sauce), Tunisian shakshuka, Turkish baklava, and more.

At home, Mama, who is one of the greatest cooks I know, embraced all these different flavors with ease, always giving the meal her own spin. She cooked fearlessly, and as a child, I took it all in.

Mama's Egyptian Kitchen

Mama's kitchen was sunny and light, with a very large window that was always open. Pantry space was limited to a few essentials: spices, olive oil (imported from another part of the Mediterranean), rice, a little pasta, dried legumes like lentils and beans, and tins of feta cheese which traveled to us from my father's family in Upper Egypt. Mama hung the garlic and onions outdoors on the balcony to keep them from spoiling. A bowl of fresh tomatoes and seasonal fruit sat in the corner.

Limited pantry space was typical in Egyptian homes. It had to do with the way people lived and shopped—which was very à la minute. Fresh produce, fish, and other items needed to make dinner were picked up that very day at the market—the idea of stocking up on the weekend for a whole week of eating was foreign. My parents, like many people of the Mediterranean, were very much guided by a farm-to-table spirit, although we did not have a fancy way to describe it.

If Baba came home with an excessive amount of whatever fruit was in season, like figs or apricots, Mama went to work making jam. Bread was another thing that my parents purchased fresh daily: five warm, fragrant, and puffy pitas per day.

After school, my brother and I did our homework at the round kitchen table while Mama cooked. It was an efficient way for her to make dinner while being available to help us with our studies. She was a chemistry teacher by profession and she took that role seriously, even at home with us kids. And even though I was

PORT SAID, CIRCA 1984

doing homework, I was also observing the magic happening in our kitchen. Maybe that's why now, when I taste something I'm cooking, I know just the right amount of cumin or allspice to add without measuring.

My parents entertained nonstop. They were always having big, festive dinners for which Mama, with the help of friends or other female members of the family, would prepare dishes for days ahead. Sometimes I got to squeeze in around the table and help stuff veggies, shell nuts for Triple Nutty Baklava (page 262), or shape Ghorayebah (page 273), a sweet bite-sized butter cookie that instantly melts in your mouth.

Other times, my dad invited friends over on a whim, and Mama, on super-short notice, would quickly pull together dinner using whatever she had on hand. The food itself was never the whole point, though. Gathering around the table was as much about the company as it was about what we served.

When the Greek Consul Mr. Yannis arrived in Port Said, Baba was one of the first people to connect with him, and they became instant friends. And when Mr. Yannis told Baba that his family had remained in Greece during his assignment in Port Said, we became his adopted family. I can't count the number of dinners we had together, with conversations on how similar or different Greek and Egyptian foods were. Mama would make stuffed grape leaves, and Mr. Yannis would shout, "Ah, dolmades!" And when she made her macaroni bechamel, Mr. Yannis would argue, "We call it pastitsio!" We loved how close our cultures are and how Mom's food made Mr. Yannis feel at home.

My Journey to America

Baba was passionate about experiential learning outside traditional academic settings, and when my brother and I were very young, he took our family on trips throughout the country, as well as to Germany, Canada, and the United States to visit family. He and Mama envisioned a future for me where I could immerse myself in all sorts of new experiences and fully master a new language.

So, their sending me to Toronto, where we had family, to finish high school at an all-girls Catholic school was a big step toward that goal. I can assure you that it was not a fun age for me to make the transition. Arabic is my first language, and at the time, I spoke the most broken English you can imagine; so I enrolled in ESL classes and hung out with the quiet ESL kids. I missed my friends and my full Egyptian life terribly, but at least I had my aunt and uncle, cousins, and my grandpa, and that was a great comfort for me.

After graduation, I enrolled at Calvin University, in Grand Rapids, Michigan. I was one of three Egyptians in a mostly Dutch-American population there at the time. My freshman year was the most difficult. Moving from Ontario, Canada, to Michigan had not been that much of a culture shock, but for the first time in my life I did not have any family around me. It was just me.

I quickly realized how short and dark I was compared to my tall, blond classmates. And, of course, my accent gave me away as "the Egyptian girl." At first, when people were curious about my background and how I had ended up in Michigan, I would tell funny stories of how my dad sold a couple of tiny pyramids and a few camels to afford my college tuition. It was a joke, of course, but a couple of girls bought it and we still laugh about that!

I adapted the way I always do, to this day: by sharing my food with anyone willing to try my cooking. My cooking skills weren't great back then, but my poor friends put up with my experiments, some of which were more successful than others.

I did not set out to have a career in food. Back then, I had many different ideas of what I would be, some of them involving media, like TV or writing, but not food. At one point I decided that maybe I'd do something in the medical field. But after my first biology lab, I went back to my room and called my parents to break the news that dissecting things was not something I cared to do. So, I studied business communications instead. One snowy January night in my junior year, some college friends and I ended up eating dinner at a Mediterranean restaurant on 28th Street, in Grand Rapids. The owners' son, Saba, happened to be managing that night. He waited on our table. I guess he liked me enough that I scored a free tabbouleh! Eventually, one of my roommates started working at the same restaurant, and through her, Saba, my now-husband, and I began to spend more time together.

Saba was born and raised in Michigan, and he is very much a Midwestern guy, but with deep Middle Eastern roots. His parents are from Jordan and his late grandmother, Teta Badia'a, was a Palestinian Christian who spent a good bit of her life between Jerusalem and Ramallah. I was attracted to Saba's quiet, thoughtful, and gentle demeanor, and I guess he didn't mind my loud personality and rowdy hair (I have since found a solution for the uncontrollable curls, thankfully!). As our relationship became more serious, Saba, knowing I missed my mother's cooking, took every opportunity to bring me food made by his mom, whom I now call Mama Dina. Her food tasted like home, and that is what sealed the deal for me; we've now been married twenty-one years.

Mama Dina's Levantine Kitchen

Mama Dina cooked nonstop, both for her family and for the family's two restaurants, which they have sold since. Her home kitchen is all Levant: rice-centered meals, roast lamb, chicken fragrant with an array of warm spices, minced Arabic salad, and hummus (see page 60) whipped to smooth perfection and finished with a big pool of olive oil in the middle.

Mama Dina is the kind of person who has a hard time simply sitting still and socializing; she can always find something to do in the kitchen. Early on in my marriage, I discovered that to spend time with her, I had to join her in her favorite place, the kitchen. So, I did!

I can easily say that she influenced the second half of my life in the most delicious of ways. In her kitchen, I got hooked on za'atar (page 25), the magical blend of wild thyme, toasted sesame seeds, and sumac, which traveled many miles to her American home from El Blad, referring to Jordan. She taught me how to make tangy, creamy labneh (page 101), tabbouleh (page 42) with the ideal ratio of parsley to bulgur, the savory hand pies that my girls adore, and more.

Mama Dina also taught me my favorite trick of peeling heaps of garlic to be used throughout the week. She would first submerge the cloves in water for a few minutes to loosen the skins, then proceed to peel, dry, and store them in jars in the fridge. I make this my practice today as well because garlic—at least in my cooking—is life!

Saba and I eventually left Michigan and moved around, from one city to another, following the path his career took us. I frequently called Mama Dina with cooking questions, and she spent time tutoring me over the phone on how to make more elaborate dishes, like her famous Palestinian Maglooba (page 233), a celebratory rice meal. I texted her pictures of the dishes as I prepared them, and she would usually send back her approval: "Good job, habibiti [darling]!"

Aside from being in the kitchens of my two mamas, I got to do some globetrotting to places around the Mediterranean and beyond, both for my job in the marketing and non-profit world and for pleasure. And while the travels were not specifically for food, that was the thing that guided my excursions; my eyes and my palate were open to new experiences, and I came home inspired and ready to implement the flavors I had sampled.

How *The Mediterranean Dish* Came to Be

After Saba's job took us to Des Moines, Iowa, I gave up my career to focus on raising our growing family. I wanted to instill in our Michigan-born girls, Dara and Hannah, an appreciation for their Egyptian and Levantine heritages, and I knew food was a good place to start. One day, Saba came home excited to tell me about this thing he'd heard about, called a "food blog." He said, "You love to cook, and you love to write; you should start a site." I had no clue what he was talking about, but he's always had big visions and I thought, *Why not? It can be a place to document recipes for my girls*. And within the hour we established TheMediterraneanDish.com.

Over the next few months, I posted recipes that I cooked for my family and friends on my tiny "hobby site." I drew from the two Egyptian and Levantine kitchens I loved, and from my travels to places like Turkey, Greece, and France, adding my own twists with modern, streamlined techniques to fit my pantry and my busy American lifestyle. People I'd never met wrote to tell me how much they enjoyed learning about my experiences growing up on the Mediterranean coast and discovering how easy it was to follow my instructions for creating dishes of things they'd only tried in restaurants, like chicken shawarma and spanakopita. I loved the feeling of inviting the whole world to join me at one big virtual table filled with the Mediterranean dishes I knew and loved, where everyone could take part in the conversation.

In 2016, Saba's work took us from Des Moines to Atlanta, Georgia, our current home. It took me all of one day to love it here. Between the sunshine and the Southern hospitality, I feel truly at home. Even during the months when we lived in an extended-stay hotel without a proper kitchen, I made use of the shabby outdoor grill and quickly formed friendships over some Charred Chicken Thighs with Dill Greek Yogurt Sauce (page 216) and assorted simple Mediterranean sides. And when we finally settled in our new suburban neighborhood, we threw casual home gatherings that were centered around platters, boards, and bowls showcasing our old family recipes and new Mediterranean-inspired experiments.

I continued to write—to share my heritage, recipes, and tips—and as traffic to my site grew, and I heard from more people who have been able to make a lifestyle change and to find joy following my recipes, the hobby became not just my full-time work but also a personal mission: to help readers cook nutritious recipes with bold Mediterranean flavors, and to do so with less stress in the kitchen and more joy at table. Today, TheMediterraneanDish.com is *the* leading site for modern Mediterranean cooking and the Mediterranean lifestyle, with millions of readers and followers across social media channels. *The Mediterranean Dish* cookbook is a natural extension of this goal.

I filled this cookbook with many of my favorite recipes that I prepare regularly, for every kind of meal and occasion, and they all celebrate the bright flavors of the Mediterranean. You will find some traditional recipes (with my own twists) and many more of my contemporary dishes that are easy to pull off any night of the week. In these pages, I aim to help you reap the joys of Mediterranean cooking anywhere—no "chefy" skills or fancy tools required.

To know that you invited me into your home, cooked my recipes, and shared them with your loved ones is the greatest reward, and I am grateful beyond measure.

So, *bon appétit*! Or, as we say in Egypt, *bel hana wel shefa*: to your joy and your health!

Let Your "Nafas" Guide Your Cooking

The *tetas* (grandmothers) where I come from, including both my mom and my mother-in-law, share this one thing in common: nafas. Others have written extensively about this word, the elusive nafas, and it is a hard thing to explain, but to help you better understand my approach to cooking upfront, I think it's important that I at least try.

Nafas, in Arabic, means "breath." It also means "soul." So, whenever you ask a teta about how much of this or that goes into her special dish, or what her secret ingredient might be, the answer will inevitably include the word *nafas*. It's not that she doesn't want to share the recipe measurements, but measuring is not a thing they do. In our culture, the thing that is most important when cooking is to do it with all you have within. Not a ton of studying or fussing over details—just your God-given intuition. Your breath. Your love. And somehow, as you give generously of yourself, the work of your hands is laced with deliciousness.

I may have inherited a tiny bit of the nafas genes because, in my cooking, I'll be the first to admit that I hate measuring things. But when I started to document the recipes on my site for my two daughters, I made myself do that measuring and eventually I got quite good at it. Soon enough, a few million other new friends started cooking my recipes, so it was necessary for me to be even more precise.

Still, in my heart, I'm not a fussy cook. I'm all about easy, one-skillet and one-pot meals that allow me to use whatever I have on hand. I play with flavors from different parts of the Mediterranean, and I don't mind a little fusion! In this spirit, I hope you'll feel free to take the recipes I've tried my best to quantify down to the letter—to ensure your success—and make them your own. I invite you to use your own nafas!

About the Mediterranean Diet

If you meet someone who was actually born and raised in that sunny part of the world where I come from, and you ask that person about the ever-so-popular "Mediterranean Diet," you'll probably get a blank, deer-in-headlights stare. That's because the word *diet* is not typically in our vocabulary. Traditionally, many of us do not sweat our food choices. Counting calories, measuring serving sizes, and using scales are not big things we do. But we don't believe in "supersize meals," either. We buy just what we need, take care not to waste, and try not to eat alone because company is the best part of a meal. While we take life seriously, we strive to do so with a joyful attitude.

In my life and on my site, I follow three "Mediterranean Diet" principles:

Eat with the seasons
Use mostly whole foods
And above all else, share

I continually stress the importance of positive lifestyle practices, including the *way* that people of the Mediterranean eat, as much as *what* we do eat. My family's meals revolve around that ubiquitous triangle graphic known as the Mediterranean Diet Pyramid, which for decades has been the global gold standard in well-being and disease prevention. The National Institutes of Health attributes this standard not to any one food or nutrient but, rather, to the many elements in our diet that contribute antioxidants and have anti-inflammatory properties, and whose ingredients work in harmony with other healthy aspects of the Mediterranean lifestyle. In my kitchen, that means meals relying heavily on seasonal, plant-based foods like vegetables, fruit, grains, legumes, and nuts, and lots of extra-virgin olive oil. (I do buy butter, but a pound might last me for months!) Lean proteins mainly from fish and poultry show up on the table a few times a week. I do make room for lamb and baklava on occasion because, my heavens, what's life without baklava?! And yes, thank goodness, we grownups allow ourselves a daily glass of wine!

The Mediterranean Diet is not a fad; and the reason its popularity never goes out of style is that pleasure, not restriction, is its central feature. This laid-back philosophy guides the chapters that follow and is designed to inspire you, not fill you with lists of do's and don'ts.

my mediterranean pantry

I know that pantry sections in cookbooks can be helpful, but they can also be overwhelming. My goal is to help you cook and eat the Mediterranean way, fearlessly and without fuss, with less stress and way more joy. So, here are two things I need you to hear now: first, cooking the Mediterranean way involves many familiar ingredients; second, you probably already have some of them on hand (check out the shopping list, pages 30–31). For those who want the nitty-gritty, let's talk more about some staples I use and how I use them.

Extra-Virgin Olive Oil: The Start of Everything Delicious!

People always ask me, "What kind of olive oil should I use?" That's a bit of a loaded question, but a very important one, so bear with me while I try to explain. Extra-virgin olive oil (EVOO) is the main fat used in many Mediterranean kitchens—the one ingredient I reach for daily and use in all my cooking. Not only does EVOO make everything it touches that much more delicious, but also many nutrition

experts regard it as arguably the healthiest oil on the planet. I am not shy with my EVOO, it's my kind of superfood, and in most of my recipes I drizzle it generously as I go.

I won't go into all the myriad claims of its benefits, but the fact is that not all olive oils are created equal. Like wine, they vary in color and have different flavor profiles and nutritional compositions, depending on the type of olives used, where and how they were harvested, and how they were processed. One of the bigger factors, however, is freshness.

I am picky about my olive oil—so much so that I've scoured the world (virtually, at least!) for the best I can find to use in my kitchen. I thank my many readers who have inspired this hunt. Now I keep an assortment of my favorites within easy reach, made from hand-picked, cold-pressed olives grown in family groves in different parts of the Mediterranean, including Greece, Spain, and Italy. To see all my favorites check out my website at TheMediterraneanDish.com.

There's so much to know about olive oil; here is a quick primer:

WHY EXTRA-VIRGIN?

"Extra-virgin" is the highest grade of olive oil, produced by a simple pressing of the olives without use of heat or chemicals. The pressed oil must have an acidity level (referring to free fatty acids) below 0.8 percent. Anything with an acidity level above this number does not qualify as extra-virgin. Plus, olive oils of 0.3 percent or less are considered top of the line. Higher-quality, lower-acid olive oils not only have a superior taste but they also retain more of the antioxidants and healthy compounds found in the olive.

CHECK THE HARVEST AND BOTTLING DATES.

I mentioned earlier that freshness is one of the bigger factors. Try to buy from a reputable source with good turnover and that carries oils from the latest harvest. Generally, once it is bottled, olive oil is best used within 24 months or so. (If you're buying from our online shop, you'll see both dates listed on our website for each olive oil we sell.)

DON'T BE CONFUSED BY OILS LABELED "PURE" OR "LIGHT."

The term "pure" signifies that the bottle contains only olive oil; however, it can be a blend of virgin oils (15 to 20 percent) with the rest being refined olive oils of lesser quality. And, no, "light" does not refer to the fat content, as all olive oil is 100 percent fat. Light olive oil is a refined oil that has a light golden hue.

SINGLE ESTATE, HAND-PICKED, COLD-PRESSED.

The acidity level, as mentioned, is one indicator of quality, but not the only one. Origin is also significant, and this is where it can get tricky. A label that says "Imported from Italy"

or "Bottled" or "Packaged" in Italy does not ensure that the olives were grown there, nor does it necessarily indicate quality—indeed, it can mean that olives grown anywhere else were pressed into oil and then that was shipped to Italy, where it was bottled. Many inexpensive oils are blends of olives of varying quality, from different countries and different groves. So, look for labels that indicate a single region or, better yet, a single estate. And look for labels that say *hand-picked and cold-pressed*. These are the oils made with olives that have been picked with love, by human hands, without chemicals, and with extra care taken to avoid bruising.

COOKING WITH OLIVE OIL.

I use all sorts of EVOO, from robust and peppery early harvest oils to fruity, milder-tasting ones. I love to bake with EVOO, too; in fact, bakers will often attest to the moistness (I can't wait till the English language gives us a better substitute for *moist*) of a cake baked with olive oil. The conventional wisdom used to be that you shouldn't use extra-virgin olive oil for frying and other high-heat cooking because it has a low smoke point and that the excess heat causes it to degrade and form harmful compounds. More recent studies show, however, that this isn't the case: quality olive oil remains quite stable at high heat and does not go rancid or lose much of its nutritional value, but excessive heat does diminish the flavor. So, for deep-frying—which I rarely do anyway—a cheaper, more neutral oil with a higher smoke point is a better choice.

OLIVE OIL FOR DRIZZLING, DIPPING, DRESSING, AND "FINISHING."

Early-harvest oils are made with olives that are picked early in the season and crushed within hours to preserve their quality, taste, and aroma; they are considered the cream

of the crop by connoisseurs. In Greece, this is known as agoureleo. These EVOOs typically have a higher level of polyphenols (antioxidants) and a robust, somewhat bitter, and peppery flavor that is wonderful in raw applications, such as salads and dips, or drizzled at the end of cooking to elevate a simple soup, a green salad, or a pan of plain roasted vegetables in an instant. They're harder to come by and more expensive than your usual supermarket oils, but well worth seeking out.

STORING YOUR EVOO.

Keep the EVOO in a cool, dark place, away from the stove and away from sunny windows. And what's the best way to keep it from ever going rancid? Consume it regularly! After opening a bottle, try to consume it within six months.

BONUS EVOO BEAUTY TIP.

I do use EVOO on my face, but that's an entirely different book to write. For now, I offer you this one quick tip: Buy yourself a little bottle with a dropper and keep a little EVOO in your bathroom. A couple drops of this magic elixir tenderly patted under the eyes could save a few Botox dollars (but consult your dermatologist first).

Herbs, Spices, and Fresh Flavors

Perhaps the most exciting part about eating the Mediterranean way is its generous use of fresh herbs, quality spices, and other natural flavorings such as citrus and aromatics. When used together, these create delicious meals without the use of too much salt or fat. Here are the flavor makers I use regularly that take me back to my roots.

TURMERIC, OREGANO, AND ALEPPO PEPPER

FRESH HERBS

My friends call me the parsley queen. That's not because I grow my own parsley—because, Lord knows, I don't have a green thumb. It's because I use copious amounts of herbs like parsley, mint, cilantro, basil, and dill in my cooking to instantly bring even the blandest dish to life. I typically include the tender part of the stems as well as the leaves, which hold even more flavor. I buy my herbs in bulk, and once they're washed and dried, I trim the ends as if I'm arranging a flower bouquet and stick them in a large jar or vase with a little bit of water. Then I cover them loosely with a recycled plastic bag and stick them in the fridge. They typically will last there for a good week or two (longer for hardier herbs like rosemary and thyme).

SPICES AND SEASONING BLENDS

A spice rack stocked with quality warm spices, dried herbs, and aromatics is a fixture in every Mediterranean kitchen. Beyond the ability to transform humble ingredients into tasty feasts, many spices have been prized for centuries for their powerful plant-derived compounds that are believed to promote good health and even help prevent disease. Most of the ones I use are probably already in your spice rack: cayenne, cinnamon, coriander, cumin, cloves, paprika (sweet and smoked), dried oregano, and ground nutmeg.

But here are a handful, like allspice or sumac, that characterize my cooking but that you may be less familiar with. I'm hoping that after trying them in my recipes, you'll wonder how you ever could have lived without them!

ALEPPO PEPPER

Aleppo pepper, or Halaby pepper, is a magical flavor maker of tangy, earthy chili flakes that offers slow-building heat and a subtle sweetness akin to the best kind of sun-dried tomatoes. It's hard to find Aleppo pepper from Syria due to the current war, so much of it is sourced from Turkey and elsewhere.

ALLSPICE

This resembles a peppery compound of cloves, cinnamon, nutmeg, and mace, but it's none of the above. Ground allspice comes from its own dried berries. A versatile spice in Eastern Mediterranean cooking, it adds depth to meat and poultry dishes, rice, and vegetarian dishes.

CARDAMOM

There are two main kinds of cardamom available—pale green cardamom sold in the husk (in pods) or ground, and black cardamom, which has a smoky taste. I mostly use ground green cardamom, but occasionally use the pods. A member of the ginger family, green cardamom has a eucalyptus-like aroma with subtle, lemony undertones that lend a fresh note to spice mixes.

SUMAC

This coarse purplish-red spice is ground from dried sumac berries. It is astringent, sour, slightly smoky, and earthy all at the same time. In the Middle East, it was often used as a replacement for a final acidic squeeze of lemon or lime, when citrus was out of season. But once you get a sense of just how versatile it is, I'm betting you'll never want to be without it. And I urge you to start with my Sumac-Rubbed Drumsticks (page 219).

TURMERIC

Maybe you've had a jar of ground turmeric hanging around for that one curry or pickle recipe. But in Eastern Mediterranean and North African cooking, we prize its mild, earthy, and somewhat musky undertones as a component in a multitude of meat dishes, pilafs, vegetable stews, and even fish. Fresh turmeric root has become widely available now as well (you can grate it like fresh ginger), although for these recipes I stick to the more convenient ground version.

Don't go overboard with turmeric; too much of it can turn a dish bitter. Turmeric needs heat to come alive. And be forewarned that it's also used as a dye and can turn your hands, clothing, and utensils bright yellow when you're working with it, though the stains should wash out.

ZA'ATAR: ZA'ATAR IS LIFE!

Pronounced za-AH-tar, this aromatic Middle Eastern blend of wild thyme, toasted sesame seeds, and sumac, in my mind, is one of the world's unique and best flavor-makers. It is earthy, herbal, nutty, and even slightly tangy. The word *za'atar* also describes the actual herb in the wild thyme family (hyssop). So, za'atar blends that stick to the traditional taste, like the one I use, will include Mediterranean wild thyme. I use za'atar regularly to season food, simply dress salads, jazz up some breakfast eggs, or serve with olive oil for dipping as part of a big mezze spread.

HOW I USE SALT AND PEPPER

All the recipes in this book were tested with Diamond Crystal kosher salt, the salt of choice in many professional kitchens and the one I use in all my cooking. Its crystals are larger than regular table salt and many other kosher salts (like Morton), and it's ideal for picking up with your fingertips for easy sprinkling, which is my preferred way to season.

I am a huge proponent of "season to taste as you go." Except for breads and other recipes where salt levels can't be adjusted during cooking, I'm not rigid in my salt measurements and suggest them only as loose guidelines. For this reason, I specify amounts of salt in the ingredient list only when it's called for once, such as in a bread or a pastry. Otherwise, I might give suggested measurements in the instructions at the various stages it's meant to be added.

When I say a generous "pinch" or "dash" of kosher salt and black pepper in my instructions, I often recommend starting somewhere around ½ to ¾ teaspoon. Again, add salt as you go, then taste and adjust to your liking.

The recipes in this book were tested with Diamond Crystal Kosher salt with suggested amounts to use as you like. If you're using a different salt, here is how you can approximately adjust salt measurements:

1 teaspoon Diamond Crystal kosher salt
= ¾ teaspoon Morton kosher salt
= ½ teaspoon table salt

And regarding black pepper, my good friends, I am way over grinding my own. If you have a fancy pepper grinder that you love to use, by all means go for it. But if you use ready-ground black pepper, enjoy the shortcut.

Acids: Citrus and Vinegar

I grew up with "green lemons," which when I moved to the states, I learned are called limes! But I do use incredible amounts of lemons and limes in my cooking, and while there are some differences in flavor—lemons being slightly sweeter and limes more on the bitter side—in

most of my recipes they can be interchanged depending on your preference. Other citrus fruits, like oranges, tangerines, and grapefruit, all have a place in Mediterranean cooking and in dessert making.

As far as vinegar goes, there are a thousand options and whole shopping aisles devoted to different varieties. But let's be real; in our home kitchens, we only have so much shelf space. I keep it simple and use mostly distilled white vinegar, white wine vinegar, red wine vinegar, and the occasional drop of balsamic vinegar. Be it a squeeze of lemon juice or a dash of vinegar stirred in at the end, a little acid could be the one ingredient that takes a dish to a whole new level of delicious.

Beans and Other Legumes

We love our beans! Dried beans, peas, and lentils have long been a reliable and affordable source of nutrient-dense, shelf-stable protein through many parts of the Mediterranean, especially where meat is avoided for religious reasons or owing to cost, freshness, or availability. I regularly use kidney beans, white beans, chickpeas, black beans, and fava beans, as well as all sorts of lentils. I use both dried and canned beans, but in all honesty, I use canned beans far more often. The exception is with hummus and falafel. For those—please, I beg of you—do start with dried chickpeas.

Pasta and Grains

A bag of dried pasta can solve the dinner dilemma any night of the week, so it's always a good idea to have some on hand. I regularly keep different shapes of pasta in my pantry.

But other grains have a big place in my heart for what they add, not just in bulk but also in nutrition and flavor. Here goes:

RICE

Standard long-grain or medium-grain white rice is the basis for most of my pilafs (especially my family's favorite, Middle Eastern Rice Pilaf with Toasted Vermicelli and Pine Nuts (page 161), as well as other sides. But I'm also a big fan of fragrant basmati rice, a staple of South Asian cooking that's also popular in parts of the Middle East. The longest grain of any rice, it cooks up nice and fluffy, and makes a simple side for virtually anything.

COUSCOUS

From the Berber word *k'seksu*, couscous looks and acts like a grain, but this North African ingredient is actually a tiny pasta of semolina flour ground from durum wheat. Nowadays, you'll find instant couscous that's already been steamed and dried; it requires little effort to prepare and can be ready in about 10 minutes. Cook it in broth and serve it as is or dress it up any way you like with herbs, spices, a little sautéed garlic in olive oil, and perhaps some colorful chopped veggies (diced red bell pepper and zucchini are my favorites). I also sometimes serve couscous as a hot breakfast cereal, sweetened with honey and dried fruits (see page 127). Larger-grained pearl couscous is also easy to

prepare. Treat it as you would a tiny pasta like orzo. It takes about 15 minutes from start to finish.

BULGUR

Also referred to as cracked wheat, bulgur is an essential ingredient in tabbouleh salad (see page 42). Like other whole grains, it's rich in fiber, vitamins, and minerals that have been shown to aid in heart health, weight loss, blood sugar control, and digestion. Bulgur is

**EXTRA NUTTY FREEKEH PILAF
WITH DRIED FRUIT, PAGE 162**

available in fine, medium, or coarse varieties and it takes anywhere from 3 minutes to 25 minutes to cook, depending on the coarseness of the grain and how it is prepared. I use different grinds for different purposes. Fine or "instant" bulgur is my choice for tabbouleh. For soups and stews, I use the coarse #3.

BARLEY, FARRO, AND FREEKEH

These are three other ancient, whole-wheat grains that turn up often in my Mediterranean cooking. Like bulgur, they're a more nutritious and filling stand-in for white rice and can usually be substituted with quinoa for those with wheat allergies (although the flavor profile is completely different). While barley and farro have a mild, earthy, and nutty flavor, freekeh, which is basically young wheat that has been harvested early while the grains are still tender and green, has a savory, smoky flavor. This is because the freekeh grains are dried and fire-roasted, then rubbed to remove the skins. As an Egyptian, I am a big freekeh fan, for sure!

If you don't find some of these grains at a supermarket near you, check out my online shop via TheMediterraneanDish.com.

Feta and Yogurt

Feta makes everything betta! If you've watched my cooking videos, you've heard me say, "Please do not use the already crumbled feta!" It's hard, dry, and sometimes too salty compared to the tangy, rich, creamy blocks stored in brine. For the record, only feta produced in Greece is permitted by the European Commission to be called "feta" as a protected, "Designation of Origin" product. That's why in Egypt, as in other Mediterranean countries, we called it "white cheese." Real Greek feta is made primarily of sheep's milk and may include up to 30 percent goat's milk. You may find some Bulgarian and French feta-style cheese made of sheep's milk, and both are fine substitutes.

As for yogurt, I'm a big fan of the thick, tangy, plain Greek yogurt, but I do also keep containers of plain whole-milk regular yogurt, which I use to make my basic labneh yogurt cheese (page 101) and for baking, or when I just need a thinner yogurt for a recipe.

Nuts and Seeds

Nut trees abound throughout the Mediterranean, and as such, nuts have played an important role in shaping the cuisine. I ate nuts practically daily when I was growing up and I still do today: as snacks, blended into dips and sauces, sprinkled on salads and vegetable dishes, folded into rice—you name it. Packed with fiber, nutrients, protein, and heart-healthy fats, they fill you up while instantly boosting the flavor and crunch factor of a dish. Walnuts, pistachios, cashews, almonds, pine nuts, and hazelnuts are the ones you'll find in my kitchen at any given time. I often buy them in bulk and store them in the freezer, where they'll retain their freshness for months.

Dried Fruits

Medjool dates, dried raisins, dried figs, dried apricots, and prunes are all great to have on hand as a healthy way to satisfy a sweet craving. I'm particularly partial to Medjool dates, which have long been a symbol of Arab hospitality and are large enough to be pitted and stuffed with nuts and other goodies, then served as a dessert on their own (see page 265). I've found that eating a couple of dates before yoga class will give me just the high-carb, mineral-rich boost I need to power me through my practice and leave me with energy to spare!

Tahini

This super-creamy, rich paste of finely ground sesame seeds has been a staple of Mediterranean households for centuries. High in protein, low in carbs, and rich in omega-3 fatty acids, tahini uses extend far beyond creamy hummus (see page 60). I use it in dressings, marinades, dips, soups, smoothies, desserts, and sauces like my Lime-Tahini Sauce (page 290), which I drizzle over many things. Quality can vary quite a bit from one brand to the next; good tahini should taste rich, luxurious, mildly nutty, and savory—not bitter and chalky. Hot tip: because the sesame oil will separate from the paste, go ahead and store your tahini jars upside down (make sure they are very tightly closed first!) in your pantry or in a cool, dry area away from direct sunlight. If you don't think you'll use it frequently, you can store your tahini in the fridge. And be sure to stir your tahini before using.

Pomegranates and Pomegranate Molasses

In Egypt, we snacked on tangy pomegranate seeds all the time, but it wasn't until I was an adult and living in the United States that I discovered the power of sweet-tart pomegranate molasses, a condiment made by reducing pomegranate juice to a sticky syrup. Now I can hardly get enough of it! I love the deep,

complex flavor it adds to drinks, sauces, marinades, dressings, and more. In a pinch, you can make your own by simmering pomegranate juice—sweetened with a little honey or sugar if you like—down to a very thick, syrupy consistency. And now that fresh pomegranates are at the supermarket throughout the year, I find all kinds of excuses for sprinkling the seeds, or arils, over salads and other dishes for a glittering, jewel-like garnish. Those little plastic containers of pomegranate arils are convenient, but sniff them before using to check for freshness.

Tomatoes, Every Which Way

Fresh, canned, roasted, stewed, or sun-dried—whatever form they come in, tomatoes are a prominent ingredient in Mediterranean cooking. To me, there's still nothing like biting into a ripe heirloom tomato in the summertime. I love sweet, multicolored cherry and grape tomatoes for salad-making, and the firmer Roma (plum) tomatoes for roasting. I've also become especially fond of the golf ball-sized Campari tomatoes; they're sweet with the right balance of acid, and a firm but delicate texture that's great for slicing into a salad or on a sandwich, or for roasting. I generally depend on those medium-sized tomatoes labeled "vine-ripened" (most likely in a greenhouse) that are sold in clusters for good results in raw and cooked dishes. While my mother would spend hours simmering fresh tomato sauce from scratch, I gladly rely on high-quality canned San Marzano whole plum tomatoes, and other canned or packaged tomato products for a saucy dish.

THE MEDITERRANEAN DISH SHOPPING LIST

This list gives you a quick at-a-glance look at some ingredients you need to begin building your Mediterranean pantry.

Dry Seasonings
Kosher salt (Diamond Crystal)

Anise seeds
Allspice (ground)
Aleppo pepper flakes
Bay leaves
Black pepper (ground and whole peppercorns)
Caraway seeds
Cardamom (pods and ground)
Cinnamon (sticks and ground)
Coriander (seeds and ground)
Cumin (seeds and ground)
Fennel seeds
Herbs, dried (dill, mint, oregano, rosemary, thyme)
Nutmeg (ground)
Paprika (sweet and smoked)
Ras el hanout
Red pepper flakes
Sesame seeds, white
Sumac
Turmeric (ground)
White pepper (ground)
Za'atar

Produce

Dry storage
Garlic
Onions (yellow, red)
Potatoes (Yukon Gold, red-skinned, baby)
Shallots
Sweet potatoes

Refrigerated
Herbs, fresh (basil, cilantro, chives, dill, mint, flat-leaf parsley, thyme, rosemary)
Leafy greens (arugula, romaine, spring mix, baby spinach)
Lemons and limes
Scallions
Seasonal fruits and vegetables

Countertop
Avocados
Bananas
Tomatoes (cherry, Campari, medium vine-ripened, heirloom)

Proteins
(Refrigerator or Freezer)
Beef (ground lean)
Chicken (whole, breasts, thighs, drumsticks)
Lamb (shanks, shoulder, rack, ground)
Seafood (fish fillets or steaks, scallops, shrimp)

Dairy & Eggs
Cheese (high-quality Greek feta, Parmesan, ricotta, mozzarella, burrata, brie, pecorino Romano, fontal or fontina)
Eggs (preferably organic, free-range)
Milk, whole dairy or plant-based alternative
Yogurt (plain whole-milk regular, whole-milk Greek)

Legumes

Chickpeas (dried and canned)
Beans, dried (fava) and canned (black-eyed
   peas, pinto, Great Northern, kidney, fava)
Lentils (brown and red)

Pastas & Grains

Rice (long-grain, basmati)
Pasta (vermicelli, spaghetti, and other
   shapes)
Couscous (fine Moroccan, large pearl)
Bulgur wheat (fine #1, coarse #3)
Farro (dry pearled, semi-pearled)
Freekeh (cracked)
Barley
Quinoa
Flour (all-purpose, chickpea flour)

Nuts, Seeds & Dried Fruits

Almonds (raw)
Cashews (raw)
Hazelnuts (raw or roasted)
Pine nuts (raw)
Pistachios (shelled, roasted)
Pumpkin seeds
Sunflower seeds
Walnuts (raw)
Fruits, dried (raisins, apricots, Mission
   figs, Medjool dates)

Oils, Vinegars & Condiments

Extra-virgin olive oil
Neutral-tasting oils (avocado,
   grapeseed, safflower)
Vinegars (balsamic, distilled white,
   white and red wine vinegars)
Pomegranate molasses
Dijon mustard (creamy)
Honey

Canned & Bottled Goods

Tahini
Artichoke hearts (jarred marinated and
   canned)

Capers (in brine)
Olives (green, kalamata, black,
   Castelvetrano)
Preserved lemons
Pickles
Red peppers, roasted
Sardines (fillets, in extra-virgin
   olive oil)
Tomatoes (canned whole, diced,
   fire-roasted, sauce, paste; sun-dried)
Tuna

Other Items

Coffee
Tea (black loose-leaf)
Hibiscus petals, dried
Wine, red and white (inexpensive but
   good enough to enjoy by the glass
   and cook with)
Dry sherry

mezze

SALADS, SPREADS, SMALL
PLATES, AND SAVORY NIBBLES

MEZZE:
THE UNOFFICIAL "WELCOME" MEAL

If you come to my house for dinner, I won't greet you with a handshake. You may get a tight hug or, if we're really close, a proper Egyptian kiss on each cheek. While I tend to the stove, you'll take a seat at my kitchen counter and immediately roll up your sleeves to dig into my bowl of The Smoothest, Fluffiest Hummus (page 60), using warm pita as a utensil.

Eventually we'll wander over to the table, and as we play catch-up, a little dish will appear, then another, and another, until the table is filled end to end with dips, bright salads, olives, pickles with just the right zing, maybe a plate of zucchini rounds sprinkled with dukkah, a few savory hand pies pulled from the freezer and quickly warmed up, and maybe an impromptu sauté of garlicky shrimp and bits of chorizo I just happen to have on hand. There is always a bottle of extra-virgin olive oil (the good stuff) close by for drizzling and dipping and small bowls of za'atar to sprinkle on things (za'atar makes everything better!).

This is mezze: small plates, shared in the most informal and unfussy way. It is the unofficial "welcome" meal.

While any of the mezze dishes in this chapter would make a fine appetizer before a main course, much as hors d'oeuvre do in other cultures, that is not the way we eat at my house. There are no separate courses or pauses. Even if the menu includes a leg of lamb or a whole roasted fish at a later point, everything just blurs together in one delicious, casual, rowdy spread filled with chatter and laughter, with everyone furiously scooping and reaching over one another and passing plates and diving in.

In some ways, mezze is a metaphor for the Mediterranean way of life: It is about breaking bread without an agenda or expectation. There is a certain intimacy, and a sense of ceasing and savoring the moment.

That's why I'm devoting the first, and largest, chapter of this book to the concept of mezze and how I carry it with me in my daily life wherever I happen to be.

Here you will find both cold salads and hot dishes to be eaten with a fork, your hands, or scooped with bread—some, like Tangy Marinated Eggplant (page 77), are true to my heritage, others, like Mid-Summer Tomato and Peach Panzanella (page 50), are inspired by influences and ingredients that surround me today. Any combination of these dishes can turn into a big buffet spread, but they can also serve simpler purposes throughout the day—as snacks, a light meal, or to complement a larger dish.

Once you embrace the spirit of mezze, there is no going back, my friend. I guarantee, you will find many ways to infuse your life with a little mezze. So, let's dig in!

everyday tomato and cucumber salad with dad's salad "whisky"

SERVES 4 TO 6

For most meals at my parents' house, my dad was in charge of the "extras": the salad, the feta plate, the pickles or olives—all the things he loved that made the meal a little more special. His "three-ingredient Mediterranean salad" literally had chopped tomatoes, cucumbers, and parsley. He seasoned it simply with salt and pepper, lime juice or vinegar, and a good drizzle of olive oil. Baba loved it when the salad sat long enough for all the juices to concentrate in the bowl. He called this delicious liquid "salad whisky" because once everyone was served and the bowl was empty, he collected the liquid in a small glass and drank it like a shot of whisky!

I inherited my love for "salad whisky" from Baba and passed it on to my girls, who now fight over who gets to drink it.

There are as many versions of this Middle Eastern salad as there are households. I like to embellish Baba's simple formula with the peppery crunch of radishes. And I load up on the fresh herbs whenever I can. To harness the "salad whisky" deliciousness, allow the salad to rest 10 minutes or so before serving. If you have any leftovers, keep in the fridge in a tightly covered container for up to one night (it gets nicely marinated, but it may lose a bit of its crunch).

3 vine-ripened medium tomatoes, cored and diced

1 English (hothouse) cucumber, diced

3 scallions, trimmed, white and green parts roughly chopped

2 or 3 radishes, diced

1 cup roughly chopped fresh flat-leaf parsley

½ cup roughly chopped fresh dill fronds

¼ cup roughly chopped fresh mint leaves

2 large garlic cloves, minced

Kosher salt and ground black pepper

1 teaspoon sumac

½ teaspoon red pepper flakes (optional)

Juice of 1 lime or lemon, plus more to taste (2 to 4 tablespoons)

Extra-virgin olive oil

1. In a large bowl, combine the tomatoes, cucumber, scallions, radishes, herbs, and garlic. Season well with salt and pepper to taste. Add the sumac and red pepper flakes (if using).

2. Dress the salad with about 2 tablespoons of the lime or lemon juice and a generous drizzle of olive oil (about 3 tablespoons). Toss to combine. Taste and adjust the seasoning, adding a splash more lime or lemon juice if you like. Allow the salad to sit about 10 minutes before serving so the flavors meld and the "salad whisky" forms.

rainbow baby bell pepper salad

SERVES 4 TO 6

I have a serious crush on those bags of adorable multicolored mini peppers you find near the packages of pre-washed lettuce in the supermarket. They're so crispy, candy-sweet, and plain fun to eat—the perfect snack for my girls. In this happy salad, I slice them into rings and toss them in a big bowl with juicy tomato wedges, briny green olives, and loads of fresh dill to add a gorgeous burst of color to the dinner table. No fancy dressing here—just a good dose of sumac, lemon juice, and extra-virgin olive oil. For an even bigger flavor, let this salad sit for 20 minutes or so before serving.

1 pound baby bell peppers, any colors, stemmed, thinly sliced into rings

6 Campari tomatoes, quartered

2 scallions, trimmed and white and green parts chopped

½ cup chopped fresh dill fronds

2 large garlic cloves, crushed

6 to 8 marinated olives (green or kalamata), pitted and roughly chopped

1 teaspoon sumac

Kosher salt and ground black pepper

Zest and juice of **1** large lemon (about **¼ cup**)

3 tablespoons extra-virgin olive oil

1. In a large bowl, combine the bell peppers, tomatoes, scallions, dill, garlic, and olives. Sprinkle with the sumac and a large pinch of salt and pepper (about ½ teaspoon each). Add the lemon zest and juice along with the olive oil and give it a good toss. Taste and adjust the seasoning.

2. Set aside for 20 minutes or so before serving to allow the flavors to meld.

cara cara orange, cucumber, and avocado salad with pomegranate seeds

SERVES 4 TO 6

I'm not really big on salads bulked up with lots of lettuce. Too often, the other ingredients get lost under piles of leaves and blankets of dressing. But a tidy bed of tender mixed greens does make an ideal backdrop for a colorful combo of my favorite winter fruits, lightly dressed in a simple vinaigrette and flecked with mildly hot Aleppo pepper to magnify the citrus flavors. I love the contrasts of creamy avocado slices, wheels of bright Cara Cara oranges, and sweet-tart pomegranate seeds. Cara Caras, which are pink-fleshed oranges on the sweeter side, work especially well in this dish (but navel oranges are a fine substitute). This festive salad will shine on your holiday table, but thankfully it's easy enough to make whenever!

Dressing

Juice of **1** large lemon (about ¼ **cup**)

2 tablespoons red wine vinegar

¼ **cup** extra-virgin olive oil

1 teaspoon Aleppo pepper flakes

Kosher salt and ground black pepper

Salad

3 cups (about **2 ounces**) baby salad greens or spring mix

3 Cara Cara or other navel oranges, peeled and sliced into wheels

½ large English (hothouse) cucumber, halved lengthwise and sliced into half-moons

1 vine-ripened medium tomato, cut into wedges

2 avocados, pitted, peeled, and cut into wedges

1 or 2 large shallots, thinly sliced crosswise

Seeds (arils) of **1** small fresh pomegranate (scant **1 cup**)

1. **Make the dressing:** In a small bowl, whisk together the lemon juice, vinegar, olive oil, Aleppo pepper, and a good dash of salt and pepper.

2. **Make the salad:** Arrange the salad greens on a platter. Add enough of the dressing to coat the leaves and toss well. Top with the oranges, cucumber, tomato, avocado, shallots, and pomegranate seeds, then drizzle with more of the dressing. Taste and adjust the seasoning to your liking.

smashed green favas and artichoke hearts

MAKES ABOUT 1 ¾ CUPS; SERVES 4 TO 6

As a child, I remember sitting at the round kitchen table with a heaping pile of fresh green fava beans in the middle. It was a fun task to open the fuzzy pods and pull out the beans, popping them directly into my mouth. In their raw form, they are crisp and earthy, with a hint of bitterness. But once blanched, the fava's true beauty and tender, creamy texture really shine.

This little dip-style appetizer is inspired by a Greek dish called *aginares me koukia* (stewed artichokes and fava). The blanched beans are skinned and slightly smashed, then doused with extra-virgin olive oil and lime juice with artichokes and fresh mint.

1 pound fresh fava beans in the pod (or **6 to 7 ounces** shelled beans; see Tip)

Kosher salt and ground black pepper

1 to 2 large garlic cloves, finely minced

1 to 2 teaspoons sumac

Juice of **1** large lime (**2 tablespoons**)

Extra-virgin olive oil

½ cup roughly chopped jarred marinated artichoke hearts

2 tablespoons finely chopped fresh chives

1 cup torn or chopped fresh mint leaves, plus extra for serving

Crusty bread, for serving

1. Pull the fava bean pods open at the seams to remove the beans. Discard the pods.

2. Fill a medium saucepan halfway with water, add 1 teaspoon salt, and bring to a boil. Prepare a bowl of ice water and set it next to the stove. Add the beans to the boiling water and cook for 3 to 5 minutes, until the beans are tender and creamy. Using a slotted spoon, transfer the beans to the ice water and let cool for 5 minutes, then drain.

3. Peel the thin white skin from the beans (if you pull the skin on one side, then gently squeeze the beans, the center should pop out). Discard the skins.

4. In a medium bowl, combine the blanched favas, the garlic, sumac, and a pinch (scant ½ teaspoon) of salt and pepper. Add the lime juice and about 2 tablespoons of the olive oil. With the back of a fork, apply some pressure to roughly mash the beans. Add the chopped artichokes, chives, and mint and mix to combine.

5. Spoon the bean and artichoke mixture onto a serving platter. Top with a generous drizzle of olive oil and additional mint. Serve with your favorite crusty bread.

TIP

One pound of fresh fava beans in their pods produces 6 to 7 ounces of beans, so buy accordingly. If you can't find fresh beans (they're usually in markets throughout the springtime), you can use about 2 cups of frozen fava beans instead; just follow the package instructions to cook them.

very green tabbouleh in lettuce boats

SERVES 6 TO 8

Unlike tabbouleh sold in plastic tubs at your local supermarket, the star of this homemade tabbouleh is not the bulgur wheat but the parsley—lots of it! Fine bulgur is what to use here, which requires less soaking time and allows the clean, verdant flavors of the salad to shine.

Tabbouleh purists will wrinkle their noses at the use of a seedless English cucumber here, but I love the added crunch. (If you use the more common American cucumbers, be sure to remove the waxy skin; cut the cucumber lengthwise in half, and remove most of the seeds before chopping.) You will need to chop the vegetables and herbs as finely as possible. A food processor works well for the herbs, but for the tomato and other vegetables, a sharp knife is essential. Parsley holds up well against the citrus in the dressing; that's why tabbouleh is even better the next day.

As their grandma Dina taught them, my girls love their tabbouleh piled onto romaine lettuce leaves—like little boats!—and it's a great way to serve tabbouleh for parties.

½ **cup** fine bulgur wheat #1

4 firm Roma (plum) tomatoes, very finely chopped

Kosher salt

1 English (hothouse) cucumber, very finely chopped

2 bunches fresh flat-leaf parsley, tough stems removed, leaves washed, well dried, and very finely chopped

12 to 15 fresh mint leaves, very finely chopped

4 scallions, trimmed, white and green parts very finely chopped

Juice of **2** large limes or **1** large lemon (about ¼ **cup**)

Extra-virgin olive oil

Romaine lettuce leaves

1. Wash the bulgur wheat and soak it in water to cover until soft, 5 to 7 minutes. Drain the soaked bulgur very well in a fine-mesh sieve, then press down on it with the back of a spoon to release any excess water.

2. Place the tomatoes in a colander and toss with a big pinch of salt (about ½ teaspoon). Set over a bowl to drain some of the excess juice, about 10 minutes.

3. Place the tomatoes, the cucumber, herbs, and scallions in a large bowl. Add the bulgur and season with salt. Mix gently. Add the lime juice and 3 tablespoons of the olive oil, and mix again. Taste and adjust the seasoning, adding a little more olive oil if you like.

4. Cover the tabbouleh and refrigerate for 20 to 30 minutes. Transfer to a serving platter and place the romaine lettuce leaves on the side for scooping. Or, for a fun presentation, scoop the tabbouleh into the lettuce leaves and arrange them on the platter.

VARIATION

Gluten-Free Version: Cauliflower Tabbouleh
In place of the bulgur wheat, use cauliflower rice. To make it, simply pulse the florets from the head of a large cauliflower in a food processor fitted with the multipurpose blade until it is the consistency of rice. Or, finely chop the florets with a sharp knife (you can also buy a bag of fresh cauliflower "rice" in many supermarket produce sections). Transfer the cauliflower to a large bowl, and make the salad.

farro, corn, and cherry tomato salad with basil vinaigrette

SERVES 4 TO 6

I love chewy, nutty farro grains as a hefty base for a salad that will hold up well in the fridge for a few days. It is extra satisfying when combined with sweet corn and kidney beans, and when brightened with a summery basil vinaigrette—hearty enough for a vegetarian lunch. You can make the vinaigrette while the farro cooks. To crank up the flavor even more, toss the salad with the vinaigrette while the farro is still a little bit warm, then leave it alone for a few minutes. The farro will drink up the vinaigrette.

1 cup pearled or semi-pearled farro

1½ cups fresh (raw or lightly cooked) or frozen and thawed corn kernels

1 cup canned kidney beans, drained and rinsed

1 cup halved cherry tomatoes

1 green bell pepper, cored and roughly chopped

Basil Vinaigrette (page 281)

Kosher salt

1. In a medium pot, cook the farro in water according to the package directions. Drain, if needed. Allow the farro to cool a little bit (it's good if the farro is still a bit warm when you dress the salad).

2. In a large bowl, combine the warm farro, the corn, kidney beans, cherry tomatoes, and bell pepper.

3. Pour the vinaigrette over the salad and toss to combine. Taste and season with salt to your liking.

romaine, arugula, and mint fattoush salad

SERVES 6

Broken, day-old pita gets a second chance as a key ingredient in a fattoush salad built with in-season vegetables and herbs you have on hand. This version is a riff on one I tried at Leyla, a modern fine-dining Lebanese restaurant on King Street in Charleston, South Carolina. Owner Dolly Awkar, who goes by the name Leyla, prepares it daily with chopped romaine and peppery arugula (in place of traditional purslane, which is hard to find in the United States), crispy bell peppers, and an array of garden-fresh veggies.

At first bite, the bold notes of citrusy sumac, fresh mint, and sweet-tart pomegranate molasses in the dressing hit me in the best way possible.

I can't decide if I'm more in love with the dressing or with the crispy bits of olive oil–fried pita. The whole combo just works for me. I always order fattoush every time I visit Leyla.

Salad

2 (6-inch) pocket-style pitas

Extra-virgin olive oil

Kosher salt

1 teaspoon sumac

About 3 hearts of romaine lettuce (8 ounces), trimmed and thinly sliced crosswise

1 cup packed baby arugula (1 to 2 ounces)

1 red bell pepper, cored, seeded, and sliced into thin batons

½ English (hothouse) cucumber, halved lengthwise, seeds scooped out, and thinly sliced crosswise (about 1 cup)

1 cup halved cherry tomatoes

1 small red onion, thinly sliced crosswise into rounds

2 or 3 radishes, thinly sliced crosswise into rounds

1 cup thinly sliced mint leaves

1 teaspoon ground black pepper

1. **Begin the salad:** Split the pita in half, separating each into 2 single-layer rounds, then tear them into bite-sized pieces. In a large skillet, heat 3 tablespoons of olive oil over medium-high heat. Add the pita and fry, tossing occasionally, until golden brown, 2 to 3 minutes.

2. Use a slotted spoon to transfer the fried pita chips to a large, paper towel–lined plate to drain. Remove the paper towel and toss the pita chips with some salt and the sumac.

3. In a large bowl, combine the lettuce, arugula, bell pepper, cucumber, tomatoes, red onion, radishes, and mint leaves. Season with a generous pinch of salt (½ to ¾ teaspoon) and the black pepper and toss well.

4. **Make the dressing:** In a small bowl, whisk together the olive oil, pomegranate molasses, lemon juice, garlic, sumac, allspice, and cinnamon.

5. **Assemble the salad:** Pour the dressing over the salad and toss well. Add the fried pita pieces and toss again to combine. Taste and adjust the seasoning, adding a bit more sumac or salt, if needed.

Pomegranate Molasses–Sumac Dressing

⅓ **cup** extra-virgin olive oil

3 **tablespoons** pomegranate
  molasses

Juice of **1** large lemon
  (about ¼ **cup**)

1 or 2 large garlic cloves, minced

1½ **teaspoons** sumac

¼ **teaspoon** ground allspice

¼ **teaspoon** ground cinnamon

TIP

It's important to toss in the pita chips just before you serve the salad so they don't lose their crunch. And if you prefer, you can toast the pita instead, as I have done for the Eggplant Fatteh with Garlicky Tahini–Yogurt Sauce (page 72).

watermelon, berry, cucumber, and feta salad with honey-lime dressing

SERVES 6

Eating watermelon never fails to take me back to childhood summers in Port Said. Friends and neighbors regularly got together early in the morning to walk over to the shore for full days in the sun. And nearly every family brought along a whole watermelon to share! It was our thing.

The kids were charged with digging holes in the sand to bury the whole watermelons to keep them cool until snack time. Then, someone would rinse the melons in the sea and cut them into large wedges. It was a glorious mess for a tiny kid like me to dig my face into a large watermelon wedge. I loved following a bite of sweet watermelon with a piece of salty, creamy gebna bieda (our Egyptian version of feta).

I still adore this sweet and salty combination—it's in my blood. Nowadays, I do a grown-up version by adding other summer produce in the mix and pulling everything together with a zesty dressing. This salad is all about quality ingredients, especially the sweet and juicy watermelon. Picking the right watermelon is a bit like going on a blind date, isn't it? Check out the tips.

Honey-Lime Dressing

2 tablespoons honey

Juice of **1 or 2** large limes (about ¼ **cup**)

Extra-virgin olive oil

Kosher salt

Salad

½ large seedless watermelon, peeled and cut into 1-inch cubes (**6 to 7 cups**)

1 English (hothouse) cucumber, cut into ½-inch cubes (about **2 cups**)

1 cup fresh blueberries

1 cup fresh raspberries

1 cup torn fresh mint leaves

1 cup torn fresh basil leaves

½ **to 1 cup** creamy Greek feta cheese, crumbled

1. In a small bowl, whisk together the honey, lime juice, 2 or 3 tablespoons of olive oil and salt to taste.

2. In a large bowl or on a serving platter with sides, combine the watermelon, cucumber, blueberries, raspberries, mint, and basil.

3. Pour the dressing over the salad and toss gently. Top with the crumbled feta and serve.

HOW TO CHOOSE THE RIPEST, SWEETEST WATERMELON

Look for a symmetrical melon that is firm and heavy for its size. Roll it around and check for the field spot (the yellowish spot where it rested on the ground while growing); it should be readily identifiable. Don't see one? That means the melon did not ripen on the vine. Lastly, and this was my dad's favorite method, give it a tap. In theory, a juicy melon should give a deep hollow sound, resonating like a tenor.

mid-summer
tomato and peach panzanella

SERVES 4 TO 6

Nothing says summer to me like my Mediterranean-meets-Georgia interpretation of panzanella, the popular Italian bread salad. I love to make this when the farmers' markets here are overflowing with the juiciest vine-ripened tomatoes and local peaches. Toasting the olive oil–drenched bread cubes helps them retain their texture and shape when added to the mix. Toss in some torn basil leaves and fresh mozzarella, and let the mixture sit a few minutes for those bread bits to soak up the juice. If you feel like playing up this number, mix in other stone fruits, like apricots, nectarines, or even plums!

½ loaf of ciabatta or other rustic Italian bread, cut into 1-inch cubes (roughly **4 heaping cups**)

Extra-virgin olive oil

Kosher salt and ground black pepper

3 or 4 vine-ripened medium tomatoes (about **1¼ pounds**), cored and cut into wedges

¼ cup red wine vinegar

2 large garlic cloves, minced

1 tablespoon fresh thyme leaves

½ teaspoon Dijon mustard

3 ripe peaches (about **1¼ pounds**), peeled, pitted, and cut into wedges

2 small shallots, thinly sliced into rounds

15 large fresh basil leaves, torn

4 to 6 ounces fresh baby mozzarella (optional)

1. Position a rack in the center of the oven. Preheat the oven to 400°F.

2. In a large bowl, combine the bread cubes with a generous amount of olive oil (about 3 tablespoons, or more as needed to coat the bread) and season with salt. Toss to make sure the bread is well coated.

3. Spread the bread cubes in a 13 × 18 × 1-inch sheet pan in a single layer (do not wash the bowl—save it for later) and bake for about 10 minutes, or until the edges get crispy and the centers turn golden but remain a bit chewy.

4. While the bread toasts, set a large colander over the bowl used for the bread. Place the tomato wedges in the colander, season well with salt, toss to coat, and set aside for a few minutes to allow the tomatoes to release their juices into the bowl.

5. Move the colander with the tomatoes to the sink for now and use the bowl with the tomato juice to make the dressing. To the tomato juices add the wine vinegar, ½ cup of the olive oil, the garlic, thyme, mustard, and a big pinch of black pepper (about ½ teaspoon). Whisk to combine.

6. Add the tomatoes to the bowl, then add the peaches, the toasted bread cubes, and the shallots, basil, and mozzarella (if using). Toss to combine. Allow the salad to sit for 20 minutes or so before serving.

greek horiatiki salad

SERVES 4 TO 6

A few years ago, I was lucky enough to visit the beautiful Greek Aegean islands of Patmos and Kos. Every part of the trip was special, but I absolutely fell in love with the friendly people and the homey, finger-licking food. I was already familiar with horiatiki, the iconic Greek salad, but it was in those small family-owned tavernas that my eyes were opened to how over-the-top delicious and surprisingly unfussy it is! This salad is all about colorful, sturdy vegetables cut into big geometric chunks (no wilted lettuce, thank you). Quality kalamata olives are a must, as is creamy sheep's milk feta, which is never crumbled but rather served in large hunks crowning the gorgeous mounds of fresh veggies.

4 vine-ripened medium tomatoes (about 1¼ **pounds**)

1 English (hothouse) cucumber, partially peeled (in stripes)

1 green bell pepper, cored and seeded

1 medium red onion

A handful of pitted whole kalamata olives

Kosher salt

½ **tablespoon** dried oregano, plus more if you like

Extra-virgin olive oil

2 **tablespoons** red wine vinegar

1 **block** (about **6 ounces**) high-quality Greek feta cheese

Crusty bread, for serving

1. Cut the tomatoes into wedges or large round slices—I like to do some of both.

2. Cut the cucumber in half lengthwise, then slice crosswise into ½-inch-thick half-moons. Slice the bell pepper into rings. Cut the red onion in half and thinly slice crosswise into half-moons (see Tip).

3. Place the tomatoes, cucumber, bell pepper, and onion in a large salad dish or shallow bowl. Add the olives. Season lightly with salt (the olives add natural saltiness) and the oregano.

4. Pour about ¼ cup of olive oil and the vinegar over the salad. Give everything a gentle toss to mix (do *not* overmix; this salad is not meant to be handled too much).

5. Break the feta into smaller blocks and arrange them on top of the salad. Add a sprinkle more of oregano, if desired. Serve with the crusty bread, if you like.

TIP

To tone down the harsh taste of the onion, you can put the slices in a bowl and cover with ice water and a bit of red wine vinegar to soak for 5 minutes or so. Drain before using in the salad.

roasted asparagus salad with cherry tomatoes, basil, and sherry vinaigrette

SERVES 4 TO 6

This pretty little salad is one of those dishes that's easy to make but delivers a big "wow" factor. It can be served at room temperature as a composed salad or a side dish. I like using thin green asparagus because it roasts quickly and makes the perfect bed for the bright tomato and basil mixture. For the cheese, I use Parmesan, but pecorino Romano or crumbled feta would be just as good; a vegetable peeler makes shaving the cheese fast and easy work.

Salad

1 pound thin asparagus, tough ends trimmed

Extra-virgin olive oil

Kosher salt

1 pint cherry or grape tomatoes, halved

15 large basil leaves, torn

⅓ **cup** shaved Parmesan cheese **(1 ounce)**, plus more as desired

Dressing

2 tablespoons sherry reserve vinegar or white wine vinegar

Extra-virgin olive oil

2 large garlic cloves, minced

1 teaspoon sumac

Kosher salt and ground black pepper

1. Position a rack in the center of the oven and preheat the oven to 400°F.

2. **Roast the asparagus:** Place the asparagus in a 13 × 18 × 1-inch sheet pan. Drizzle with 1 tablespoon of the olive oil (or enough to coat the stalks) and sprinkle with a big pinch of salt (about ½ teaspoon). Toss the asparagus to coat well with the oil and spread out in the pan in one single layer. Place in the oven and roast for about 15 minutes, or until the asparagus is tender to your liking. Remove from the oven and allow the asparagus to cool briefly.

3. **Make the dressing:** In a medium bowl, combine the vinegar, 2 to 3 tablespoons of the olive oil, the garlic, and sumac. Whisk in salt and black pepper to taste. Add the tomatoes to the dressing and toss to coat. Add the basil and gently toss again.

4. **Assemble the salad:** Arrange the roasted asparagus on a serving platter, top with the tomato and basil mixture and the dressing, then sprinkle with the shaved Parmesan.

two peas and a potato salad

SERVES 4 TO 6

I'm not much for the mayo-heavy potato salads, so this is my go-to version, amped up with chickpeas, green peas, fresh herbs, and capers, then tossed together in a garlicky Dijon dressing. I use a combination of Yukon Gold and red-skinned baby potatoes, but you can make this with just larger Yukon Gold potatoes as well—but make sure to quarter them before boiling. Potato salad is one of those dishes you should make 1 to 2 hours before serving and let sit in the fridge to build flavor. Heck, you can make it one day ahead and keep it in a covered container in the fridge.

Salad

1½ pounds baby potatoes, halved (or quartered, if large)

Kosher salt

1 cup frozen peas

1 (15-ounce) can chickpeas, drained and rinsed

⅓ cup finely chopped red onion

½ cup roughly chopped fresh flat-leaf parsley

⅓ cup roughly chopped fresh dill fronds

2 tablespoons drained capers

Dijon Dressing

⅓ cup extra-virgin olive oil

2 tablespoons white wine vinegar

2 teaspoons Dijon mustard

1 large garlic clove, minced

1 teaspoon Aleppo pepper flakes

½ teaspoon sumac

½ teaspoon ground coriander

Ground black pepper

1. **Boil the potatoes:** Place the potatoes in a large saucepan, cover with cold water by 2 inches, and stir in about 1 teaspoon salt. Bring to a boil, then reduce the heat to a gentle simmer. Cook the potatoes for 15 minutes, or until just tender but still somewhat firm. Add the frozen peas and chickpeas and cook for another 7 minutes, or until the potatoes are cooked through and tender but not mushy (you can test by poking a potato with a fork or pairing knife; it should go through without resistance). Drain well.

2. **Make the dressing:** In a large bowl, place the olive oil, the vinegar, Dijon mustard, garlic, Aleppo pepper, sumac, coriander, and a big pinch of black pepper (about ½ teaspoon). Whisk to combine.

3. **Assemble the salad:** Add the potatoes, peas, and chickpeas to the bowl. Season lightly with salt and toss to coat with the dressing. Add the red onion, parsley, dill, and capers. Give everything one more toss to combine.

4. Cover the bowl with plastic wrap and chill the potato salad for 1 hour to allow the flavors to meld. Remove from the fridge and let it rest at room temperature for about 20 minutes before serving.

not-your-deli's tuna salad

**SERVES 8 AS PART OF A MEZZE WITH PITA CHIPS,
OR MAKES ENOUGH FILLING FOR 4 SANDWICHES**

This sassy tuna salad truly defies expectations. First, it ditches heavy mayonnaise in favor of a zippy Dijon-lime dressing (yes, I'm a big fan of Dijon). Loads of fresh herbs, crunchy veggies, and briny kalamata olives add dazzle and dimension. And I am picky about my tuna; I mostly turn to responsibly caught low-mercury tuna. I'm not embarrassed to admit that tuna salad–stuffed pita pockets are sometimes what's for dinner!

Dijon Dressing

2½ **teaspoon**s Dijon mustard

Grated zest of **1** lime, plus juice of 2 limes (about ¼ **cup** juice)

⅓ **cup** extra-virgin olive oil

1 **teaspoon** sumac

Kosher salt and ground black pepper

½ **teaspoon** red pepper flakes (optional)

Tuna Salad

3 **(5-ounce)** cans quality albacore tuna, drained (preferably packed in olive oil)

2 celery stalks, finely chopped

½ English (hothouse) cucumber, finely chopped, or peeled and seeded garden cuke

4 **or 5** small radishes, finely diced

3 scallions, trimmed, white and green parts finely chopped

½ medium red onion, chopped

½ **cup** pitted and halved kalamata olives

1 **cup** chopped flat-leaf parsley

½ **cup** fresh mint leaves, torn

1. **Make the dressing:** In a small bowl, whisk together the mustard, lime zest, and lime juice. Add the olive oil, the sumac, about ½ teaspoon each of the salt and black pepper, and the red pepper flakes (if using), and whisk until well blended.

2. **Make the salad:** In a large salad bowl, place the tuna, celery, cucumber, radishes, scallions, red onion, olives, parsley, and mint leaves. Mix gently with a wooden spoon.

3. Pour the dressing over the tuna salad. Mix again to make sure the salad is evenly coated with the dressing. Taste and adjust the seasoning as needed.

4. Serve the salad immediately or cover and refrigerate for just a few minutes to allow the flavors to meld.

the smoothest, fluffiest hummus

MAKES ABOUT 3 CUPS; SERVES 6

Something magical happens when you blend chickpeas with earthy, rich tahini. But my mother-in-law Dina, who made tubs of it almost daily, has some tricks up her sleeve for making the best hummus I've ever tasted. First, you must cook the chickpeas until very tender (even canned chickpeas can use a little simmer!)—a little baking soda aids in softening the skins and makes them easier to peel. Some think that peeling the chickpeas is an unnecessary step, but what a difference it makes! And, yes, adding ice cubes via the top of the food processor while it's running is the final key to whipping up this puree into a consistency as smooth and fluffy as freshly churned ice cream.

1¼ cups dried chickpeas

1½ teaspoons baking soda

1 or 2 large garlic cloves, minced

3 or 4 ice cubes

⅓ cup tahini paste, plus more as desired

Kosher salt

Juice of **1** large lemon (about **¼ cup**), plus more as desired

Hot water (optional)

Extra-virgin olive oil

Sumac

Warm pita bread, for serving

1. Place the chickpeas in a large bowl and cover with at least 3 cups water (the chickpeas should be submerged by 3 or 4 inches). Soak overnight.

2. The next day, drain the chickpeas and place them in a medium pot. Pour enough cool water into the pot to cover the chickpeas by about 2 inches. Bring to a boil over high heat, then reduce the heat and let simmer anywhere from 40 minutes to 1 hour (the cooking time will depend on their freshness), until the chickpeas are cooked through and very tender; as they cook, skim off any foam that forms on top. Drain the chickpeas. Set aside a few spoonfuls of the cooked chickpeas for serving later and return the rest to the pot.

3. Add enough hot water to the pot to cover the cooked chickpeas. Add the baking soda and set aside for 20 minutes (this helps loosen the skins).

4. Drain the chickpeas in a colander. Take a handful of chickpeas at a time and rub them between your hands under running water to remove the skins, then place the peeled chickpeas in the bowl of a food processor fitted with the multipurpose blade. (Don't worry if you don't remove all the skins, and if you skip this step, your hummus will still taste good; it will just have more of a rustic texture.)

5. Add the garlic to the food processor, then puree the chickpeas until a powder-like mixture forms. While the processor is running, add the ice cubes, tahini, ½ teaspoon salt, and the lemon juice through the top opening. Blend until it is the consistency of soft-serve ice cream, 4 to 5 minutes.

6. Taste the hummus and if needed, add more salt, tahini, or lemon juice until you reach the taste you're after. Transfer the hummus to a small serving bowl or plate, and use the back of a spoon to make a wide well in the center. Add a generous drizzle (about 2 tablespoons) of the olive oil, sprinkle to taste with the sumac, and add the reserved chickpeas to the middle. Enjoy with warm pita bread. (The hummus can be refrigerated in an airtight container for up to 3 days.)

VARIATION

Shortcut: Canned-Chickpea Hummus

If you don't have the time to soak and cook dried chickpeas, you can use 3 cups of canned chickpeas that have been drained and rinsed. Even though canned chickpeas do not need cooking, boiling them in water to cover by at least 2 inches for 20 to 30 minutes will soften them and produce a creamier hummus (this is a cheater's way to imitate the results of cooking chickpeas from scratch). From there, peel the chickpeas and follow the recipe as written.

meanest loaded hummus dip

MAKES ABOUT 3 CUPS; SERVES 6

When you top creamy hummus with boldly seasoned minced lamb, chopped tomatoes and red onions, plenty of parsley, and a handful of toasted pine nuts—well, that is just an epic mezze situation! But I'll unapologetically confess that there have been many times I served this very layered hummus dip for dinner. Why not? For best results, start with The Smoothest, Fluffiest Hummus (page 60), but in a pinch you can use a tub of quality store-bought hummus (this is a no-judgment zone).

Spiced Meat Topping

Extra-virgin olive oil

1 small red onion, coarsely chopped

½ large green bell pepper, cored, seeded, and coarsely chopped

2 large garlic cloves, minced

8 ounces ground lamb

Kosher salt and black pepper

1 teaspoon ground allspice

½ teaspoon sumac

¼ teaspoon ground cinnamon

½ cup canned tomato sauce

For Serving

The Smoothest, Fluffiest Hummus (page 60), or 12 ounces quality store-bought hummus

Extra-virgin olive oil

1 Roma (plum) tomato, chopped

½ cup chopped flat-leaf parsley

3 tablespoons fresh pomegranate seeds (arils)

3 tablespoons toasted pine nuts (optional)

Warm pita bread or homemade pita chips (page 91)

1. **Make the topping:** In a medium nonstick skillet, heat 1 tablespoon of olive oil over medium-high heat until shimmering. Add most of the onion, reserving 1 to 2 tablespoons for later. Add the green pepper and garlic, then cook for 5 to 7 minutes, stirring regularly, until vegetables are softened.

2. Add the lamb and cook, stirring often, about 8 minutes, until fully browned. Carefully drain any excess fat from the skillet by pushing the meat to one side and carefully tilting the skillet in the opposite direction over a heat-safe bowl (to discard when cooled). Return the skillet to the stove and season the meat with a big pinch of salt and black pepper (about ½ teaspoon each), then add the allspice, sumac, and cinnamon. Stir in the tomato sauce and cook for another 4 minutes or so, stirring occasionally. Taste and adjust the seasoning.

3. **Serve the hummus:** Spread the hummus in a wide serving bowl or on a small platter. Drizzle with about 2 tablespoons of olive oil. Top with the spiced meat, then add the tomatoes, parsley, and remaining onion. Sprinkle with the pomegranate seeds and the pine nuts (if using). Serve immediately with warm pita, flatbread, or pita chips.

chunky sardine spread with cilantro, lime, and shallots

MAKES ABOUT 2 ½ CUPS; SERVES 6

Canned sardines are generally accessible and relatively affordable, but this is one case where, as your friend, I urge you to pay a little bit more for quality, wild-caught sardines; you'll get better flavor and fewer preservatives (always compare labels).

I adore the pungent flavor of omega 3–rich sardines packed in extra-virgin olive oil. Here, I break those little fish up (bones and all) and toss them with a few fresh herbs, some olives, and a good squeeze of lime juice. This recipe makes a punchy spread for some warm crostini, or could even be tossed with toasted orzo for a light meal.

2 (4-ounce) cans sardines packed in extra-virgin olive oil (such as Wild Planet or King Oscar)

1 cup roughly chopped fresh cilantro

½ large red bell pepper, cored and chopped

2 scallions, trimmed, white and green parts roughly chopped

6 to 10 green Castelvetrano olives, pitted and chopped

Kosher salt and ground black pepper

Red pepper flakes (optional)

Juice of **2** large limes (about ¼ **cup**)

Crostini, for serving

1. Place the sardines and about 1 tablespoon of the canning oil in a medium bowl. Using a fork, break up the sardines into smaller chunks.

2. Fold in the cilantro, bell pepper, scallions, and olives. Season to taste with salt and black pepper, and if you like heat, a bit of red pepper flakes. Add the lime juice. Mix to combine.

3. Serve over crostini for an appetizer or toss with orzo for a small meal.

citrus-avocado dip
with walnuts, feta, and herbs

MAKES ABOUT 2 HEAPING CUPS; SERVES 6

You wouldn't expect to see something that looks like guacamole on a Middle Eastern mezze menu. And even as I write about it, I am experiencing a little guilt—like I'm cheating on my favorite creamy hummus! But one taste of this seemingly out-of-place dip should make it clear why it's perfectly welcome at this party. Oranges are the first hint of a Mediterranean connection, and they play together flawlessly with their avocado co-star: one is bright and juicy, and the other is rich and velvety. Feta, walnuts, and fresh herbs seal the deal! Serve this extra-sassy, flavor-packed dip with either your favorite chips or crostini, or pile it on top of warm toast (everyone loves an avocado toast!), or serve it as a fun side dish with some grilled fish (page 180).

2 navel oranges, peeled and
  diced

2 large avocados (or 3 smaller),
  pitted, peeled, and diced

½ **cup** finely chopped red onion

½ **cup** finely chopped fresh
  cilantro

½ **cup** finely chopped fresh mint
  leaves

½ **cup** coarsely chopped
  walnuts, toasted

Kosher salt and ground black
  pepper

¾ **teaspoon** sumac

Pinch of cayenne pepper

Juice of **1** large lime (about
  2 tablespoons)

Extra-virgin olive oil

1 to 2 ounces Greek feta cheese,
  crumbled (**¼ to ½ cup**)

Chips or crostini, for serving

1.   Place the oranges, avocado, red onion, cilantro, mint, and walnuts in a large bowl. Season with salt and pepper (about ½ teaspoon each), the sumac, and cayenne.

2.   Add the lime juice and 2 tablespoons of the olive oil. Toss gently to combine. Top with the feta and serve with chips or crostini.

matbucha

SERVES 6

Matbucha, pronounced mat-BOO-kha, is a cooked salad—almost more of a dip—with Maghrebi origins. I'm obsessed with this comforting blend of roasted peppers, slow-cooked tomatoes, and warm spices such as paprika and coriander; once you try it, I think you'll be, too. Making it the traditional way can be a long ordeal, and instead of investing hours in peeling fresh tomatoes and cooking them down to their concentrated essence, I substitute canned San Marzano tomatoes, which have a rich, sweet flavor that shines in this dish. Using both sweet and hot peppers, and roasting them over an open flame, adds subtle layers of spice and smokiness. Of course, this is wonderful with pita or warm bread, but try tossing it with rice or couscous, as well—and a couple tablespoons of matbucha over scrambled eggs is never a bad idea!

Extra-virgin olive oil

5 large garlic cloves, minced

1 (28-ounce) can whole peeled tomatoes, preferably San Marzano, with juices

1 teaspoon sweet paprika

1 teaspoon ground coriander

¾ teaspoon Aleppo pepper flakes

½ teaspoon ground cumin

Kosher salt and ground black pepper

1 large green bell pepper

1 large red bell pepper

1 or 2 medium jalapeño peppers

Easy Homemade Pita Bread (page 99) or flatbread, for serving

1. In a large saucepan, heat ⅓ cup of olive oil over medium heat until shimmering. Add the garlic and cook, stirring constantly, until it turns fragrant and golden, about 30 seconds. Add the tomatoes and their juices. Season with the paprika, coriander, Aleppo pepper, cumin, and a good dash of salt and black pepper.

2. Break up the tomatoes a bit with a wooden spoon. Raise the heat to medium-high and bring the tomatoes to a boil for 3 minutes or so, then reduce the heat to medium-low and allow the tomatoes to simmer, stirring occasionally, until the liquid has reduced and the tomatoes have cooked down some, about 20 minutes.

3. Meanwhile, roast the bell peppers and jalapeños according to one of the methods described on page 68. When cool enough to handle, peel away the charred skin, remove the stems and seeds (if you like a little kick to your matbucha, leave the jalapeño seeds), and roughly chop.

4. Add the chopped bell peppers and jalapeños to the tomato mixture and simmer, stirring occasionally, until the mixture is cooked down and beautifully concentrated, another 15 to 20 minutes. Allow the matbucha to come to room temperature before serving with pita or flatbread or storing in the fridge.

Recipe continues

HOW TO ROAST PEPPERS

GAS STOVE METHOD: Turn a burner or two to high and set each pepper directly on the flame. Use a pair of tongs to turn the peppers until the skins are completely blackened on all sides and the peppers feel soft, about 15 minutes. Transfer the peppers to a large bowl, cover with plastic wrap for 5 to 10 minutes, then slip off the skins.

GRILL METHOD: Heat a gas grill to high or prepare a charcoal grill for direct heat and set the peppers over direct heat. Transfer the peppers to a large bowl, cover with plastic wrap for 5 to 10 minutes, then slip off the skins.

BROILER METHOD: Set an oven rack about 4 inches below the heat source. Arrange the peppers in a baking dish or sheet pan large enough to hold them (make sure there is space between them so they don't steam). Place the peppers in the oven and broil, using tongs to flip them from one side to another, until blackened and soft, 20 to 25 minutes. Transfer the peppers to a large bowl, cover with plastic wrap for 5 to 10 minutes, then slip off the skins.

fig, walnut, and olive tapenade

MAKES 1 PACKED CUP; SERVES 4

Tapenade is a classic olive-based spread from Provence that sounds like it should be a fancy hors d'oeuvre, yet it's so darn easy to make. This version was inspired by a handful of dried figs that sat in my pantry begging to be used. After plumping them up in hot water for a few minutes, I threw the softened figs into the food processor along with some olives, walnuts, and other staples I had on hand. I whizzed them into a savory snack that's a little salty, a little sweet, and hard to stop eating!

½ **cup** (packed) dried Mission figs (about **3 ounces**)

½ **cup** (packed) pitted kalamata olives

½ **cup** walnut halves

1 small garlic clove, chopped

Juice of ½ lemon (about **2 tablespoons**), plus more if needed

Extra-virgin olive oil

Kosher salt and ground black pepper

Crackers or crostini, to serve

1. Place the figs in a small bowl and cover them with boiling water. Let soak for 5 to 10 minutes, until they are soft. Drain, remove any tough stems, and roughly chop.

2. In a small food processor fitted with the multipurpose blade, place the softened figs and add the olives, walnuts, garlic, lemon juice, and ⅓ cup of olive oil. Season lightly with salt and black pepper. Run the processor for 2 to 3 minutes, pausing to scrape down the side of the bowl as needed, until the mixture is a paste. Taste and adjust the lemon juice and seasoning.

3. Spoon the tapenade into a small serving bowl and accompany with your favorite crackers or crostini. (Tapenade can be refrigerated in an airtight container or mason jar for up to 2 weeks.)

savory baked feta

SERVES 6

Baking a block of high-quality feta is a real treat the world finally discovered (thank you, TikTok)! My Greek friends call it feta bouyiourdi. The blast of heat from your oven will not fully melt the feta, but it will transform it into a luscious spread that's absolutely addictive. It makes a festive presentation when baked with bright veggies and savory herbs, and when bathed in good olive oil. For serving, all you need is some crusty bread.

½ medium red onion, sliced ¼ inch thick

½ large green bell pepper, cored, seeded, and sliced into ¼-inch-thick rounds

½ **cup** halved cherry tomatoes

6 kalamata olives, pitted and halved

2 **teaspoons** dried oregano

2½ **teaspoons** red pepper flakes (optional)

3 **or 4** fresh thyme sprigs (optional)

Extra-virgin olive oil

1 (8-ounce) block high-quality Greek feta cheese, preferably packed in brine

Fresh mint leaves, for garnish (optional)

Crusty bread (see Tip)

1. Position a rack in the center of the oven. Preheat the oven to 400°F.

2. Arrange the onion, bell pepper, cherry tomatoes, and olives on the bottom of a 6- to 8-inch skillet or baking dish. Sprinkle with 1 teaspoon of the oregano and a big pinch of red pepper flakes (if using), then add some of the thyme sprigs. Drizzle with 2 tablespoons or so of the olive oil.

3. Place the feta on top and season the feta with the remaining dried teaspoon oregano, red pepper flakes (if using), and thyme sprigs. Drizzle another 2 or 3 tablespoons of olive oil on top and brush the sides of the feta with some more of the oil.

4. Set the baking dish in a large sheet pan that can hold it (this makes it easier to handle) and place in the oven. Bake for 25 to 30 minutes, until the cheese softens and gains a bit of color. If you'd like a little more color, run it under the broiler for a minute or two, watching very carefully to make sure the cheese doesn't burn.

5. Serve with crusty bread or the pita chips.

TIP
If you're serving this with sliced bread, give the bread slices a brush of extra-virgin olive oil, spread them on a sheet pan, and toast in the oven briefly, turning over partway through, while the feta is baking.

eggplant fatteh
with garlicky tahini-yogurt sauce

**SERVES 8 OR MORE AS PART OF MEZZE, OR
4 TO 6 AS A VEGETARIAN MAIN COURSE**

This popular Middle Eastern dish is another fun way to use crispy pita chips, layered with melty roasted eggplant cubes, pine nuts, chickpeas, and a creamy tahini-yogurt sauce. At my house, we call these "Mediterranean nachos." You can serve this eggplant fatteh as a vegetarian main dish or as an appetizer for a small crowd.

Eggplant Fatteh

2 globe eggplants (about
    1 pound each)

Kosher salt

2 **(6-inch)** pocket-style pita
    loaves

Extra-virgin olive oil

¼ **cup** pine nuts

¼ **cup** slivered almonds

1 teaspoon sumac

1 teaspoon Aleppo pepper flakes

½ **cup** fresh pomegranate seeds
    (arils; see page 29)

1 **(15-ounce)** can chickpeas,
    drained

Tahini-Yogurt Sauce

1 **cup** plain whole-milk regular
    yogurt (not Greek)

3 **tablespoons** tahini

2 or 3 large garlic cloves,
    crushed

Juice of ½ large lemon
    (**2 tablespoons**), plus more
    as desired

1 **cup** torn fresh mint leaves

Kosher salt

1. **Begin the fatteh:** Trim and partially peel the eggplants so the skin is striped. Cut the eggplants into 1-inch cubes. Toss the eggplant with about 1½ teaspoons salt and let sit in a colander for about 20 minutes while you prepare the rest of the ingredients.

2. Position a rack in the center of the oven. Preheat the oven to 425°F.

3. Split the pita into single layers and put them directly on the oven rack to toast for 3 to 5 minutes, until lightly browned and crispy, watching carefully that they don't burn. Set aside until cool enough to handle, then break into smaller pieces.

4. In a small skillet, heat 1 teaspoon of the olive oil over medium heat. Add the pine nuts and toast until lightly browned, 2 to 3 minutes, shaking the pan occasionally, then use a slotted spoon to transfer them to a paper towel to drain.

5. Add the slivered almonds to the skillet and toast over medium heat, tossing occasionally, until lightly browned, 2 to 3 minutes. Drain on the same paper towel as the pine nuts.

6. **Prepare the sauce:** In a small bowl, combine the yogurt, tahini, garlic, lemon juice, and half the mint. Season with big pinch of salt (about ½ teaspoon). Whisk until smooth and spreadable. (If it seems too thick, thin with a little more lemon juice or water.)

7. **Roast the eggplant:** Using a paper towel, pat the eggplant dry. Scatter the eggplant cubes in a 13 × 18 × 1-inch sheet pan in a single layer. Drizzle with ¼ cup olive oil (more if needed) and toss until well coated. Roast the eggplant for 20 to 25 minutes, until tender and charred in some parts, tossing once midway through, making sure the eggplant cubes remain in a single layer. Remove from the oven, sprinkle with the sumac and Aleppo pepper, and toss to coat.

8. **Assemble the fatteh:** Place the crispy pita pieces on a rimmed serving platter or in a shallow casserole dish. Layer the rest as follows: roasted eggplant, half the pomegranate seeds, the chickpeas, and half the toasted nuts. Add dollops of the tahini-yogurt sauce and smooth the top with the back of a spoon. Finish with the remaining mint, nuts, and pomegranate seeds. Add a drizzle of olive oil, if you like. Serve at room temperature.

saucy mini soutzoukakia with bell peppers

SERVES 6 TO 8 AS PART OF MEZZE, OR 4 AS A MAIN COURSE

Say it with me: soo-tzoo-KAH-kyah! These tasty meatballs also go by another name, *Izmir kofte*. In this recipe, they are emboldened with onions, garlic, parsley, and a unique spice combo, the star of which is cumin. But Yiayia Helen, who I met at an Atlanta Greek festival, taught me one secret ingredient that yields the juiciest meatballs: toasted bread soaked in water (or milk). As it turns out, my mom does the same. Works like a charm! When I make soutzoukakia for dinner, I shape them into giant ovals and serve them over vermicelli rice (see page 161). But these smaller, saucy soutzoukakia are perfect for a hearty mezze.

Mini Meatballs

1 slice bread (**1 ounce**), toasted medium brown

⅓ **cup** water

1 **pound** lean ground beef

1 small yellow onion, finely chopped

3 garlic cloves, minced

1 large egg, lightly beaten

2 **teaspoons** ground cumin

½ **teaspoon** ground cinnamon

1 teaspoon dried oregano

½ **cup** finely chopped fresh flat-leaf parsley

Kosher salt and ground black pepper

1 **tablespoon** extra-virgin olive oil, plus more for baking dish

Chunky Tomato Sauce

2 to 3 tablespoons extra-virgin olive oil

6 mini bell peppers (**6 ounces** total), any color, cored, seeded, and thinly sliced crosswise

1. **Begin the meatballs:** To a small bowl add the toasted bread and cover with the water; let soak until very soft, about 10 minutes. Squeeze the liquid from the bread and discard the water.

2. Crumble the soaked bread into a large bowl. Add the beef, onion, garlic, egg, cumin, cinnamon, oregano, and parsley. Add a big pinch of salt and black pepper (about ½ teaspoon each). Drizzle with 1 tablespoon of the olive oil. Knead the meat mixture until well combined. Cover the bowl with plastic wrap and place in the refrigerator to chill.

3. Position a rack in the center of the oven and preheat the oven to 400°F.

4. **Make the sauce:** In a medium saucepan or large skillet, heat the olive oil over medium-high heat until shimmering. Add the bell peppers and cook, tossing regularly, until the peppers gain a little bit of color, 3 to 5 minutes. Transfer the peppers to a medium bowl.

5. Reduce the heat to medium, then add the onion and garlic and cook, stirring regularly and adjusting the heat so the garlic softens but does not burn, 2 to 3 minutes. Add the wine and cook until reduced by about half, then add the tomatoes, cinnamon, and cumin. Season lightly with salt and black pepper to taste. Bring to a boil, then turn the heat to low and simmer, partly covered, for 15 minutes. Add the cooked bell peppers to the skillet and stir. Taste and adjust the seasoning to your liking.

1 small yellow onion, finely
chopped

2 large garlic cloves, minced

½ **cup** dry red wine

1 **(16-ounce)** can diced tomatoes
with juices

½ **teaspoon** ground cinnamon

½ **teaspoon** ground cumin

Kosher salt and ground black
pepper

Crusty breads, for serving

6. Form and cook the meatballs: Lightly brush the bottom
of a 9 × 13-inch baking dish with a little olive oil.

7. Take the meat mixture out of the fridge. Wet your hands
and scoop out portions of 1 to 2 tablespoons and form
the mixture into small oval-shaped meatballs. You should
make 18 or so, depending on size. Arrange the meatballs in
the baking dish.

8. When the sauce is ready, carefully pour or spoon it
over the meatballs. Place the baking dish in the oven and
bake until the meatballs are well cooked through, about
30 minutes. Check partway through to make sure the sauce
is not dry, and if needed, add a little water to the bottom
of the dish. Remove the meatballs from the oven and finish
with a generous drizzle of olive oil. Serve with assorted
crusty breads.

tangy marinated eggplant

SERVES 6 AS PART OF MEZZE OR AS A VEGETARIAN SIDE DISH

Ever since I was a little girl I've loved my mama's fried eggplant, but this lighter roasted version, spiked with a garlicky lime and vinegar dressing, briny capers, and finely chopped jalapeños, is right up there with it. And, yes, the wisest thing to do is to dress the roasted eggplant wedges while they are still hot, so they'll absorb as much flavor as possible, and then allow them to sit and marinate at room temperature for a few minutes and up to one hour before serving. I use baby eggplants (or Italian eggplants) here, but if not available, use the smallest globe eggplants you can find (which have fewer seeds and are less bitter-tasting). When buying eggplants, also check the condition of the stem end; it should look fresh and green.

Extra-virgin olive oil

3 mini eggplants (about **1 pound**), trimmed and cut into wedges

Kosher salt

3 or 4 large garlic cloves

1 or 2 jalapeño peppers, finely chopped (seeds removed for less heat)

1 tablespoon drained capers

Juice of **2** large limes (about **¼ cup**)

1 tablespoon distilled white vinegar

¾ teaspoon sumac

¼ cup chopped fresh mint leaves

1. Position one rack in the center of the oven and another rack 4 to 5 inches from the heat source. Preheat the oven to 400°F. Lightly brush a 13 × 18 × 1-inch sheet pan with a little of the olive oil.

2. Place the eggplant, flesh side up, on a work surface or large tray. Season generously with salt (about 1½ teaspoons) and set aside to "sweat" for about 20 minutes while the oven is preheating.

3. Using paper towels, pat the eggplant dry, removing excess water and salt. Arrange the eggplant in the sheet pan, flesh side facing up. Brush generously with about 3 tablespoons of the olive oil (or more if needed to coat all the pieces), and roast for 25 to 30 minutes, until fork-tender. For a little more color (which I highly recommend), set the oven to broil and place the eggplant on the top rack under the heat source for the last 1 to 2 minutes, watching carefully (it should gain a nice deep, golden-brown color but it should not burn).

4. While the eggplant roasts, pound the garlic and jalapeños into a chunky paste for the dressing using a mortar and pestle. (Or, mince the garlic and jalapeño as finely as you can and transfer to a medium bowl.) Add the capers, lime juice, vinegar, and 3 tablespoons of olive oil; whisk to combine.

5. As soon as the eggplant is cooked through, carefully transfer the pieces to a large bowl. Sprinkle with the sumac, then pour the vinaigrette over the eggplant and add the fresh mint. Using a pair of tongs, give the hot eggplant a gentle toss to coat. Set aside to marinate for 20 minutes, then serve at room temperature.

pan-grilled zucchini with dukkah and fresh herbs

SERVES 4 AS PART OF MEZZE OR AS A VEGETARIAN SIDE DISH

Two things take these simple pan-grilled zucchini to flavor-bomb level: nutty, spicy dukkah and a lime-tahini sauce. Together, they add richness and depth of flavor, finished with just enough brightness from a good squeeze of lime juice. You'll want the zucchini here to have some char, while maintaining a bite.

3 medium zucchini (or summer squash), trimmed and cut on the diagonal into ½-inch discs

Kosher salt

Extra-virgin olive oil

Juice of ½ lime (about **1 tablespoon**), plus more as needed

2 tablespoons roughly chopped fresh flat-leaf parsley

4 to 5 tablespoons Dukkah (page 282)

Lime-Tahini Sauce (page 290), for drizzling

1. Place the zucchini slices in a large bowl and season with a big pinch of salt (about ½ teaspoon). Drizzle with 2 tablespoons of the olive oil and toss to coat.

2. Heat a large cast-iron pan or griddle over medium-high heat. When the griddle is hot, add the zucchini in one layer (do this in batches, if you need to). Cook on each side for about 4 minutes, until lightly browned and the zucchini has softened a bit but still holds its shape.

3. Transfer the zucchini back to the bowl, and add the lime juice and parsley. Toss to combine. Sprinkle with 2 tablespoons of the dukkah and toss; taste, adding more lime juice and olive oil, if you like.

4. Arrange the zucchini on a serving platter and sprinkle some more dukkah on top. Drizzle with the lime-tahini sauce and serve.

spanish-style garlic shrimp with potatoes

SERVES 4 TO 6 AS MEZZE, OR 3 AS A LIGHT MAIN COURSE

Gambas al ajillo, or Spanish garlic shrimp, is one of my favorite quick tapas! I mean, big, juicy shrimp swimming in a tangy, garlicky olive oil sauce—what could be better? When I posted the shrimp recipe on Instagram, Bruce, who had been following my feed, shared a variation from his trip to Barcelona, where some local restaurants add cubes of boiled potatoes. So, here's to Bruce for the brilliant addition of tender potatoes! I used to serve it with neatly sliced toasted bread, but I've since discovered that hefty rustic bread, roughly torn does a better job of soaking up the tasty sauce.

Large, plump shrimp work best for this recipe. Still, even the largest shrimp will cook fast, so watch them carefully to avoid overcooking. The key is to remove the shrimp from the heat as soon as the flesh turns pearly-pink. And remember too that, in this case, the shrimp will continue to cook in the hot sauce after you remove it from heat.

2 or 3 medium Yukon Gold or other yellow potatoes, peeled and cut into cubes or small chunks

Kosher salt

1 pound large to jumbo shrimp (thawed, if frozen), peeled and deveined

½ cup extra-virgin olive oil

10 large garlic cloves, roughly chopped

1 teaspoon red pepper flakes (or to taste)

1 teaspoon sweet paprika

2 tablespoons dry sherry or dry white wine

Juice of ½ large lemon (about **2 tablespoons**)

½ cup roughly chopped fresh flat-leaf parsley

Crusty bread, for serving

1. Place the potatoes in a medium saucepan and cover with cold water by an inch or two. Add about 1 teaspoon of salt. Bring to a boil over high heat, then turn the heat to low and simmer until the potatoes are cooked through and tender enough to be pierced with a fork without resistance, 5 to 8 minutes, depending on their size. Drain the potatoes.

2. Pat the shrimp dry and season lightly with salt. Toss well.

3. In a large nonstick skillet, heat the olive oil over medium heat until shimmering. Add the garlic and red pepper flakes. Cook over medium heat, stirring frequently, until the garlic begins to turn golden, 30 seconds to 1 minute.

4. Add the shrimp and the paprika. Cook, tossing frequently, just until the shrimp turn pink, up to 3 minutes or so, depending on size. Immediately remove the skillet from the heat.

5. Add the sherry or wine and lemon juice and stir. Add the boiled potatoes and stir to combine. Sprinkle and toss with the parsley.

6. Transfer the shrimp and potatoes with their sauce to a serving bowl. Serve immediately, with crusty bread.

sizzling shrimp and chorizo

SERVES 4 TO 6 AS MEZZE

This dish came together on a whim when our good friends Molly and Charlie dropped by for dinner one night, and I needed to rustle up an appetizer on the spot. Luckily, I happened to have a bag of frozen small shrimp and some dried Spanish chorizo on hand. I quickly chopped up a bunch of garlic and a scallion, and threw them together in a sauté pan with a big glug of olive oil and a splash of the wine we were drinking. Then I showered the sizzling finished dish with chopped cilantro. My little crowd of critics enjoyed this dish so much that I decided to put it in the book for those times you need something super quick.

2½ ounces dried Spanish chorizo, chopped into small bits

3 tablespoons extra-virgin olive oil

1 scallion, trimmed, white and green parts thinly sliced

4 or 5 large garlic cloves, minced

½ cup dry white wine

1 pound small shrimp (thawed, if frozen), peeled and deveined

¼ cup roughly chopped fresh cilantro

Crusty bread wedges, for serving

1. Heat a large nonstick skillet over medium-high heat. When hot, add the chorizo and cook, stirring occasionally, until it has some color and crisps up a bit, 3 to 5 minutes.

2. Add the olive oil, scallion, and garlic. Stir for 30 seconds or so, then reduce the heat to medium and add the wine. Cook for 2 to 3 minutes, until the wine reduces by about half.

3. Add the shrimp and cook, stirring, just until the shrimp turn pink, 2 to 3 more minutes, being careful not to overcook them.

4. Turn the heat off, add the cilantro, and stir. Serve with crusty bread wedges.

two-bean makhlouta
with bulgur and lamb

SERVES 6 TO 8 AS MEZZE, OR 4 AS A MAIN COURSE

Makhlouta (pronounced makh-LOO-tah, and yes, you make the *kh* sound as if you were clearing your throat) literally means "mixed" or "mixture" in Arabic. It is a hearty and warmly spiced winter dish from the mountains of Lebanon that combines several grains and legumes, and sometimes meat. I added diced bits of lamb here, which are totally optional, but the lamb makes this dish even more hearty and satisfying. More traditional makhlouta recipes are brothy, more like a grain stew (not this version—mine is more of a pilaf with beans and bulgur) and most call for cumin, which is an important flavor-maker, but I do like to add a little allspice mainly to season the lamb.

Really, makhlouta is a meal in its own right, and I love it with a side of Romaine, Arugula, and Mint Fattoush Salad (page 46). The two dishes together are like a flavor party in your mouth!

Remember to use coarse (#3 grind) bulgur here. The finer kind will not work in this recipe.

⅔ **cup** coarse bulgur wheat #3

Extra-virgin olive oil

8 ounces boneless lamb shoulder or leg, trimmed of fat and diced very small

Kosher salt and freshly ground black pepper

¾ **teaspoon** ground allspice

1 large yellow onion, finely chopped

1 or 2 large garlic cloves, minced

3 tablespoons tomato paste

1½ **cups** water

1 (15-ounce) can red kidney beans, drained and rinsed

1 (15-ounce) can chickpeas, drained and rinsed

1½ **teaspoons** ground cumin

Roughly chopped fresh flat-leaf parsley, for garnish

1. Rinse the bulgur well and put it in a medium bowl. Cover with water and let soak for about 15 minutes. Drain well.

2. In a large saucepan with a lid, heat 1 tablespoon of the olive oil over medium-high heat until shimmering. Add the lamb. Season with a big pinch of salt and black pepper (about ½ teaspoon each), and the allspice. Brown the meat, stirring frequently, 5 to 7 minutes. Transfer to a plate.

3. To the same saucepan add 2 more tablespoons of the olive oil. Add the onion and garlic and cook over medium heat, stirring frequently, until the onion softens and turns yellow.

4. Add the tomato paste and water, stir, then add the kidney beans and chickpeas. Stir in the browned meat and the bulgur. Add the cumin and season with another big pinch of salt and black pepper (about ½ teaspoon each).

5. Bring the mixture to a boil, then turn the heat to low. Cover the saucepan and cook until the liquid has been fully absorbed and the bulgur is cooked through and tender, 15 to 20 minutes. Garnish with the parsley and serve.

fatayer
(spinach and onion hand pie triangles)

MAKES 18 TO 20 HAND PIES

Mama Dina (by now you must know that's my mother-in-law) makes these little Middle Eastern pastries—triangles of yeast-risen dough stuffed with a tangy mixture of sumac-seasoned spinach and onions—by the dozens. Her freezer is stocked with big bags of these savory treats for whenever any of her five adult "kids" stop by. As we were getting ready to head to the airport the last time we visited her, she handed me a bag of about 40 frozen pies. "Here, for the road," she said with a smile, and I stuffed them into my backpack for our two-hour flight back to Atlanta.

I've adapted and shrunk the recipe a bit for our small family, but I always make enough to have extras for the freezer, ready to warm up for a snack or a light lunch, maybe with a side of Greek Horiatiki Salad (page 53) or Everyday Tomato and Cucumber Salad (page 36).

I typically use my Basic Savory Dough recipe (page 90) for making these savory pies, which takes an hour and a half, but in a pinch I have used store-bought pizza dough.

1 pound fresh baby spinach, roughly chopped

Kosher salt

Extra-virgin olive oil

1 large yellow onion, finely chopped

1½ tablespoons sumac

1 teaspoon ground black pepper

¼ teaspoon ground allspice

Juice of **1 large** lemon (about **4 tablespoons**)

All-purpose flour, for rolling the dough

1 recipe Basic Savory Dough (page 90)

1 large egg, lightly beaten

1. Place the spinach in a large colander and sprinkle with 1 teaspoon salt. Toss, then let rest for 5 minutes.

2. In a large nonstick skillet, heat 1 tablespoon of olive oil over medium-high heat until shimmering. Add the onion and cook, stirring frequently, until softened and gaining some color, about 5 minutes. Remove to a medium bowl and drain any excess liquid from the skillet.

3. Return the skillet to the stove and heat another tablespoon of olive oil over medium-high heat. Add the spinach, in batches if necessary, and cook, stirring frequently, until it just wilts, about 1 minute.

4. Return the wilted spinach to the colander to cool. When cool enough to handle, wrap the spinach in a clean tea towel and squeeze it over the sink to get rid of as much excess liquid as you can (this step is very important).

5. Add the spinach to the bowl with the onion. Add the sumac, black pepper, allspice, and lemon juice. Mix well to combine. Taste and adjust the seasoning to your liking.

6. On a clean, lightly floured surface, roll out the dough to a ¼-inch thickness. Using a glass or a 4-inch cookie cutter, cut the dough into 4-inch circles; collect any scraps and reroll to cut more circles. Cover the circles with a clean towel and let rest for 5 to 10 minutes.

7. Position a rack in the center of the oven. Preheat the oven to 400°F. Lightly brush two 13 × 9 × 1-inch sheet pans with a little olive oil and set aside.

8. Set a small bowl of water beside the pans (you'll use this for wetting your fingers as you work with the dough). Put 2 packed (flat, not heaping) tablespoons of the spinach mixture in the middle of each circle of dough and bring up the edges at three points toward the middle to make a peak, forming a triangular package. Lightly wet your fingers and press the edges of the dough together firmly on the sides and at the top to seal.

9. Arrange the pies in a single layer on the sheet pans. Brush the tops with the beaten egg. Bake until lightly golden brown, 12 to 15 minutes.

sfiha (open-faced mini meat pies)

MAKES 14 MINI PIES

My curly-haired tween, Hannah, who is not a big eater but can down a few of these in minutes, calls these "little pizzas." Adults love them, too! Sfiha (sfeeha), also known in some Middle Eastern parts as *lahm bi al ajeen*, meaning "meat in the dough," are basically open-faced mini meat pies. Like Fatayer (page 86), you can bake up a big batch and store them in the freezer, then reheat some for a quick snack (follow the freezing and reheating tips, opposite). This spicy meat topping is fairly popular in many parts of the Levant, though not typically finished with pomegranate seeds (a little creative license for a pop of color). You'll also see other creative toppings made with labneh, cheese, za'atar, and more.

All-purpose flour, for rolling the dough

1 recipe Basic Savory Dough (page 90)

2 vine-ripened medium tomatoes, finely chopped

1 small yellow onion, finely chopped

1 jalapeño pepper, finely chopped (seeds removed for less heat)

10 ounces lean ground beef

3 tablespoons tahini

2 tablespoons tomato paste

Extra-virgin olive oil

1 teaspoon Aleppo pepper flakes

1 teaspoon ground allspice

½ teaspoon ground cinnamon

Kosher salt and ground black pepper

1 tablespoon fresh lemon juice

2 to 3 tablespoons toasted pine nuts (optional)

2 to 3 tablespoons fresh pomegranate seeds (arils; optional)

1. On a clean, lightly floured surface, roll out the dough to a ¼-inch thickness. Using a small ramekin, or even the top of a yogurt tub as your guide, cut the dough into 4½-inch circles; collect the scraps and reroll to make more circles.

2. Cover the circles of dough with a clean towel and set aside to rest for 30 minutes.

3. Meanwhile, make the filling. Put the chopped tomatoes in a fine-mesh sieve and set it over a bowl to let the tomatoes drain their excess liquid for about 10 minutes. Add the onion and jalapeño to the sieve and let drain for a few more minutes. Using the back of a spoon, push down on the mixture to press out excess liquid.

4. Transfer the tomato mixture to a medium bowl. Add the ground beef, tahini, tomato paste, and 1 tablespoon of olive oil. Add the Aleppo pepper, allspice, cinnamon, 1 teaspoon salt, 1 teaspoon black pepper, and the lemon juice. Mix until well combined.

5. Position a rack in the center of the oven and preheat the oven to 450°F. Lightly brush two 13 × 18 × 1-inch sheet pans with a little olive oil.

6. Arrange the dough circles in the sheet pans. Add 2 tablespoons of the meat mixture to the middle of each dough circle. Using the back of a spoon, lightly spread the mixture over the dough, leaving a small ¼-inch-wide border around the edge. Bake until the edges turn crisp and golden brown, 10 to 15 minutes.

7. Serve these hot or at room temperature, and if you like, add a sprinkle of toasted pine nuts or pomegranate seeds on top just before serving.

TIPS FOR SAVORY PIES

Reminder, if you plan to make the Basic Savory Dough (page 90) for the crust as I do, budget about an hour and a half for making the dough. But if you don't have the time, store-bought pizza dough is a fine shortcut.

To freeze the pies you have baked, arrange them on a large sheet pan and place in the freezer for 1 to 2 hours, until fully frozen. Transfer the frozen pies to a zippered bag or freezer container. Close tightly and store in the freezer for up to two months.

To reheat frozen pies, simply arrange them on a large sheet pan in a single layer and warm them on the center rack of a preheated 350°F oven until warmed through.

basic savory dough

MAKES ENOUGH FOR 14 (4½-INCH) MINI PIES

I use this easy dough for mini savory pies like Sfiha (page 88) and Fatayer (page 86). Making it is a snap when using a stand mixer fitted with a dough hook, but you can also give your muscles a little workout and knead by hand, if you prefer; see the notes below.

2¼ teaspoons (one ¼-ounce package) active dry yeast

Scant **1 teaspoon** sugar

1 cup warm milk, or more if needed

3½ cups all-purpose flour

1 teaspoon kosher salt

⅓ cup grapeseed or other neutral-tasting oil, plus more for the bowl

1. In a small bowl, combine the yeast, sugar, and ½ cup of the warmed milk. Stir briefly. Set aside for about 10 minutes to activate (the mixture should bubble and develop a yeasty aroma).

2. In the bowl of a stand mixer fitted with the dough hook, combine the flour and salt using the lowest speed setting. Slowly add the ⅓ cup oil, then the yeast and milk mixture, and finally the remaining ½ cup milk. Increase the speed to medium-low and knead until the dough begins to form. If there are dry bits in the bottom of the bowl, add a tiny bit of additional milk or water (no more than 1 tablespoon at a time) as necessary as you continue mixing. Mix until the dough has formed into a smooth and slightly sticky ball, 3 to 5 minutes.

3. Lightly grease a large mixing bowl with 1 tablespoon of oil.

4. Form the dough into a ball and place it in the bowl. Cover the bowl tightly with plastic wrap and set in a warm place for the dough to double in size, about 1½ hours.

5. Punch the dough down and knead briefly to deflate. Then use the dough to make savory pies or pizza.

NOTE

To knead the dough by hand, combine the dough ingredients in a large bowl and stir as instructed. Knead by hand in the bowl for a few minutes, until the mixture begins to form a shaggy dough, then turn it out onto a clean floured surface and knead for about 10 to 12 minutes, adding a tiny bit of milk or water if it appears dry (no more than 1 tablespoon at a time). You want a smooth and slightly sticky ball of dough. Follow the rest of the recipe from step 3.

the best, crispiest pita chips

MAKES 32 CHIPS

Crispy homemade pita chips baked with extra-virgin olive oil and your seasoning of choice are perfectly addictive by themselves, whether for a snack, added to a little mezze platter, or with any of the dips and spreads in this chapter! I also love using them in place of croutons in soups.

When I make Easy Homemade Pita Bread (page 99), I often turn the leftovers into baked chips. But you can use any kind of pita you like. I prefer pocket pitas, which you can split at the seam in half so that you have a thinner layer to work with.

Adjust the heat here according to the thinness of your bread (I give two options). And watch the pita chips carefully so you can take them out just as they turn a nice golden brown.

2 (6-inch) pocket-style pitas, store-bought or Easy Homemade Pita Bread (page 99)

Extra-virgin olive oil

Kosher salt

Seasoning of choice (I often use za'atar, sumac, or even dukkah; see recipe, page 282)

1. Position the rack in the center of the oven and preheat the oven to 375°F for thin pitas or 425°F for thicker pitas.

2. Prepare a large sheet pan (do not line with parchment or foil—direct contact with the hot pan produces crispier, more evenly colored pita chips).

3. Split each pita in half horizontally, following the seam with a sharp knife or kitchen shears so that you end up with 4 single rounds of pita.

4. Brush the pita rounds generously and evenly on both sides with some olive oil and sprinkle each round with salt and other seasonings of your choice.

5. Using a knife, cut each round first in half and then cut each half in half again for 4 portions. Cut each portion in half again, to yield 8 triangles.

6. Arrange the pita triangles on the sheet pan in a single layer. Bake until crisp, from 5 to 10 minutes, checking occasionally to turn over the pita triangles that have gained color, until they all are crispy and golden brown to your liking.

7. Let the pita chips cool completely before serving or packing for storage. As they cool, they will get even crisper and become sturdier. Pita chips stored in a closed container at room temperature will keep for 3 days to up to 1 week. In my experience, for fresher, best-tasting pita chips, 3 days is better. (Honestly, these are addictive; they've never lasted this long in my house!)

savory roasted chickpeas

MAKES ABOUT 3 ½ CUPS

When roasted in the oven, chickpeas magically transform into an amazing crunchy, salty, gluten-free snack. Hit them up with spices right when they come out of the oven—I find the spices cling better to the hot chickpeas. You can use canned chickpeas in this recipe, but be sure to drain and dry them well before roasting. For even crispier chickpeas, soak I cup of dried chickpeas in plenty of water for 24 hours, then drain and dry them well (do not cook them), and follow the recipe as written. And if you want to go the extra mile, peel them before you roast them (I confess I don't peel my chickpeas for this recipe).

2 (15-ounce) cans chickpeas, drained and rinsed

Extra-virgin olive oil

Kosher salt

Seasonings of choice

1. Use some paper towels to pat the chickpeas completely dry. Line a large sheet pan with more paper towels and spread the chickpeas on top. Let thoroughly dry, 10 to 20 minutes more.

2. Meanwhile, position a rack in the center of the oven and preheat the oven to 400°F.

3. Transfer the dry chickpeas to a bowl, remove and discard the paper towels from the sheet pan, then return the chickpeas to the pan. Drizzle the chickpeas with a generous amount of olive oil (about 2 tablespoons, or enough to coat the chickpeas well) and sprinkle with about I teaspoon salt. Toss the chickpeas, making sure they are well-coated with the olive oil, then spread the chickpeas evenly on the sheet pan in a single layer.

4. Roast the chickpeas, shaking the pan every 10 minutes or so for even cooking, until they turn a deep golden brown and their exterior is nice and crispy, anywhere from 25 to 35 minutes.

5. Immediately season the chickpeas with the seasoning of your choice. Though crispiest while still hot, they are still tasty (if somewhat chewier) when cooled. (Cooled roasted chickpeas can be stored in a mason jar for up to 5 days. Leave the lid a bit loose so the chickpeas can breathe—this helps keep them crispy for longer.)

eggs, breads, and breakfasty things

MORNING RITUALS

They say breakfast is the most important meal of the day. That was true for me growing up in Port Said, not so much because of the food but more for what this predictable little ritual meant for our family. We greeted each new day together, even if only for a quick five minutes, standing around the kitchen table as we got our backpacks ready for school. Every breakfast began with my dad's prayer, short and sweet, with his palms lifted to heaven in gratitude. "Father, a new day you have given us. Thank you."

On weekday mornings, he assembled breakfast while my mom took charge of waking us kids up (my brother usually needed a few pulls before he was ready to leave his warm bed). Those hurried breakfasts typically consisted of savory things that were simple but fortifying: a hard-boiled egg with a side of sliced tomato and cucumber (yes, salad for breakfast), a pita sandwich stuffed with gebna bieda—creamy white cheese, the Egyptian version of feta—and a few olives or little cups of tangy strained yogurt from our favorite dairy shop, topped with a drizzle of honey or jam.

"Father, a new day you have given us. Thank you."

Baba was obsessed with winter oranges. He bought them in excess and woke up way before the rest of us to squeeze them by hand (using a manual juicer) into tall glasses. I can still picture the delight on his face as he watched me take the first sip and nod my head in approval. He was so proud of his one-ingredient juice.

On more leisurely weekends, which for us in that part of the world were Friday mornings, our breakfasts often turned into wholesome feasts that could include a little bit of everything: Ful Mudammas (stewed fava beans; page 102) simmered overnight in our special pear-shaped pot called qidra, crispy fresh falafels picked up at the nearest local joint (where falafel, or ta'amayieh, is something of an art form), herby omelets we call "eggah" (see page 112), salads and olives galore, and any number of Mama's homemade jams to smear on pita or Breakfast Sweet Rolls (page 120).

Many of these dishes are a part of my family's breakfast ritual today, and I've added quite a few of my own favorites, as well. A stack of pita on the table that I have made or picked up from a nearby Middle Eastern bakery is ever present— for breakfast, as for every other meal.

Some weekend mornings, I make the Ful Mudammas using canned fava beans for a major shortcut, spiked with my own blend of seasonings, like cumin, garlic, and chiles. I might whip up some eggs into a cozy, glorious mess like Batata Harra and Egg Scramble (page 116) that's never Instagram-worthy but has everyone's mouth watering anyway. Or, I'll sauté sweet potatoes with

chickpeas and whatever veggies I have on hand to serve as a bed for poached eggs, giving my little Mediterranean twist on the American breakfast skillet (see page 124). My curly-haired tween Hannah gets extra-excited about falafel mornings, when I blend up a batch of the herby chickpea mixture and we work together to turn them into balls, frying them up and popping them straight into our mouths before they even have a chance to make it to the table! No less exciting to her and her big sister Dara are my easy Breakfast Pitas with Soft-Boiled Eggs and Labneh (page 108)—not your average breakfast sandwich.

To be clear, of course I don't set up a big morning feast every day, nor every weekend. On rushed mornings, you might catch me munching on a slice of Banana-Walnut Bread with Dates (page 272), or leaning over the sink with a piece of bread smeared with hummus, or eating a Spanikopita Egg Muffin (page 115) that's left over from a batch purposefully made to last for days, while Saba brews coffee and everyone else eats whatever they've found for themselves at the kitchen counter. Even as we do our own thing, we are gathered in one place, intentionally, for a few precious moments in the morning, and I get to see the faces I love most before my day begins. That, to me, is the gift of breakfast.

easy homemade pita bread

MAKES 7 OR 8 PITAS

Back in Port Said, the bread of choice for my parents was always pita or aish baladi (the more rustic, country version made with whole bran), picked up early every morning from the forn (the traditional bakery with a domed clay oven). Years after I moved to the United States, I was so thrilled to learn how easy it was to make pita in my own kitchen with just a few basic ingredients—no special forn needed. You can make this bread using either your standard oven or a cast-iron skillet on the stovetop. (The raw dough can be refrigerated up to a week and baked fresh in minutes, plus baked pita freezes well; see the Make-Ahead Tip on page 100).

My girls are hooked on freshly made pita dipped in extra-virgin olive oil flavored with za'atar (see page 25). Give it a try, and if you're like me, you may never go back to store-bought pita again.

1 cup lukewarm water (around 95°F)

2 teaspoons (a little less than one ¼-ounce package) active dry yeast

½ teaspoon sugar

3 cups all-purpose flour

1 teaspoon kosher salt

Extra-virgin olive oil

1. Pour the water into a large bowl. Add the yeast and sugar and stir until dissolved. Add ½ cup of the flour and stir again. Place the mixing bowl in a warm place, uncovered, until the mixture bubbles and forms a loose sponge, about 15 minutes.

2. Add the salt, 2 tablespoons of olive oil, and about 2 cups of the remaining flour. Stir until the mixture forms a shaggy mass (at this point, the dough has little to no gluten development and just looks like a sticky mess and you can easily pull bits off). Dust the dough with a little of the remaining ½ cup flour, then knead the mixture inside the bowl for about 1 minute to incorporate any stray bits.

3. Dust a clean work surface with just a bit of the remaining flour. Knead lightly for a couple minutes, until the dough is smooth. Cover and let the dough rest for 10 minutes, then knead again for a couple more minutes. The dough should be a bit moist; if it's too sticky you can help it with a little dusting of flour.

4. Wipe out the bowl, coat it lightly with a little olive oil, and return the dough to the bowl. Turn the dough a couple times in the bowl to coat with the oil. Cover the bowl tightly with plastic wrap, then lay a clean kitchen towel over the top. Put the bowl in a warm place. Let sit until the dough rises to double in size, about 1 hour.

Recipe continues

5. You have two options for baking the pita. To bake the pita in the oven, position a rack in the center of the oven and place a heavy-duty baking sheet or large cast-iron skillet on the center rack. Preheat the oven to 475°F. If you are cooking the pita on the stovetop, have ready a large cast-iron skillet.

6. Punch to deflate the dough and place it on a clean work surface. Divide the dough into 7 or 8 equal pieces and shape them into balls. Cover with a towel and let them rest for about 10 minutes. Meanwhile, if you are cooking the pita on the stovetop, start heating the skillet over medium-high heat.

7. Using a floured rolling pin, roll one of the balls into a circle that's 8 or 9 inches wide and about ¼ inch thick. Lift and turn the dough frequently as you roll so that the dough doesn't stick to your counter too much. (If the dough starts to stick, sprinkle on a tiny bit of flour.) If the dough starts to spring back as you roll, set it aside to rest for a few minutes, then continue rolling. Set the flattened circle aside and repeat with the other balls of dough. (Once you get going, you can be cooking one pita while rolling another, if you can manage it.)

8. *To bake pita in the oven:* Working in batches, place 2 rolled-out pitas directly on the hot baking sheet. Bake for 2 minutes on one side, and then, using a spatula or a pair of tongs, carefully turn each pita over to bake for 1 minute on the other side. The pita will puff nicely and gain a faint golden color, which means it's ready. Remove from the oven and cover the baked pitas loosely with a clean towel while you repeat the process with the rest of the pitas.

To cook pita on the stovetop: Test the heat of the skillet by adding a couple drops of water; the skillet is ready when the beads of water sizzle immediately. Drizzle a tiny bit of olive oil into the pan and wipe off any excess. Working with one pita at a time, lay a rolled-out pita on the skillet and bake for 30 seconds, until bubbles start to form. Using a spatula, flip the pita over and cook until large toasted spots appear on the underside, 1 to 2 minutes. Flip again and cook another 1 to 2 minutes. The pita should puff and gain a little color when it's ready. Keep the cooked pita covered loosely with a clean towel while you work on the remaining pitas.

9. Baked pita breads are best enjoyed fresh and hot out of the oven. That said, homemade pita will store well for a few days in an airtight bag; just warm the pitas in your oven or toaster oven, or even over an open flame, before serving. You can also turn the pitas into pita chips (see page 91). You can also freeze baked pitas for up to 3 months; reheat the frozen pitas on a large sheet pan (or directly on the oven rack) in a 350°F oven until soft and warmed through.

MAKE AHEAD TIP
Pita dough can be prepared ahead and refrigerated for up to 1 week. Once the dough has risen, separate it into portions and place them on a lightly oiled tray or in a large bowl, then cover tightly with plastic wrap. You can bake one ball or however many pitas you need at a time, keeping the rest of the dough covered in the fridge.

VARIATIONS
For whole wheat pita, try equal parts whole wheat flour and all-purpose flour (1½ cups each). For gluten-free, try Bob's Red Mill gluten-free all-purpose baking flour.

homemade labneh

MAKES ABOUT 1 ¼ CUPS

If Greek yogurt is strained yogurt, then labneh is basically extra-strained yogurt; in fact, I think of it as the best form of cream cheese—tangy, thick, and extra creamy. Labneh is made simply by straining whole milk yogurt (quality full-fat cow's milk yogurt or goat's milk yogurt) so it loses most of its liquid and turns into cheese. After 24 hours of straining, the yogurt will thicken a bit and you can use it at this point; but if you wait a few more hours, it will be even creamier and tangier (48 and up to 72 hours, if you like). At this point you can pack it into an airtight glass container and store it in the fridge for up to two weeks.

I love being able to reach for labneh in the fridge to smear on toast or use in sandwiches. It's also excellent tossed with some herbs and drizzled with a generous bit of rich and peppery extra-virgin olive oil like I do with my Herbed Labneh (page 293).

1 quart (32 ounces) plain whole-milk regular yogurt (not Greek)

¾ teaspoon kosher salt

1. In a medium bowl, combine the yogurt and salt.

2. Set a fine-mesh sieve large enough to hold the yogurt over a large bowl. Line the sieve with lightweight cheesecloth or a muslin towel large enough that the edges hang over the bowl.

3. Pour the yogurt mixture into the lined sieve. Fold the towel's overhang gently over the yogurt to cover it. Refrigerate for 24 to 48 hours to allow the yogurt to drain most of its liquid. Store your homemade labneh in the fridge in a tightly closed container for up to 2 weeks (or longer if you pour a good bit of olive oil over the top to seal it, preventing air from spoiling it).

VARIATION

Labneh Balls

For another way to store the labneh, try my mother-in-law Dina's labneh balls (this works best for thicker labneh that's been drained for 48 to 72 hours). Form the labneh into small balls about 1 tablespoon in size. Place the labneh balls in a large sterilized airtight jar and pour extra-virgin olive oil over them to cover by about ½ inch. Cover the jar tightly and leave at room temperature in a cool, dark place for up to 3 weeks (or longer if the labneh balls remain covered with the oil).

ful mudammas

SERVES 4

Ful (pronounced "fool") mudammas is a protein-packed breakfast staple throughout the Middle East, but it's actually considered Egypt's national dish. And this Egyptian girl can't live without a weekly dose of her poor man's porridge, made of stewed fava beans (or broad beans) seasoned with cumin. Ful mudammas was my dad's specialty. He routinely simmered a pot of fava beans on the stove and then stored them in their cooking liquid in the fridge for use throughout the week. I take a shortcut by using canned fava beans—adding in small chunks of tomatoes, fresh parsley, and a zippy lemon sauce with mashed garlic and jalapeños. By the way, you can use chickpeas or even pinto beans if you can't find favas (not the same flavor but still delicious). Pita bread (page 99) is a must to sop up the delicious bean porridge.

Beans

2 (15-ounce) cans plain fava beans, rinsed and drained

½ cup water

Kosher salt

½ to 1 teaspoon ground cumin

Lemon-Garlic Sauce

1 or 2 jalapeño peppers, roughly chopped (seeds removed for less heat; reserve a few slices for garnish)

2 large garlic cloves, roughly chopped

Juice of **1** large lemon (about **¼ cup**)

For Serving

Extra-virgin olive oil

1 cup roughly chopped fresh flat-leaf parsley

1 vine-ripened medium tomato, diced

Pita bread, sliced fresh veggies of choice, and olives

1. **Cook the beans:** In a 10-inch cast-iron skillet or heavy saucepan, combine the fava beans and the water. Cook over medium-high heat, stirring occasionally, until the beans are heated through, 5 to 7 minutes.

2. Season the beans to taste with salt and the cumin. Use a potato masher or fork to mash the beans until they look like a chunky stew.

3. **Make the sauce:** Mash the hot peppers and garlic into a rough paste with a mortar and pestle, or with a few pulses in a small food processor, then add the lemon juice and stir to combine. (This sauce is meant to be chunky.)

4. **Serve the dish:** Pour the sauce over the warm fava beans. Add a generous drizzle of the olive oil. Top with the parsley, tomato, and a few reserved slices of jalapeño peppers, if you like. Serve with the pita bread, sliced vegetables, and olives on the side.

I DON'T REMEMBER
A LIFE WITHOUT FALAFEL

I have the sweetest memories of the falafel from Mr. Bishay's falafel joint in the heart of Port Said's busy Souq El Hamidi. Dad and I often visited on weekend mornings, when we did our big souq excursions. You could smell Mr. Bishay's fragrant falafels from miles away, and he always served them with the biggest smile. While the two men caught up on life, I stood on a chair to get a good view of the falafel being mixed in the large, ancient processor. One of the guys working the fryer would always hand me a paper cone with a few hot falafels to snack on; they were so herby and fluffy, and are something I still crave.

I began working on my own falafel game soon after I got married.

As in many parts of the Middle East, Egypt has had a big falafel scene, and there is a bit of friendly rivalry among falafel makers. Some, like Mr. Bishay (who has since passed away), sold super-crispy falafel balls on the smaller side that you couldn't help popping in your mouth right out of the paper cone. Others sold larger, flat-ish falafel patties coated with sesame seeds—those are more fit for dinner with all the sides and fixin's. And of course, all the falafel makers had their own signature spin on the falafel pita, like the falafel supreme—an insane pita pocket pregnant with falafel, fries, fresh herbs, diced veggies, pickles, hot peppers, and a generous drizzle of tahini.

I began working on my own falafel game soon after I got married, watching my mother-in-law Dina make big batches of them both at home and at the restaurants she ran in Michigan. She makes hers with chickpeas, as is customary in Levantine kitchens, while the Egyptian falafel I grew up with (known as ta'amyieh) are made from split fava beans. But the seasonings—cumin, coriander, lots of garlic and herbs—are pretty similar.

No, making falafel at home is not the same as eating them freshly fried, on the streets of the Middle East. But it is the closest thing to it (and a lot closer than those packaged falafels sold in a fancy health food market).

anytime falafel

MAKES 24 FALAFEL BALLS

There are no rules for how to eat falafel: Pop them right into your mouth, dip them in some hummus, or stuff them into a pita pocket along with my Everyday Tomato and Cucumber Salad with Dad's Salad "Whisky" (page 36) and a generous drizzle of Lime-Tahini Sauce (page 290). Heck, you can add a couple of falafels next to your scrambled eggs in place of Tater Tots. You can make them ahead, too: make the recipe through step 5, then arrange the raw falafel balls on a sheet pan lined with parchment paper and freeze for 1 to 2 hours, until hardened. Transfer the frozen falafel balls to a container or zippered plastic bag and return to the freezer; they will keep in the freezer for up to 1 month. You can cook them directly from the freezer following the recipe from step 6 on.

SOME FALAFEL WISDOM FOR BEGINNERS

- There are no shortcuts. That is why I almost always make falafel ahead of time (remember, you can freeze uncooked falafel balls or patties for up to 1 month).
- Canned chickpeas are not an option. Raw, dried chickpeas that have been soaked overnight are necessary for the falafels to hold their shape. So, budget your time accordingly!
- Don't fry up the falafel until you're ready to serve them! Cold falafel are not a good look.
- And, yes, baked falafel are an option, but I won't lie to you—fried are far better.

2 cups dried chickpeas (not canned or already cooked chickpeas)

½ teaspoon baking soda

1 cup fresh flat-leaf parsley leaves

¾ cup fresh cilantro leaves

½ cup fresh dill fronds

1 small yellow onion, quartered

7 or 8 large garlic cloves, peeled and left whole

1 tablespoon kosher salt

1 tablespoon ground black pepper

1 tablespoon ground coriander

1 tablespoon ground cumin

1 teaspoon cayenne pepper (optional)

1 tablespoon chickpea flour or all-purpose flour (I prefer the taste of chickpea flour, but either will work)

1 teaspoon baking powder

2 tablespoons toasted sesame seeds

Neutral-tasting oil, for frying (any with a high smoke point)

Lime-Tahini Sauce (page 290), for serving

1. One day in advance, place the dried chickpeas and baking soda in a large bowl and fill with water to cover the chickpeas by at least 2 inches. Soak for 18 to 24 hours. When ready, drain the chickpeas and pat them dry.

2. Add the chickpeas, parsley, cilantro, dill, onion, garlic, salt, black pepper, coriander, cumin, cayenne (if using), and chickpea flour to the bowl of a large food processor fitted with the multipurpose blade. Pulse a few seconds at a time, scraping down the sides of the bowl periodically, until the mixture is like coarse meal, but not pasty. To test the consistency, try rolling a spoonful into a small ball. If it doesn't hold together (it's okay if it's a little crumbly), give it a few more pulses and try again. Be careful not to over-process.

3. Transfer the falafel mixture to a large container and cover tightly. Refrigerate for at least 1 hour, or up to overnight, until ready to cook. This will help the mixture firm up so it's easier to shape.

4. Just before shaping and frying, stir the baking powder and sesame seeds into the falafel mixture until thoroughly incorporated.

5. Scoop up 1 tablespoonful of the falafel mixture and, using your hands, form into a small ball or a $\frac{1}{2}$-inch-thick patty (it helps to have wet hands as you form the falafels, so they do not stick). Set on a baking sheet and repeat with the rest of the mixture, keeping them spaced on the baking sheet. Do not pack or flatten them too much, as you want them to still be fluffy when they're cooked.

6. Line a large plate with paper towels. Fill a small saucepan about half full with the oil and heat the oil over medium-high until it bubbles softly. (If you use a deep-frying thermometer, the oil temperature should read 350°F.)

7. Test one falafel by carefully adding it to the bubbling oil using a slotted spoon. The oil should keep bubbling gently when the falafel is added; if not, the oil is not hot enough yet. Proceed with frying the rest of the falafels, adding them carefully without crowding the pan and working in batches, as needed. Let them fry until crispy and medium brown on the outside and cooked through (they should be light green in color and fluffy on the inside), about 5 minutes.

8. Place the fried falafel patties on the paper towel-lined plate to drain. Serve hot with the lime-tahini sauce.

breakfast pitas
with soft-boiled eggs and labneh

MAKES 4 SANDWICHES

I am always on the lookout for fun, family-friendly breakfasts that don't take hours to prepare. Here, soft-boiled eggs with bright and perfectly jammy yolks join peppery arugula, juicy tomatoes, mellow avocado slices, and tart and creamy labneh in the ultimate breakfast sandwich situation. What more can you ask for in a hand-held meal that is great for eating on the go? A good dash of Aleppo pepper adds extra zing without overwhelming the delicate flavors within. If you prefer your yolks hard-cooked, allow the eggs to cook 3 minutes longer.

4 large eggs, cold from the fridge

Kosher salt

Aleppo pepper flakes

2 (6-inch) pita breads, cut in half crosswise to make 4 pita pockets

Labneh, homemade (see page 101) or store-bought

2 cups baby arugula

1 ripe large heirloom tomato, sliced into rounds

1 avocado, pitted and thinly sliced

1. In a saucepan large enough to hold the eggs in one layer, fill at least halfway with water and bring to a boil over medium-high heat. Gently lower the eggs into the boiling water, one by one. Add more water, if needed, to cover the eggs. Cook for exactly 6½ minutes, adjusting the heat to keep the water at a gentle boil.

2. Meanwhile, prepare a medium bowl with cold water and ice cubes, and set it next to the stove. When the eggs are finished, use a slotted spoon to transfer them gently to the ice water and chill them for about 2 minutes.

3. Gently crack the cooled eggs and peel them under running water. Cut each egg in half lengthwise and season with salt and a generous pinch of Aleppo pepper.

4. Open each pita pocket and spread a bit of labneh on the bottom side. Divide the arugula, tomato, and avocado slices among the pita pockets. Season with salt and a bit of Aleppo pepper. Add one egg to each pita pocket.

baked sunny side up eggs
with sweet peppers and onion

SERVES 6

Here is an efficient way to make a killer brunch centerpiece: sheet-pan eggs! Nestle whole eggs in a medley of roasted bell peppers and onion slices on one large sheet pan and bake; it's a great-tasting dish that is easy enough for everyday but also delivers on the wow factor.

Don't be afraid to change up this recipe to suit your taste, using other spices or veggies you have on hand. Zucchini, yellow squash, carrots, and scallions are a few good options here. Just make sure that all the pieces are cut to approximately the same size, so they will roast evenly and finish at the same time.

1 green bell pepper, cored, seeded, and thinly sliced

1 orange bell pepper, cored, seeded, and thinly sliced

1 red bell pepper, cored, seeded, and thinly sliced

1 medium red onion, halved and thinly sliced crosswise

Kosher salt and ground black pepper

2 teaspoons dried oregano

1 teaspoon Aleppo pepper flakes or other sweet chile seasoning

1 teaspoon ground cumin

Extra-virgin olive oil

6 large eggs

½ cup chopped fresh flat-leaf parsley

1 Roma (plum) tomato, cored and diced

Crumbled feta cheese (optional)

Crusty bread, for serving

1. Position a rack in the center of the oven and preheat the oven to 400°F.

2. Place the bell peppers and onion in a large bowl. Season with salt and black pepper to taste. Add 1 teaspoon of the oregano as well as the Aleppo pepper and the cumin. Drizzle with olive oil, then toss the vegetables to make sure they are well coated with the oil and spices.

3. Transfer the vegetable medley to a 13 × 18 × 1-inch sheet pan. Spread in one layer, then roast until the peppers have softened, about 15 minutes.

4. Remove the pan from the oven and with a large spoon, form 6 wells in the roasted veggies. Carefully crack an egg into each well, keeping the yolks intact. (It helps to crack each egg into a small dish first, then slide it carefully into the well.)

5. Return the pan to the oven and bake until the egg whites are just set, about another 8 minutes. (I like my yolks a bit runny, so cook a minute or two longer if you prefer harder eggs.)

6. Season the eggs with salt and pepper to taste. Sprinkle the remaining teaspoon of oregano over all, then garnish with the parsley, tomato, and a sprinkle of feta (if using). Serve immediately, with your favorite crusty bread.

caramelized cauliflower, onion, and parsley eggah

SERVES 4 TO 6

The baked omelets I grew up with are very similar to Italian frittatas, but with more Middle Eastern flavors and often a pinch of baking powder—a trick I learned from my mom to fluff up the eggs a bit. We call them "eggahs," and the ones I recall from my childhood were loaded with parsley, but I like to experiment with other fillings. My current favorite is a savory combination of deeply caramelized cauliflower and onion, with the heady warmth of sumac, cumin, and turmeric—okay, and a little parsley for good measure! Make sure you cut up the cauliflower into very small florets, and while it may seem like you're using a lot of extra-virgin olive oil, the cauliflower and onion need it to cook down to their proper melt-in-your-mouth tenderness.

½ **cup** extra-virgin olive oil

1 head of cauliflower, trimmed and separated into bite-sized florets

1 medium yellow onion, halved and thinly sliced

Kosher salt and ground black pepper

1½ **teaspoons** sumac

1 **teaspoon** ground cumin

¾ **teaspoon** ground turmeric

6 large eggs

⅓ **cup** whole milk or plant-based alternative

½ **cup** roughly chopped fresh flat-leaf parsley

½ **teaspoon** baking powder

1. Position a rack in the center of the oven and preheat the oven to 350°F.

2. In a 10-inch cast-iron or other heavy oven-safe skillet, heat the olive oil over medium-high heat until shimmering but not smoking.

3. Add the cauliflower and onion, and season with a generous pinch of salt and black pepper (about ¾ teaspoon each), as well as 1 teaspoon of the sumac, ½ teaspoon of the cumin, and ½ teaspoon of the turmeric.

4. Cook, stirring occasionally, until the cauliflower is tender and well caramelized (it should be quite tender and golden brown in color with some charred spots), about 20 minutes.

5. In a medium bowl, whisk together the eggs, milk, parsley, and baking powder with a big pinch of salt and black pepper (about ½ teaspoon each), as well as the remaining ½ teaspoon sumac, ½ teaspoon cumin, and ¼ teaspoon turmeric.

6. Pour the egg mixture over the cooked cauliflower and onion. Transfer the skillet to the oven and bake until the eggs settle and are no longer runny, 8 to 12 minutes.

spanakopita egg muffins

MAKES 8 MUFFINS

These egg muffins take inspiration from the savory Greek pastry spanakopita, which is loaded with spinach, creamy feta, fresh parsley, and mint. But obviously this version is not a flaky phyllo pastry. Instead, I make an egg mixture with similar flavors and pour it into a muffin pan to bake. I like to make these egg muffins ahead to enjoy for breakfast-on-the-go, and you can freeze them too, which is great when you need breakfast (or a high-protein snack) at a minute's notice. A pinch of baking powder will make the egg muffins nice and airy.

Extra-virgin olive oil

8 large eggs

1 teaspoon dried oregano

½ teaspoon ground black pepper

½ teaspoon sweet paprika

¼ teaspoon baking powder

Kosher salt

1 (6-ounce) package frozen chopped spinach, thawed and completely drained (wring out any water)

½ small yellow onion, finely chopped (about **½ cup**)

1 cup roughly chopped fresh flat-leaf parsley

3 tablespoons chopped fresh mint leaves

3 large garlic cloves, minced

1 (4-ounce) block feta cheese, crumbled (**1 cup**)

1. Position a rack in the center of the oven and preheat the oven to 350°F. Generously brush the bottom and sides of 8 cups of a muffin tin with olive oil. (If your muffin tin has more than 8 cups, fill any remaining cups with water.)

2. In a medium bowl with a spout, combine the eggs, oregano, black pepper, paprika, baking powder, and a pinch of salt. (Using a bowl with a spout makes pouring the mixture into the muffin tin so easy.) Whisk well, then add the spinach, onion, parsley, mint, garlic, and feta. Whisk until the mixture is well blended.

3. Pour the egg and spinach mixture to fill each muffin cup about three-fourths of the way (make sure you leave enough room for rising). Bake for 25 to 30 minutes, until the eggs are fully set. Let cool briefly, then run a butter knife around the edge of each muffin to loosen. Remove from the pan and serve, or store for later.

NOTES

MAKE AHEAD: If you're not planning to serve the egg muffins immediately, let them cool completely in the tin, then carefully pop the egg muffins out of the tin and store them in a glass container with a tight lid or a zippered plastic bag. They'll keep in the fridge for 3 to 4 days. Or, you can individually wrap them in foil and freeze them for up to 2 months.

REHEATING: There are two ways to reheat these egg muffins. If you are heating them from frozen, wrap the muffins individually in foil (not too tightly) and heat in a 300°F oven until warmed through. Or, remove them from the foil wrap and microwave them on low (setting 3 out of 10) and heat briefly; they need only 15 to 20 seconds (if they are frozen, they may take 60 seconds). Be careful not to overheat them or they can turn rubbery.

batata harra and egg scramble

SERVES 4 TO 6

Batata harra is the Arabic translation for "spicy potatoes," and these show up in many forms on the Middle Eastern table, usually as a hot side or mezze plate. Here, I cut the potatoes super-small and sauté them in some olive oil with onions and warm seasonings, plus scrambled eggs for a hefty brunch. I like mine with just enough kick to wake up the taste buds, and a splash of lime juice and fresh herbs to temper the heat. You can adjust the spice level to your liking by using less or more of the fresh and dried chiles.

Extra-virgin olive oil

5 Yukon Gold or other yellow potatoes (**1½ pounds**), peeled and cut into ½-inch cubes

1 medium yellow onion, roughly chopped

1 to 2 teaspoons red pepper flakes

1 teaspoon ground coriander

¼ teaspoon ground turmeric

Kosher salt and ground black pepper

4 large garlic cloves, minced

1 or 2 hot chiles, such as serrano or jalapeño, sliced crosswise (seeds removed for less heat)

Juice of ½ lime (about **1 tablespoon**)

½ cup roughly chopped fresh cilantro

¼ cup roughly chopped fresh dill fronds

5 large eggs

1. In a large nonstick pan with a lid, heat ¼ cup of olive oil over medium-high heat until shimmering but not smoking. Add the potatoes, onion, red pepper flakes, coriander, and turmeric. Season with salt and black pepper. Stir with a wooden spoon to combine. Cook the potato mixture over medium-high heat, stirring frequently, allowing the potatoes and onion to gain some char as they soften, about 15 minutes.

2. Add the garlic and sliced chiles. Stir to combine. Turn the heat to low, cover the pan, and cook, stirring occasionally, until the potatoes can be easily pierced with a fork, about 15 minutes. Add the lime juice, cilantro, and dill. Give the potatoes a toss. Turn the heat off but keep the lid on so the potatoes stay warm.

3. In a large nonstick skillet, heat 1 tablespoon of olive oil over medium-low heat until just shimmering. Break the eggs directly into the pan and cook, undisturbed, until a thin layer of cooked egg appears around the edge of the skillet, 1 to 2 minutes.

4. With a wooden spoon, begin to scramble the eggs until barely set, 1 to 2 minutes. The eggs should still look wet on the top. Season lightly with salt and black pepper.

5. Transfer the eggs to the pan of potatoes, mix everything, and serve immediately.

chickpea and spinach shakshuka with lime–tahini sauce

SERVES 4

This Tunisian dish of eggs braised in a chunky, spicy tomato sauce has been a favorite of many North African and Middle Eastern cultures for centuries, and it has morphed into a bazillion variations. I add my spin by augmenting the customary tomato–bell pepper–onion mixture with chickpeas and spinach, and by lacing it with tahini sauce. I'll admit that the addition of tahini sauce was at first a happy accident; but it was so good that now I'm all in with this combo! The recipe has a bit of a kick, but if you prefer your shakshuka mild, simply omit the jalapeño. Serve it right from the pan with a side of good bread.

¼ **cup** extra-virgin olive oil

1 small yellow onion, chopped

1 red bell pepper, cored, seeded, and roughly chopped

½ green bell pepper, cored, seeded, and roughly chopped

1 jalapeño pepper, finely chopped (seeded for less heat)

Kosher salt and black pepper

3 large garlic cloves, minced

5 or 6 vine-ripened medium tomatoes, roughly chopped

1 **cup** canned chickpeas, drained and rinsed

1½ **teaspoons** Aleppo pepper flakes, plus extra

¾ **teaspoon** ground cumin

¼ **cup** water

Lime–Tahini Sauce (page 290; optional)

3 **cups** (packed) baby spinach (2½ ounces)

4 large eggs

½ **cup** chopped flat-leaf parsley

1. In a large sauté pan with a lid, heat the olive oil over medium-high heat until shimmering but not smoking. Add the onion, bell peppers, jalapeño (if using), and ¾ teaspoon salt. Cook, stirring occasionally, until the onion and peppers are softened and lightly colored, about 5 minutes.

2. Add the garlic, tomatoes, chickpeas, Aleppo pepper, cumin, ½ teaspoon of black pepper, and the water. Stir to combine, then taste and adjust the seasoning. Bring to a boil, then lower the heat to medium-low and cook, stirring occasionally, until the tomatoes have formed a thick sauce, 20 to 25 minutes. (If using the tahini sauce, prepare it while the tomatoes are cooking.)

3. When the tomatoes are saucy, add the spinach, stir, and cook until fully wilted, about 3 minutes. Using the back of a spoon, make 4 wells in the mixture. Crack an egg into each well and sprinkle the eggs with a pinch each of salt and Aleppo pepper.

4. Cover the sauté pan and cook until the egg whites are set (the yolks should still be runny), about 4 minutes. Uncover and drizzle a good 4 to 6 tablespoons of the tahini sauce (if using) all over the shakshuka. Sprinkle with the parsley and serve.

MAKE-AHEAD TIP
You can prepare the tomato mixture a night or two in advance. Store it in the fridge in an airtight container. You can also make the tahini sauce ahead of time and store it in the fridge. When you're ready, warm the tomato mixture in a large skillet, make the wells and add the eggs, and cook as directed in the recipe.

breakfast sweet rolls

MAKES 14 ROLLS

Airy and slightly sweet, these sesame seed–crusted rolls taste almost like an indulgent brioche, except that they have no butter at all! Every time I eat them, I think of Easter Monday in Egypt, when families would picnic in the parks or on the beach, welcoming the spring season with baskets of these rolls and pastel-colored eggs. My girls and Saba love them so much that whenever my mom visits us in Atlanta, she makes large batches of them to store in the freezer. I learned to make them from her over Facetime one Saturday morning. (Thank God for technology!)

Happily, even for a non-baker like myself, these rolls are easy to get right. You do need to be patient enough to allow the dough to rise properly, so budget about 3 hours or so for that. We love them with a drizzle of honey or a smear of Mama's Citrus-Carrot Jam (page 128).

¼ **cup** warm water

⅓ **cup** plus ½ **teaspoon** sugar

3 **teaspoons** active dry yeast (1 package plus ¾ **teaspoon**)

3½ **cups** all-purpose flour

1 **teaspoon** baking powder

½ **cup** whole milk or plant-based substitute, at room temperature

½ **cup** plain whole-milk regular yogurt (not Greek) or plant-based substitute, at room temperature

1¼ **teaspoons** vanilla extract

½ **cup** grapeseed or other neutral-tasting oil, plus more for pan

1 large egg yolk, at room temperature

½ **teaspoon** distilled white vinegar

2 **tablespoons** raw sesame seeds

1. In a measuring cup, combine the warm water with the ½ teaspoon sugar. Gently fold in the yeast, without stirring. Cover the cup with a small plate or towel and set aside until foamy and bubbly, 5 to 10 minutes.

2. Meanwhile, in a large bowl, combine the flour and baking powder.

3. In a medium bowl, combine the milk, yogurt, and 1 teaspoon of the vanilla. Stir in the remaining ⅓ cup sugar.

4. Pour the wet yogurt mixture over the dry flour mixture and stir with a wooden spoon to combine. Fold in the yeast mixture. At this point, the dough will be wet and sticky.

5. Transfer the dough to a stand mixer fitted with the dough hook. Mix on the lowest setting until a soft, somewhat wet dough forms, 2 to 4 minutes.

6. Grease the bottom of a large bowl with a bit of grapeseed oil. With lightly oiled hands, form the dough into a ball and set inside the bowl. Cover the bowl with plastic wrap and place in a warm area to double in size, about 1 hour.

7. Brush 1 or 2 baking sheets with a bit of the oil. Divide the dough into 14 equal parts and roll into a small ball. Arrange the dough balls on the baking sheet(s), making sure they are spaced 2 to 3 inches apart. Cover with a clean kitchen towel and place in a warm area to double in size again, about 2 hours.

8. When ready to bake, position a rack in the center of the oven and preheat the oven to 350°F.

9. In a small bowl, whisk the egg yolk with the vinegar and the remaining ¼ teaspoon vanilla. Brush the risen rolls with the egg-yolk mixture and then sprinkle the tops with the sesame seeds. Bake the rolls on the middle rack until they turn a light golden brown, 20 to 25 minutes.

HOW TO BUILD
A MEDITERRANEAN BREAKFAST BOARD

I love brunch with my girlfriends, and I find that a Mediterranean brunch board makes all of us happy and lets me hang with them at the table to visit and graze, rather than keeping me in the kitchen cooking and serving. I take a bit of a mezze approach, pairing dips like hummus with hearty falafel and halved hard-boiled eggs for a pop of bright yellow. I like to add two to three cheeses to the board. My go-tos for the cheese component are chunks of feta, a bowl of labneh, fresh mozzarella, Middle Eastern braided mozzarella (I'm lucky to have a grocer near me that sells it), or burrata (in a bowl, as it does get messy when poked with a knife). After adding these heartier anchors, I fill in the rest of my breakfast board with bright and fresh items, like a bowl of tabbouleh salad, sliced fresh veggies (tomatoes, cucumbers, radish, carrots, whatever else I have on hand), and extras like olives, pickles, and other marinated veggies.

It's always nice to add a little something sweet to cleanse the palate, like a small bowl of honey or jam, and always have fresh fruit—whatever is in season. By now you know that nothing happens without pita around here, and for this modern grazing board, I like slicing the bread into wedges to tuck into any gaps that I see on the board. My brunch board is always different, depending on what I have on hand. That's the beauty of this situation—I get to clean out my fridge!

za'atar sweet potato and chickpea breakfast hash

SERVES 4

Potato hash is a very American thing that I love and appreciate for the humble and comforting dish that it is. This hash takes on a Mediterranean twist: cubed sweet potatoes are cooked in extra-virgin olive oil with red onion, bell pepper, and chickpeas, and are well seasoned with coriander, paprika, za'atar, and other warm spices. You can prepare the eggs any way you like to serve on top of the hash, but for me, cutting into a perfectly poached egg and allowing some of that yolk to run over the sweet potatoes is just magic.

3 tablespoons extra-virgin olive oil

1 medium red onion, chopped

2 small sweet potatoes (about 1½ pounds total), peeled and cut into ½-inch cubes

1 **cup** canned chickpeas, drained and rinsed

Kosher salt and ground black pepper

1 **teaspoon** ground coriander

½ **teaspoon** ground cumin

½ **teaspoon** sweet paprika

½ **teaspoon** ground turmeric

2 large garlic cloves, minced

1 large red bell pepper, cored, seeded, and chopped

1 **tablespoon** za'atar, plus more as desired

1 **teaspoon** distilled white vinegar

4 large eggs

1. In a 12-inch cast-iron skillet, heat the olive oil over medium-high heat until shimmering but not smoking. Add the red onion, sweet potatoes, and chickpeas. Season with a big pinch of salt and black pepper (about ½ teaspoon each). Add the coriander, cumin, paprika, and turmeric. Stir to combine. Cook, stirring frequently, until the onion is nicely caramelized and the sweet potatoes have softened quite a bit, 10 to 15 minutes.

2. Reduce the heat to medium. Add the garlic and bell pepper. Continue to cook, stirring frequently, until the pepper has softened and the potatoes are now cooked through, another 5 to 10 minutes. Sprinkle with the za'atar.

3. Meanwhile, bring a medium pot of water to a steady simmer over medium-low heat and add the vinegar. Break each egg into a small bowl or ramekin. Stir the simmering water gently and carefully slide each egg in; the egg whites should wrap around the yolk. Cook for 3 minutes exactly, then remove the eggs from the simmering water using a slotted spoon and put them on a paper towel to drain briefly. Season with a pinch of salt, pepper, and a little more za'atar.

4. Divide the sweet potato hash among 4 bowls and top each with a poached egg. Serve immediately.

sweet and nutty couscous in milk

SERVES 4

This couscous cereal situation was something I was playing with here in my Atlanta kitchen one morning while thinking back to my childhood. Cold, sugary cereal was not a thing for us growing up; breakfast was mostly a savory meal. But we occasionally ate grains like barley as you would oatmeal: cooked into a warm porridge, often slightly sweetened with honey and finished with a dash of cinnamon.

For this version, I toast instant couscous in ghee (clarified butter, but regular unsalted butter is fine if that's what you have on hand). Then I scoop the fluffy grains into serving bowls, sprinkle them with brown sugar and nuts, and pour some hot milk over the top.

Feel free to jazz this up as you like—with the optional shredded coconut or some dried fruits, with honey in place of the brown sugar, or with a non-dairy milk. Because it's made with the smallest-size couscous available that's already been steamed and dried, it's a snap to prepare on a hectic morning. Yet this couscous is so comforting and indulgent that I've been known to serve it as a little holiday breakfast while we're still in our jammies and are curled up on the couch. Feel free also to substitute other grains for the couscous—even grits (for my Southern friends)!

⅓ **cup** roughly chopped hazelnuts

⅓ **cup** roughly chopped pistachios

⅓ **cup** roughly chopped walnuts

1½ **cups** water

1½ **cups** Moroccan instant couscous

2 **tablespoons** ghee or unsalted butter

Dark brown sugar

⅓ **cup** shredded coconut (optional)

Whole milk or non-dairy alternative, warmed

1. In a small skillet, combine the nuts and toast over medium heat, tossing regularly until they gain a little color. Place the toasted nuts in a small bowl.

2. In a medium saucepan, bring the water to a boil over high heat. Add the couscous, stir, then immediately turn the heat off. Cover the saucepan and let sit undisturbed for 10 minutes (the couscous will double in size). Fluff the couscous with a fork.

3. In a medium nonstick skillet, heat the ghee over medium-high heat until melted. Add the couscous and toast for 3 to 5 minutes, stirring occasionally (the couscous should gain some color and crisp up a bit).

4. Divide the toasted couscous among 4 cereal bowls. Top each with a sprinkling of brown sugar and shredded coconut (if using). Add the nuts, then pour a bit of the warmed milk into each bowl and dig in!

mama's citrus-carrot jam

MAKES 1 ½ TO 2 CUPS

Of all the jams Mama made for us when we were growing up—fig, date, apricot; you name it—she was most known for her orange and cinnamon-scented carrot jam. This is an easy recipe requiring familiar ingredients most of us carry year-round. But don't expect a smooth jam—this one has a rustic texture almost like a coarse marmalade. I especially love it with Breakfast Sweet Rolls (page 120). It's tasty if you eat it immediately, but if you give it time in the fridge (it keeps for a couple weeks), it gets even better.

1 pound carrots, trimmed, peeled, and cut into large chunks

1 cup sugar

1 tablespoon grated orange zest

1 cup orange juice

½ cup water

Juice of ½ large lemon (about **2 tablespoons**)

3 whole cloves

¼ teaspoon ground cinnamon

1. Put the carrot pieces in the bowl of a food processor fitted with the multipurpose blade. Cover and process until the carrots are finely chopped. (You should end up with about 3 cups finely chopped carrots.)

2. Transfer the carrots to a medium saucepan and add the sugar, orange zest, orange juice, and water. Stir to combine and bring to a boil over medium-high heat.

3. Lower the heat to medium-low or low to maintain a gentle simmer and cook for 45 minutes, stirring occasionally.

4. Add the lemon juice, cloves, and cinnamon, stir again, and simmer for another 30 to 45 minutes, until most of the liquid has evaporated and the carrots have broken down and softened to a coarse fruit-like mixture.

5. Remove from the heat and spoon the carrot jam into small mason jars (see Note). Use the back of a spoon to push down on the jam so that a bit of the syrup rises to the top. Cover tightly with the lids, let cool, then store the jars in the fridge for 2 to 3 weeks or in the freezer for up to 6 months.

NOTE
Although mason jars do not have to be sterilized for this refrigerator jam, do be sure they are very clean. I wash my canning jars with soap and cold water, then dry them in a warm (150°F) oven for about 15 minutes, or until fully dry.

meatless mains, soups, and sides

FOR THOSE WHO
WORK IN ACRES, NOT IN HOURS

Baba never carried a shopping list. More often than not, Mama would ask him something like, "If you have time to stop at the souq, bring me some produce." No further instruction. (I know! I wouldn't dare send Saba to the store without a detailed list of what exactly to bring back and how much of it. Let's just say, it wouldn't be good for our marriage.)

Khoudar was the word she used, meaning "greens," but the word encompasses all produce. Hand in hand, Baba and I would go on a fun "hunt" for what looked good at the souq that day. And whatever goodies we brought home, Mama unpacked them as if she were a contestant on the TV show *Chopped* unpacking a mystery basket, but she always magically turned it into a delicious meal.

Even though I do not have access to the farmers' market year-round, still one of my favorite things to do is to shop for produce. And I still approach it like a hunt, the same way I did when I was a child. But when I'm shopping for produce these days, I am also reminded of Baba's words about taking care of the farmers and souq merchants: "They feed us, and so we need to make sure they too are fed." Eating with the seasons, as much as we can, is one of the simple Mediterranean principles I grew up with—and how I honor those who work in acres, not in hours. It's also delicious, sustainable, and economical.

I'm lucky that my girls love their veggies; as a family, we do eat vegetarian several times a week. In this chapter, I've included some of my favorite vegetarian sides, like Mushroom, Veggie, and Feta Phyllo Purses (page 151), Blistered Plum Tomatoes with Burrata, Basil, and Pomegranate Molasses (page 152), and Melty Sweet Potato Rounds with Honeyed Tahini and Toasted Sesame Seeds (page 159). But the great thing about Mediterranean cooking is that the use of vegetables truly goes well beyond small sides. You can play up seasonal produce in a big all-veg casserole like the Messy Vegetable Briam (page 135), toss them with a little pearled couscous or spaghetti for the perfect pasta night, or pair your greens with your beans to create the perfect warm-your-belly soup, like my Garlicky Spinach and Chickpea Soup with Lemon and Pecorino Romano (page 148). I hope this chapter will inspire you to add more color to every meal.

messy vegetable briam

SERVES 4 TO 5 AS A MAIN COURSE, 8 AS A SIDE DISH

Many years ago, at a small restaurant on the Greek island of Patmos, my dining posse and I asked the older couple who owned the place to surprise us with their best homemade dish. They brought out a rustic, blistered vegetable casserole and warm bread for sopping up the saucy, garlicky goodness. Similar to Provence's ratatouille and other related dishes throughout the Mediterranean, briam melds eggplant, zucchini, tomatoes, and potatoes (which are roasted to succulent, stewy perfection with plenty of good olive oil and fragrant herbs and spices). You can slice the vegetables into rounds and arrange them in neat rows, or just toss them together in a large baking pan and call it good. A bed of rice or warm rustic bread is all you need to complete the meal, although a small plate of feta and some olives won't hurt.

1 medium globe eggplant (about **1 pound**), partly peeled to create a striped pattern and cut into 1-inch pieces

Kosher salt

2 medium zucchini (about **1 pound**), cut into 1-inch pieces

3 medium Yukon Gold or other yellow potatoes (about **1 pound**), peeled and cut into 1-inch pieces

1 large red onion, cut into 1-inch pieces

5 large garlic cloves, minced

2 teaspoons dried oregano

1 teaspoon sweet paprika

1 teaspoon ground black pepper

½ **teaspoon** ground cumin

½ **cup** roughly chopped fresh flat-leaf parsley

Extra-virgin olive oil

1 **(28-ounce)** can crushed tomatoes

Crumbled feta cheese, olives, bread, or rice, for serving

1. Place the eggplant in a large colander in the sink. Sprinkle with about 1 teaspoon salt. Toss and let the eggplant sit to "sweat out" its bitterness for 20 to 30 minutes, then rinse briefly with water and dry well with paper towels.

2. Position a rack in the center of the oven and preheat the oven to 400°F.

3. Place the eggplant, zucchini, potatoes, and red onion in a large bowl. Add the garlic, oregano, paprika, black pepper, cumin, and a big pinch of salt (about ½ teaspoon). Add the parsley and ⅓ cup of olive oil, and give the vegetables a good toss to make sure they're evenly coated with the oil and spices.

4. Spread half the tomatoes in a 9 × 13 × 2-inch baking pan (or 4-quart baking dish). Arrange the vegetables evenly over the tomatoes. Cover the vegetables evenly with the remaining tomatoes. Drizzle generously with more olive oil. Cover the pan with foil, making sure the foil is not touching the vegetables, and bake for 45 minutes. Carefully remove the foil and continue to bake until the vegetables are very tender and caramelized in some parts, about another 30 minutes.

5. Serve with feta cheese, olives, and your favorite crusty bread, or over a bed of rice or other grain.

roasted bell pepper boats
with orzo and basil vinaigrette

This is a quick and modern take on Mahshi (page 230), or stuffed vegetables. The peppers are roasted until tender, and then filled with an herby warm orzo pasta. No one is ever mad when I serve them as a vegetarian main, but they also make a great side next to something meaty or even grilled fish.

Extra-virgin olive oil

5 large bell peppers, any colors, halved lengthwise, cored, and seeded

2 teaspoons dried oregano

Kosher salt and ground black pepper

¾ cup orzo pasta

1 cup cooked or canned chickpeas, drained

1 cup cherry tomatoes, halved

1 large shallot, minced

¼ cup chopped pitted kalamata olives

¼ cup toasted pine nuts (optional)

⅓ cup Basil Vinaigrette (page 281), plus more to taste

⅓ cup crumbled creamy feta cheese (from a 2-ounce block)

1. Position a rack in the center of the oven and preheat the oven to 400°F. Brush a large baking dish with about 1 tablespoon of olive oil.

2. Brush the peppers generously on all sides with some olive oil and arrange them in a single layer, cut side up, in the baking dish. Season with the oregano and a big pinch of both salt and black pepper (about ½ teaspoon each). Roast the peppers until they are tender, 30 to 35 minutes.

3. Meanwhile, bring a large pot of salted water to a boil and cook the orzo according to package instructions or until al dente, about 8 minutes. Drain well.

4. In a medium bowl, combine the orzo, chickpeas, tomatoes, shallot, olives, and pine nuts (if using). Drizzle with the vinaigrette, then toss to combine. Taste and add more of the vinaigrette to your liking.

5. Spoon the orzo mixture into the pepper halves. Sprinkle a little feta on top and serve.

greek-style baked butter beans

SERVES 4 AS A MAIN COURSE, 8 AS A SIDE DISH

A while back, I got an email from a reader named Dorothy, who was asking about gigandes plaki, a tender baked-bean casserole with loads of olive oil that her favorite Greek restaurant in Vancouver used to serve. Any idea of turning humble beans into a satisfying family meal gets me excited so I went to work on this recipe for Dorothy! Since the traditional gigandes (giant) beans can be hard to source, I typically go with the largest canned white beans I can find. This satisfying dish makes a great vegetarian main, or you can serve it at room temperature over crusty bread as part of a mezze spread for a larger crowd. This recipe makes a good amount and will keep well in the fridge for 4 days or so in a tightly closed container.

Extra-virgin olive oil

1 large yellow onion, roughly chopped

2 large carrots, peeled and roughly chopped

2 celery stalks, roughly chopped

4 large garlic cloves, minced

Kosher salt

1 (28-ounce) can diced tomatoes, with juices

¾ cup water

½ cup chopped flat-leaf parsley, plus more for garnish

1 tablespoon fresh thyme leaves

1½ teaspoons dried oregano

½ to 1 teaspoon red pepper flakes

½ teaspoon ground black pepper

¼ to ½ teaspoon ground cinnamon

1 dried bay leaf

2 (15-ounce) cans butter beans, drained and rinsed (or the largest beans you can find)

Creamy feta cheese, crumbled

Rustic bread, for serving

1. Position a rack in the center of the oven and preheat the oven to 375°F. In a large oven-safe skillet, heat ¼ cup of olive oil over medium-high heat until shimmering. Add the onion, carrots, celery, and garlic. Season with a big pinch of salt (about ½ teaspoon). Cook, stirring frequently, until the vegetables soften, 5 to 7 minutes.

2. Add the tomatoes with their juices and the water. Season with another big pinch of salt (about ½ teaspoon). Add the parsley, thyme, oregano, red pepper flakes, black pepper, cinnamon, and bay leaf.

3. Stir in the beans and cook for 5 minutes over high heat. At this point, taste and adjust the seasoning to your liking, then transfer the mixture to the oven and bake until thickened and the top layer turns a light golden brown, 25 to 30 minutes.

4. Remove and discard the bay leaf. Finish the dish with a drizzle of olive oil, a pinch of parsley, and a good sprinkle of feta. Serve with rustic bread.

egyptian moussaka

SERVES 4 AS A MAIN COURSE

Don't get me wrong, I totally dig Greek moussaka, with its rich meat filling and indulgent layer of creamy bechamel. But my first love is for the humbler *sha'abi* (local) moussaka of my childhood: layers of eggplant and green peppers in a pool of a garlicky, vinegar-spiked tomato sauce. This was one of my mom's specialties, and I remember begging for it at least once a week.

2 medium globe eggplants (about **2 pounds** total)

Kosher salt and ground black pepper

Extra-virgin olive oil

2 green bell peppers, cored, seeded, and sliced into 2-inch-wide strips

4 large garlic cloves, minced

1 (**28-ounce**) can whole San Marzano tomatoes, with juices

½ **teaspoon** ground coriander

½ **teaspoon** sweet paprika

½ **teaspoon** red pepper flakes, plus more to taste

2½ **tablespoons** distilled white vinegar

Warm pita bread, for serving

1. Position a rack in the center of the oven and preheat the oven to 400°F.

2. Trim the ends of the eggplant and partially peel them lengthwise to make a striped pattern, then slice them lengthwise into ½-inch-thick slabs. Season the eggplant well on both sides with salt (1 to 1½ teaspoons) and arrange the slabs in a single layer on a large tray or other clean surface. Let them sit for 20 to 30 minutes. Using a paper towel, dry the eggplant slabs and wipe away any excess salt.

3. Brush the eggplant slabs on both sides with about ¼ cup of olive oil and arrange them in a single layer in two 13 × 18 × 1-inch sheet pans. Brush the bell pepper slices with a little olive oil on both sides and place them next to the eggplant. Bake until both the eggplant and the bell pepper are soft and pliable, about 20 minutes.

4. Meanwhile, in a large skillet, heat ¼ cup of olive oil over medium heat until shimmering. Add the garlic, immediately reduce the heat to low, and cook, stirring regularly, until fragrant and light golden, adjusting the time and heat as needed to avoid burning, about 1 minute.

5. Add the tomatoes and their juices to the skillet and season with a generous pinch of salt and black pepper (about ¾ teaspoon each). Add the coriander, paprika, and red pepper flakes, then stir and raise the heat to medium-high. Bring the sauce to a boil and boil for 5 minutes, then reduce the heat and let simmer on low heat until the eggplant and bell peppers have finished par-baking, another 10 to 15 minutes. Add the vinegar and stir.

6. Nestle the eggplant and bell peppers in the sauce and cook over medium heat for another 15 to 20 minutes, until the sauce has thickened and turned a deeper red. Serve warm, with pita bread.

summer squash roll-ups with herbed ricotta and walnut stuffing

SERVES 4 AS A MAIN COURSE

When we lived in Des Moines, Iowa, I was lucky enough to have friends with green thumbs. One summer in particular, my friend Wendy, whose husband owned a landscaping business, regularly gifted me with giant zucchini from their abundant garden. I'd go to town coming up with creative ways to keep them from going to waste: I'd slice them into rounds and sauté them in good olive oil; I'd hollow them out and stuffed them with meat and rice; I'd char them on the grill and finish them with an herby dressing. And, yes, I would sometimes slice them thinly lengthwise and then roll the planks up with cheese and bake them.

Here I do just that, stuffing them with a ricotta and walnut filling that makes this dish comforting, hearty, and somewhat fancy. It's also fairly easy to prepare. Any medium or larger zucchini or summer squash will work for this, so long as they are cylindrical rather than crookneck. Use the sharpest knife you have, or even a mandoline, for thin and even slices. Once roasted for a little bit, the squash will be pliable enough to roll up. For a layer of smoky flavor, you can also quickly char the squash slices on the grill. My garlicky, herb-loaded Busy Mama's Spaghetti Sauce (page 288) pairs beautifully with this (make it in advance), but if you go with store-bought marinara, you won't hurt my feelings.

Squash

Extra-virgin olive oil

1½ **pounds** zucchini or straight-neck summer squash (about 4 medium or 3 large), ends trimmed, then sliced lengthwise into ¼-inch slabs

Kosher salt

2 **cups** Busy Mama's Spaghetti Sauce (page 288), or your favorite store-bought marinara sauce

Finely chopped fresh flat-leaf parsley, for garnish

Finely chopped fresh basil, for garnish

1. Position a rack in the center of the oven and another above or below it. Preheat the oven to 400°F. Have ready two 13 × 18 × 1-inch sheet pans and an 8 × 11 × 2-inch baking dish.

2. **Prepare the squash:** Lightly brush the sheet pans with some olive oil. Arrange the zucchini slabs on the pans in a single layer. Season lightly with salt and brush the tops with some olive oil. Bake one sheet pan on the center rack and the other on the other rack until the squash is pliable but still firm, taking care that it does not turn mushy, 5 to 10 minutes. Set aside to cool briefly. Leave the oven on.

3. **Make the stuffing:** In a medium bowl, beat the egg with a fork, then add the ricotta, Parmesan, walnuts, garlic, oregano, parsley, basil, and a pinch each of salt and black pepper. Add about 1 tablespoon olive oil and mix with a spoon until well combined.

Herbed Ricotta and Walnut Stuffing

1 large egg

1 cup ricotta

½ **cup** grated Parmesan cheese

¼ **cup** finely chopped walnuts

1 large garlic clove, minced

½ **teaspoon** dried oregano

½ **cup** finely chopped fresh
   flat-leaf parsley

¼ **cup** finely chopped fresh basil

Ground black pepper

Crusty bread, for serving

4. Assemble and bake the squash rolls: Spread about ¾ cup of the spaghetti sauce in the baking dish. Spoon about 1 tablespoon of the stuffing on each squash slice and spread gently with the back of a spoon to cover the slabs evenly. Starting with the short end closest to you, roll the squash slices into pinwheels (rolls). Arrange the pinwheels in the baking dish, seam side down. Drop dollops of any leftover cheese mixture in between the roll-ups and spoon the remaining sauce on top.

5. Bake the squash rolls on the middle rack of the oven until the squash is fully cooked and very tender (the ricotta mixture may ooze out the sides, which is just fine), 15 to 20 minutes. Remove from the oven and let sit for 5 to 10 minutes. Sprinkle with the parsley and basil, and serve with crusty bread.

fasolia

SERVES 4 AS A MAIN COURSE, 6 AS A SIDE DISH

When you take a bite of these braised green beans, the beans will be neither crispy nor mushy, but instead will be super tender with a velvety finish.

The fasolia I grew up with were slowly braised with tomatoes and plenty of herbs and spices, and often incorporated bits of minced meat, as well. For a vegetarian take on this dish, I augment it instead with yellow potatoes for substance and carrots for a contrasting pop of color and sweetness. Served over Middle Eastern Rice Pilaf with Toasted Vermicelli and Pine Nuts (page 161), it's a meal in itself, but also pairs well as a side dish with chicken, lamb, or any meaty main.

Extra-virgin olive oil

1 large yellow onion, finely chopped

5 large garlic cloves, minced

2 teaspoons dried oregano

1 teaspoon ground cumin

1 (28-ounce) can whole peeled tomatoes (preferably San Marzano), with juices

1 dried bay leaf

1½ pounds fresh green beans, trimmed and cut into 1½-inch pieces (frozen cut green beans work well also)

3 medium Yukon Gold or other yellow potatoes (about **1 pound**), cut into ½- to ¾-inch pieces

3 large carrots, peeled and diced

1 cup water

Kosher salt and ground black pepper

Juice of **1** large lemon (about **¼ cup**)

½ cup roughly chopped fresh flat-leaf parsley

Rustic bread or rice, for serving

1. Position a rack in the center of the oven and preheat the oven to 300°F.

2. In a large Dutch oven or oven-safe pot with a lid, heat ¼ cup of the olive oil over medium heat. Add the onion and cook, stirring occasionally, until tender, 5 to 7 minutes. Add the garlic, oregano, and cumin. Cook, stirring frequently, until fragrant, another 2 minutes.

3. Add the tomatoes, bay leaf, green beans, potatoes, carrots, and water. Season to taste with salt and black pepper. Raise the heat and simmer for 15 minutes, stirring occasionally.

4. Cover and transfer the pot to the oven. Bake until the sauce thickens slightly and the beans and potatoes can easily be cut with the side of your fork, about 35 minutes or so. (It's a good idea to check once partway through cooking, adding a little bit of water if needed.)

5. Remove and discard the bay leaf. Stir in the lemon juice, parsley, and a generous drizzle of good olive oil (about ¼ cup or so). Serve with your choice of rice or rustic bread to sop up the sauce!

cheesy cauliflower fusilli with pine nuts

SERVES 4 AS A MAIN COURSE

No, I didn't replace traditional semolina pasta with a gluten-free alternative made from cauliflower to create this recipe. I'm not that trendy, and I still like my carbs. I just happened to have a half-used box of pasta in my pantry and found that I could stretch the pasta into a meal for the whole family by bulking it up with tasty bits of cauliflower that were caramelized in garlic-infused olive oil. Use a short, curly pasta (like fusilli or rotini), which will hold on to the cheesy coating of salty pecorino Romano cheese and melty, nutty Italian fontal.

Kosher salt

1 large head of cauliflower (2 to 2½ pounds), trimmed of leaves and quartered

8 ounces fusilli or other short, curly pasta

Extra-virgin olive oil

2 small garlic cloves, smashed

½ teaspoon red pepper flakes, plus more for serving

2 ounces pecorino Romano cheese, finely grated (scant **¾ cup**), plus more for serving

2 ounces fontina or fontal cheese, grated (**½ cup** packed), plus more for serving

⅓ cup pine nuts, lightly toasted

1. In a large pot, bring about 10 cups of water to a boil over high heat and season well with about 2 tablespoons salt. Carefully add the cauliflower to the boiling water and cook for 5 minutes. Using tongs, remove the cauliflower and set it on a large plate to cool.

2. Bring the water back to a boil and add the pasta. Cook for about 7 minutes, until tender but not fully cooked. Using a ladle, transfer 3 cups of the pasta cooking water to a bowl. Drain the pasta.

3. Chop the cooled cauliflower into very small pieces (not quite as small as cauliflower rice, though).

4. In a large nonstick pan over medium heat, heat 6 tablespoons of the olive oil until shimmering. Add the garlic, stirring frequently until it turns golden brown, 1 or 2 minutes.

5. Discard the garlic and raise the heat to medium-high. Add the cauliflower and red pepper flakes and cook, stirring occasionally, until the cauliflower turns a deep golden brown (I like to have some charred bits as well), about 15 minutes.

6. Reduce the heat to medium and add the pasta along with ¼ cup of the reserved pasta cooking water. Cook for 4 minutes or so, tossing frequently until the pasta is cooked to al dente; add a little more water if needed. Stir in the pecorino Romano and add about ½ cup more of the pasta water. Then add the remaining cheese and stir until all the cheese is melted and the pasta is well coated with it. Drizzle with a little more olive oil and stir. Taste and adjust the seasoning.

7. Transfer the pasta to bowls and top with the pine nuts. Serve with more cheese and red pepper flakes on the side.

fire-roasted tomato, freekeh, and black-eyed pea soup

SERVES 4 TO 6 AS A MAIN COURSE

Freekeh (see page 28) is young green wheat whose stalks are burned in the production process to remove the chaff—you can definitely detect a slight smoky taste to the grain. Here I pair it with black-eyed peas and add aromatics and canned fire-roasted tomatoes to subtly play up the smoky flavor of the freekeh. Don't worry; if you buy a whole package of freekeh to make this soup, I promise I'll give you more ways to use it, including my Extra-Nutty Freekeh Pilaf with Dried Fruit (page 162) or my Fish and Freekeh Casserole (page 177). I like my soup rib-sticking thick, if you prefer it thinner, add one or two more cups of broth.

1½ **cups** cracked freekeh

3 **tablespoons** extra-virgin olive oil

1 medium yellow onion, roughly chopped

2 celery stalks, roughly chopped

2 large carrots, peeled and roughly chopped

4 large garlic cloves, minced

Kosher salt

1 (14.5-**ounce**) can diced fire-roasted tomatoes

1 (14.5-**ounce**) can black-eyed peas, drained and rinsed

6 **cups** low-sodium vegetable broth or chicken broth, plus more as needed

1 **teaspoon** ground black pepper

1 **teaspoon** sweet paprika

¾ **teaspoon** ground cumin

2 **or** 3 fresh thyme sprigs

¼ **cup** roughly chopped fresh flat-leaf parsley

1. Rinse the freekeh under running water, then put it in a bowl and cover with cold water. Set aside for 30 minutes, or until tender.

2. Meanwhile, in a large Dutch oven, heat the olive oil over medium heat until shimmering. Add the onion, celery, carrots, garlic, and a generous pinch of salt (about ¾ teaspoon). Cook, stirring regularly, until softened, about 5 minutes.

3. Drain the freekeh and add it to the pot. Stir in the tomatoes, black-eyed peas, and broth. Add the black pepper, paprika, cumin, and thyme sprigs.

4. Bring to a boil and cook for 4 minutes, then reduce the heat to low and simmer, partially covered, until the freekeh is fully cooked (it should be tender and slightly chewy), about 20 minutes.

5. Just before serving, remove the thyme sprigs and stir in the fresh parsley.

harissa, red lentil, and tomato soup

SERVES 4 TO 6 AS A MAIN COURSE

Red lentils have a sweet, nutty taste and a creamy consistency that I find so soothing in vegetable stews and soups like this one. A dollop of harissa—the iconic North African paste of chiles and warm spices—stirred in at the end adds a little extra heat and a layer of tang and umami. If you've ever thought of lentils as bland or boring, trust me, you won't after you give this easy one-pot meal a try.

I highly recommend you make Homemade Harissa Paste (page 286), but in a pinch you can use quality store-bought harissa (and by quality here I mean that you wouldn't mind eating the stuff straight from the jar).

Extra-virgin olive oil

1 medium yellow onion, roughly chopped

2 large garlic cloves, minced

3 medium carrots, peeled and roughly chopped

2 celery stalks, roughly chopped

Kosher salt and ground black pepper

1 teaspoon ground coriander

½ teaspoon ground cumin

¼ teaspoon ground turmeric

2 vine-ripened medium tomatoes, chopped

3 tablespoons tomato paste

1½ cups red lentils, rinsed

4 cups vegetable stock

1 cup water

2 to 4 tablespoons Homemade Harissa Paste (page 286), or quality store-bought harissa

Juice of 1 large lime (about 2 tablespoons)

½ cup roughly chopped fresh cilantro

Crusty bread, for serving

1. In a medium Dutch oven or pot, heat 3 tablespoons of the olive oil over medium-high heat until shimmering. Add the onion, garlic, carrots, and celery and season with a big pinch of salt and black pepper (about ½ teaspoon each). Reduce the heat to medium and cook the vegetables for 5 to 7 minutes, tossing regularly until they soften.

2. Add the coriander, cumin, and turmeric to the pot and stir to coat the vegetables. Stir in the tomatoes and tomato paste and cook for another 5 minutes over medium heat, then add the lentils, vegetable stock, and water.

3. Raise the heat to medium-high and bring to a boil, then boil for 5 minutes. Turn the heat to medium-low, cover partially with the lid, and simmer for 20 to 25 minutes, until the lentils are tender and creamy. Check occasionally and add a little more stock or water if the soup gets too thick for your liking.

4. Stir in the harissa, 1 tablespoon of the lime juice, and the cilantro. Taste and adjust the seasoning, and if needed add the remaining tablespoon lime juice. Serve hot with your favorite crusty bread.

garlicky spinach and chickpea soup with lemon and pecorino romano

SERVES 4 AS A MAIN COURSE

If someone were to dare me to make a kick-butt Mediterranean dinner using pantry scraps, this chickpea soup would be it. Canned chickpeas and baby spinach are the stars, supported by onions, fresh garlic, a few spices, and the all-essential fresh lemon juice. I love that this soup begins all North African with warm notes of things like coriander and cumin and ends Italian style, with a pour of extra-virgin olive oil (the good stuff) and a shower of grated pecorino Romano cheese. If you skip the cheese, you will not know what you're missing; it rounds out the flavor in the best way possible.

2 (15-ounce) cans chickpeas

Extra-virgin olive oil

1 large yellow onion, roughly chopped

4 or 5 large garlic cloves, minced

Kosher salt

1 teaspoon ground cumin

1 teaspoon ground coriander

¾ teaspoon sweet paprika

½ teaspoon red pepper flakes

½ teaspoon ground black pepper

4 cups vegetable stock or low-sodium chicken broth

2 cups (packed) fresh baby spinach (2 to 3 ounces)

½ cup roughly chopped fresh flat-leaf parsley

1 large lemon, cut in half

½ cup grated pecorino Romano cheese

Crusty bread, for serving

1. Drain the chickpeas, reserving ½ cup of their liquid.

2. In a large pot, heat 3 tablespoons of the olive oil over medium heat until shimmering. Add the onion and garlic and season with a big pinch of salt (about ½ teaspoon). Cook over medium heat, stirring regularly, until fragrant, about 5 minutes. Add the cumin, coriander, paprika, red pepper flakes, and black pepper and cook, stirring regularly for about 30 seconds.

3. Add the chickpeas and stir to coat with the spices. Using a potato masher or the back of a sturdy fork, roughly mash the chickpeas (you're just looking to break some of the chickpeas).

4. Add the stock and the reserved chickpea liquid. Raise the heat and bring to a boil, then boil for 5 minutes. Turn the heat down to medium-low and partly cover the pot with the lid. Simmer the chickpeas for 30 minutes.

5. Turn the heat off. Stir in the spinach and parsley, and let the soup sit for 1 minute, until the spinach wilts. Squeeze half a lemon over the soup, stir, and taste, adding more lemon juice to your liking.

6. Transfer the soup to serving bowls and top each bowl with a drizzle of olive oil and a bit of grated pecorino Romano cheese. Serve with crusty bread.

mushroom, veggie, and feta phyllo purses

SERVES 6 AS A SIDE DISH

If you haven't used it much, let me start by saying: do not fear phyllo! I know the paper-thin sheets can be intimidating to work with, but this recipe is a fun one to try because you don't have to worry about a perfectly shaped pastry. Here, the sheets are whimsically wrapped around an herby mixture of tender sautéed veggies and feta. Once baked, what might have looked like a crumbly mess magically turns into a crispy little purse—a delightful, savory surprise for company!

Extra-virgin olive oil

1 pound baby bella mushrooms, roughly chopped

1 large red bell pepper, cored, seeded, and roughly chopped

1 medium zucchini, roughly chopped

1 small yellow onion, roughly chopped

2 large garlic cloves, minced

Kosher salt

1 teaspoon ground black pepper

1 teaspoon dried oregano

½ cup roughly chopped fresh flat-leaf parsley

½ cup creamy feta cheese, crumbled (from a 2½-ounce block)

18 frozen phyllo sheets (about half a 1-pound box), thawed if frozen

1. Position a rack in the center of the oven and preheat the oven to 375°F.

2. In a large nonstick skillet, heat 3 tablespoons of the olive oil over medium-high heat until shimmering. Add the chopped mushrooms, bell pepper, zucchini, onion, and garlic. Season with a big pinch of salt (about ½ teaspoon), the black pepper, and oregano. Cook for about 25 minutes, tossing occasionally, until the veggies soften and fully release their liquid (there should be no liquid in the pan when you're done). Stir in the parsley and feta, then set aside.

3. Unroll the phyllo sheets on a work surface and cover with plastic wrap, then top with a lightly dampened cloth. (This will keep the phyllo from drying out and breaking while you work.)

4. Line a large sheet pan with parchment paper and lightly brush with some olive oil. Place 3 sheets of phyllo on top of each other in the sheet pan and brush the top sheet with a little olive oil.

5. Place 4 generous tablespoons of the veggie mixture in the middle of the phyllo. Pull the sides of the phyllo up and gather at the top (yes, it will crumble and that is okay). Brush the top layer of phyllo, including the crumbled top, with a little olive oil.

6. Set this first "purse" of phyllo in one corner of the sheet pan. Repeat 5 more times to make a total of 6 phyllo purses stuffed with the mushroom and veggies mixture.

7. Bake for 25 minutes, or until the purses are golden brown and crispy.

blistered plum tomatoes with burrata, basil, and pomegranate molasses

SERVES 6 AS A SIDE DISH

It's safe to admit that I have a legit tomato obsession, but I have to say that blistered tomatoes—intense with flavor and perfectly collapsed in their juices—are one of my favorite ways to get my tomato fix. This little number mingles with burrata (mozzarella's softer, oozier cousin) to make a fun side dish—but don't be shy to toss it all together with your favorite pasta and call it dinner! And if you don't plan to use the roasted tomatoes right away, hold the burrata and basil and let the tomatoes cool completely, then store them in your fridge in an airtight container for up to 4 days. You can stir them into soups or add them to toasted bread that's been slathered with Herbed Labneh (page 293).

2 pounds small Roma (plum) tomatoes, halved

3 large garlic cloves, minced

2 teaspoons fresh thyme leaves

1 teaspoon Aleppo pepper flakes

Kosher salt and ground black pepper

¼ cup extra-virgin olive oil

1 to 2 tablespoons pomegranate molasses or prepared balsamic glaze (a sweetened reduction of balsamic vinegar)

4 to 6 ounces burrata cheese

¼ cup torn fresh basil leaves

1. Position a rack in the center of the oven and preheat the oven to 425°F.

2. Place the tomato halves in a large bowl. Add the garlic, thyme, Aleppo pepper, and a big pinch of salt and black pepper (about ½ teaspoon each). Drizzle with the olive oil and toss well to combine.

3. Transfer the tomatoes to a 13 × 18 × 1-inch sheet pan. Spread the tomatoes, flesh side up, in a single layer. Roast for 30 to 45 minutes, until the tomatoes have collapsed to your desired doneness.

4. Allow the tomatoes to cool a little bit, then transfer them with their juices to a serving platter. Drizzle with the pomegranate molasses or balsamic glaze. Tear the burrata into pieces and add on top, and finish with the torn basil leaves.

roasted roots with herbed labneh and preserved lemon

SERVES 6 AS A SIDE DISH

Roasted root veggies deliver all kinds of comfort—all you have to do to coax out their God-given sweetness is to coat them with some good olive oil and let them linger in a hot oven until they're tender, with perfectly caramelized edges. That's what this recipe gives you—and more. As soon as they emerge from the oven, sprinkle them with mellow, buttery roasted garlic and bits of tangy preserved lemon, then serve them with some herby labneh for a dollop of cool, creamy indulgence in every bite.

4 small Yukon Gold or other yellow potatoes, peeled and cut into 1½-inch pieces

2 large carrots, peeled and cut into 1½-inch pieces

1 large golden beet, peeled, trimmed, and cut into 1½-inch pieces

1 large red onion, cut into 1½-inch pieces

Kosher salt and ground black pepper

1½ **teaspoons** Aleppo pepper flakes

¼ **cup** extra-virgin olive oil, plus more as needed

2 large red beets, peeled, trimmed, and cut into 1½-inch pieces

1 head of garlic

1 or 2 Easy Preserved Lemons (page 285), cut into small pieces, to serve

Herbed Labneh (page 293), to serve

1. Position a rack in the center of the oven and preheat the oven to 425°F.

2. In a large bowl, combine the potatoes, carrots, golden beet, and red onion pieces. Season well with salt and black pepper. Add 1 teaspoon Aleppo pepper and the olive oil. Toss to coat well. Transfer the veggies to a 13 × 18 × 1-inch nonstick sheet pan and arrange them in a single layer.

3. In the same bowl, place the red beets and season with a small pinch of salt and pepper (about ¼ teaspoon each) and remaining ½ teaspoon Aleppo pepper. Add a drizzle of olive oil and toss to coat. Transfer to the sheet pan.

4. Peel off the outermost papery skin of the garlic but leave the head intact. Slice the top of the garlic head off (¼ to ½ inch from top), leaving the cloves exposed. Make sure all the cloves have some portion exposed so that they properly roast. Place the garlic head on a piece of foil and drizzle the garlic with about 1 tablespoon olive oil and massage the oil over the exposed clove tips. Close up the foil around the garlic head and place it in the sheet pan.

5. Roast the veggies for 30 minutes, then use a pair of tongs to carefully turn them over and return them to the oven to roast for another 10 to 15 minutes, until the vegetables are quite tender and charred in some places.

6. Transfer the roasted vegetables to a serving platter. Pop the roasted garlic cloves out of the head and give them a rough chop. Sprinkle the garlic and the preserved lemons all over the vegetables. Then dollop the labneh on top in different places and serve with the remaining labneh on the side.

the crispiest red-skinned potatoes with dukkah or spicy walnut-cilantro chili sauce

SERVES 6 AS A SIDE DISH

Sometimes, it is just nice to serve your meal with a side of satisfying potatoes—especially, when roasted according to this genius method I learned from J. Kenji Lopez-Alt. In one of his food science-y videos, he first parboiled the chunked raw potatoes in water with a little baking soda, which causes the pectin in the potatoes to break down, resulting in more surface area that will crisp up to golden-brown perfection, while keeping the insides meltingly tender. Game changer! Now, to dress the potatoes up, try some nutty Dukkah (page 282) or Spicy Walnut-Cilantro Chili Sauce (page 287).

Kosher salt

½ **teaspoon** baking soda

3 **pounds** red-skinned potatoes, scrubbed and quartered (or halved, depending on size)

¾ **teaspoon** ground black pepper

5 **tablespoons** extra-virgin olive oil

Dukkah (page 282) or Spicy Walnut-Cilantro Chili Sauce (page 287), for serving

1. Position a rack in the center of the oven. Preheat the oven to 450°F. When the oven is hot, place a 13 × 9 × 1-inch sheet pan on the middle rack.

2. Using a large pot, bring about 8 cups of water to a boil. Add 1 tablespoon salt and the baking soda. Carefully add the potatoes and bring back to a boil. Cook until you can easily stick a fork in a potato piece without meeting much resistance, 10 to 15 minutes after the water returns to a boil. Drain the potatoes in a large colander and let them sit for 5 minutes or so to allow excess moisture to evaporate.

3. Return the potatoes to the pot and season with a big pinch of salt (about ½ teaspoon) and the black pepper. Drizzle the olive oil over the potatoes and give the pot a few good shakes to make sure the potatoes are well coated.

4. Wearing oven mitts, carefully take the hot sheet pan out of the oven and spread the potatoes in a single layer in the pan. Return the pan to the oven and roast the potatoes for 20 minutes, undisturbed.

5. Carefully take the sheet pan out of the oven again and, using tongs, turn the potatoes over. Return them to the oven and roast for another 30 minutes or so, turning and shaking them a couple of times during cooking, until they are crisp all over, turning a deep golden brown.

6. Transfer the potatoes to a serving platter and either toss with a few tablespoons of dukkah or drizzle with the chili sauce.

melty sweet potato rounds with honeyed tahini and toasted sesame seeds

SERVES 8 TO 10 AS AN APPETIZER, 4 TO 6 AS A SIDE DISH

The secret to getting melty-tender sweet potatoes? First, cover tightly with foil and roast them so the steam will work its magic to soften the potatoes' insides. Then uncover them and roast until nicely browned, concentrating and intensifying their natural flavors. As soon as they come out of the oven, hit the sweet potatoes with the magical honeyed tahini and some toasted sesame seeds. Then pass them around on a platter for everyone to eat with their fingers and watch them disappear! (If by chance you don't use all the honeyed tahini, it's extra indulgent when smeared on your breakfast toast—you may just ditch PB&J forever. And if you don't have leftover honeyed tahini, you may want to consider doubling it next time!)

Extra-virgin olive oil

3 medium sweet potatoes, scrubbed and cut into ¾-inch-thick rounds

Kosher salt

½ **cup** tahini, well stirred

¼ **cup** honey

¼ **cup** toasted sesame seeds

1. Position a rack in the center of the oven. Preheat the oven to 425°F. Line a 13 × 9 × 1-inch sheet pan with foil and brush generously with olive oil.

2. Arrange the sweet potato rounds in the pan in a single layer. Generously brush the tops of the rounds with olive oil and season with a big pinch of salt (about ½ teaspoon). Cover the pan tightly with another piece of foil.

3. Roast the potatoes for 30 minutes, then remove the top foil and discard. Return the potatoes to the oven and roast for another 15 to 20 minutes, until the bottoms turn golden brown. Carefully flip the rounds over to roast on the other side for an additional 10 minutes or so. When finished, the potatoes should be melty-tender and charred nicely on both sides. Let the sweet potatoes cool briefly for 5 minutes.

4. In a small bowl, combine the tahini and honey and stir well. If the mixture is thick, warm it up for a few seconds in the microwave. (You want it to be runny enough to drizzle over the potatoes.)

5. Using a spatula, transfer the sweet potato rounds to a serving platter. Drizzle the honeyed tahini over the sweet potatoes and top with a generous sprinkle of sesame seeds. Serve immediately.

raquel's falafel-inspired roasted veggie bowls

SERVES 4

My brilliant editor and friend Raquel Pelzel and I are equally obsessed with falafel. I asked her to share an easy recipe that her family loves, and I'm so glad she shared this one:

I love falafel, but I'm not gonna lie—I'm too lazy to make and fry them! These bowls satisfy my falafel cravings completely—in a fraction of the time. For the chickpeas, I use Suzy's method on page 92 in step 4 of the recipe. If I have fresh herbs like thyme and sage, I'll chop some up and add them in, too.

For the roasted vegetables

¼ **cup** extra-virgin olive oil

12 garlic cloves, minced

1 **tablespoon** ground cumin

1 **tablespoon** ground coriander

1½ **teaspoons** fine salt or
    1 **tablespoon** kosher salt

1 head of cauliflower, cut into
    bite-sized florets

10 **ounces** cremini mushrooms,
    stemmed and quartered

For the bowls

Cooked long-grain white rice
    (about 4 cups)

Crispy Chickpeas (page 92) or
    1 (**15-ounce**) can chickpeas,
    drained and rinsed

2 Persian cucumbers, chopped

1 **cup** quartered cherry or grape
    tomatoes

¼ red bell pepper, finely chopped

2 scallions, thinly sliced

2 **tablespoons** chopped curly
    parsley

Lime-Tahini Sauce (page 290)

1. Preheat the oven to 425°F.

2. In a large bowl whisk together the olive oil, garlic, cumin, coriander, and salt. Add the cauliflower and mushrooms and toss to coat well in the oil and spices. Transfer to a parchment paper-lined sheet pan and toast until very tender and brown, 25 to 30 minutes, stirring midway through. Remove from the oven and set aside.

3. Divide the rice among 4 bowls. Top with cauliflower and mushrooms, then add a sprinkle of chickpeas, cucumbers, tomatoes, bell pepper, scallion, and parsley. Drizzle with the lime-tahini sauce and serve.

middle eastern rice pilaf with toasted vermicelli and pine nuts

SERVES 6 AS A SIDE DISH

This simple vegan mixture of white rice and toasted vermicelli is the everyday starch in many parts of the Middle East, and it's the one side I make more often than anything else. The pine nuts are optional, but they add another dimension of flavor and texture that complements pretty much anything I choose to serve this with. As easy as it is to make, there are a few important steps to achieve the fluffiness and balanced taste. Check out the tips!

2 cups medium-grain or long-grain white rice

Extra-virgin olive oil

1 cup vermicelli pasta, broken into 1- or 2-inch pieces

Kosher salt

3½ cups water

½ cup pine nuts (optional)

Tips for perfect rice

First, rinse the rice well to get rid of any excess starch, which would cause it to become sticky and clumpy. Second, soak the rice in cold water for 20 minutes; this shortens the cooking time so that the interior of the grain cooks through before the exterior loses its shape. Third, season the rice with salt at the beginning; this evenly flavors the grains as they cook. And last, when the rice is fully cooked, let it rest, covered, for 10 to 15 minutes or so, then fluff it with a fork.

1. Put the rice in a large bowl and rinse very well under cold running water (the water should run clear). Cover the rice with fresh water and soak until you can easily break a grain of rice between your thumb and index finger, about 20 minutes. Drain well.

2. In a medium nonstick saucepan, heat 2½ tablespoons of the olive oil over medium-high heat until shimmering. Add the vermicelli and cook, stirring continuously, to toast it evenly until it turns a nice golden brown, watching carefully so it does not burn.

3. Add the drained rice and stir briefly to coat with the oil. Season with a big pinch of salt (about ½ teaspoon). Add the water and bring to a boil, then boil until the water significantly reduces to just barely covering the rice.

4. Reduce the heat to low, cover the saucepan, and simmer until the rice is fully cooked, about 20 minutes. Turn the heat off and leave the rice covered in its pot for 10 to 15 minutes, then uncover and fluff with a fork.

5. Meanwhile, if using the pine nuts, heat a little bit of olive oil in a small skillet set over medium heat. Add the pine nuts and stir constantly, adjusting the heat to make sure the pine nuts turn a nice golden brown without burning, about 2 minutes. Watch carefully, as the nuts can burn fast.

6. Transfer the rice to a serving platter and top with the toasted pine nuts.

extra nutty
freekeh pilaf with dried fruit

SERVES 4 TO 6

Of all the Mediterranean grains I use—and I use a lot of them—I have a bias toward freekeh. Besides rice, it is probably the grain I associate most with my Egyptian childhood. Aside from freekeh soup (see page 144), which was a winter staple, the chewy, smoky, green wheat grains made their way to the dinner table in other ways, too. Even our celebratory Christmas turkey was stuffed with freekeh. I didn't much care for turkey as a kid, but I loved the stuffing. As an adult, I discovered that the combo of freekeh and toasted nuts makes a comforting dish to serve with many things—a little something special in place of rice. When I tested this recipe, my collaborator Susan and her husband Ralph were over for dinner. As we sampled it, we agreed that adding a little hint of sweetness in the form of dried fruit bits would take this freekeh dish to the next level. I got up and threw a bunch of raisins on top. And that did it!

2 cups cracked freekeh

Extra-virgin olive oil

1 medium yellow onion, roughly chopped

2 celery stalks, roughly chopped

2 large garlic cloves, minced

1 teaspoon ground cumin

½ **teaspoon** ground coriander

Kosher salt

2½ **cups** vegetable stock or low-sodium chicken broth

1 cup raw blanched almonds

1 cup raw blanched hazelnuts

⅓ **cup** shelled pistachios

⅓ **cup** dried fruit, such as raisins, chopped apricots, or chopped figs, or a combination

2 tablespoons roughly chopped fresh flat-leaf parsley

1. Rinse the freekeh and put it in a bowl. Cover with water and soak for 30 minutes, until tender.

2. In a pot, heat ¼ cup of the olive oil over medium-high heat until shimmering. Add the onion, celery, and garlic and cook for 5 minutes, tossing regularly and making sure the garlic does not burn.

3. Add the freekeh and season with the cumin, coriander, and a big pinch of salt (about ½ teaspoon). Add the stock and raise the heat to bring it to a rolling boil. Lower the heat and cover the pot, then simmer until the freekeh has fully absorbed the stock and is tender, 20 to 30 minutes.

4. In a medium skillet, heat 1 tablespoon of the olive oil over medium heat. Add the almonds, hazelnuts, and pistachios and cook, stirring constantly and watching carefully, until toasted, 3 to 5 minutes.

5. Transfer the freekeh to a serving platter and top with the chopped nuts, dried fruit, and parsley.

olive oil and garlic spaghetti with artichokes and olives

SERVES 4 AS A MAIN COURSE

If it's pasta night at my house and I give the girls a choice, they will pick this recipe every single time. That's how much they love it. The idea comes from the Naples classic, spaghetti aglio e olio, where noodles are cooked until al dente—tender but still firm to the bite—and then coated with garlic-infused olive oil. It might be served with no more than a shower of fresh parsley or a pinch of red pepper flakes. But for a complete vegetarian main, I like to sneak in a few of my favorite staples: yellow grape tomatoes, marinated artichoke hearts, and olives. Key to this dish is excellent olive oil, which is only briefly warmed through—not quite cooked—to preserve its delicate flavor. Just as important: Don't allow the garlic to brown as it warms in the oil, as that will bring an unwelcome bitterness to the dish. Keep this spaghetti dinner vegetarian or, if you like, toss in some cooked shrimp or grilled chicken at the end.

Kosher salt and ground black pepper

1 pound thin spaghetti

Extra-virgin olive oil

4 large garlic cloves, crushed

1 cup roughly chopped fresh flat-leaf parsley

2 cups halved yellow grape tomatoes

3 scallions, trimmed, white and green parts chopped

1 cup drained and quartered jarred marinated artichoke hearts

¼ cup halved pitted kalamata olives

2 to 3 ounces creamy feta cheese, crumbled (about ½ **cup**)

1 cup torn fresh basil leaves, plus more if desired

Grated zest of 1 lemon

½ teaspoon red pepper flakes (optional)

1. Bring a large pot of salted water to a rolling boil, add the pasta, and cook according to package instructions, until the spaghetti is al dente, 7 to 8 minutes.

2. When the pasta is almost ready, heat about ½ cup of the olive oil in a large, heavy skillet over medium heat. Turn the heat to low, add the garlic and a pinch of salt, then cook for 10 seconds, stirring frequently, taking care not to let the garlic burn. Add the parsley, tomatoes, and scallions and stir. Cook until just warmed through, about 30 seconds.

3. Drain the pasta and return it to the pot. Pour the warmed olive oil sauce over the pasta, then season to taste with salt and black pepper. Add the artichoke hearts, olives, feta, basil, lemon zest, and red pepper flakes (if using), and toss one more time.

4. Transfer the spaghetti and sauce to serving bowls and add a little more basil to your liking. Serve immediately.

toasted pearl couscous and summer vegetable medley

SERVES 4 TO 6 AS A SIDE DISH

Pearl couscous is a tiny pearl-shaped pasta that can transform a few produce items into a one-pot meal. Before adding the boiling water to the couscous, I toss the beads around in a pan with a generous bit of olive oil and then watch them turn a beautiful golden brown as they develop a toasty, nutty flavor I love. This dish can stand alone as a light vegetarian main, or as a side with fish or chicken. Kate, who tested it, said "My pickiest child didn't even try to weed out the veggies!" That's when I knew this dish was a keeper.

Extra-virgin olive oil

2 cups pearl couscous

3 cups boiling water

Kosher salt

8 ounces baby bella mushrooms, trimmed and halved

1 medium zucchini, ends trimmed, halved lengthwise, and sliced into ¼-inch pieces

1 medium yellow squash, ends trimmed, halved lengthwise, and sliced into ¼-inch pieces

2 medium shallots, thinly sliced into rings

2 large garlic cloves, minced

Scant **1 teaspoon** ground black pepper

½ teaspoon ground coriander

½ teaspoon ground cumin

Grated zest of 1 lemon

1 cup roughly chopped fresh flat-leaf parsley

1 cup roughly chopped fresh mint leaves

1 tablespoon chopped fresh thyme leaves

1. In a medium saucepan, heat 2 tablespoons of the olive oil over medium-high until just shimmering. Add the couscous and toast until golden brown, stirring regularly, 3 to 5 minutes.

2. Add the boiling water and season with big pinch of salt (about ½ teaspoon). Bring to a boil, then turn the heat to low, cover, and simmer until the couscous is fully cooked and all the water has been absorbed, 12 to 15 minutes.

3. Meanwhile, in a large nonstick skillet, heat 1 tablespoon of the olive oil over medium-high heat. Add the mushrooms and season to taste with salt. Cook, stirring occasionally, until the mushrooms are lightly browned, about 5 minutes. Transfer the mushrooms to a plate.

4. In the same skillet, add another drizzle of olive oil and then the zucchini, yellow squash, shallots, and garlic. Season to taste with salt. Cook over medium-high heat, stirring frequently, until the vegetables soften and gain some color, 5 to 7 minutes.

5. Return the mushrooms to the skillet. Add the couscous, black pepper, coriander, and cumin. Stir to combine. Finally, stir in the lemon zest, parsley, mint, and thyme. Taste and adjust the seasoning, then serve.

from the sea

IF YOU GIVE A KID A FISH

I learned to bait a hook before I can remember (not sure I was ever good at it). Maurice, one of our neighbors, was a bit of a fly-casting expert, and he knew all the secret places to fish. There were many to choose from—along the Mediterranean, the Suez Canal, and so on. He often took me and my brother with his family at some ungodly hour of the morning to one of his favorite spots outside the city. We each got our own fishing pole and a bucket of sardines or other small fish for bait, and we had contests to see who could catch the most. I don't remember if there was a reward for the winner, but it was still loads of fun. At the end of a long day, we'd trudge home exhausted, my face crusty with salt and my curls full of sand—nothing a hot shower couldn't fix. Maurice's wife, Aziza, or my mom would swiftly clean our fish haul under running cold water, scraping the scales off, removing the fins, and gutting and simply seasoning it for a quick sear, like I do with the trout (page 187).

You get the point: I am a fish kid.

Then there were the long days, playing in the sand, by the seashore where my friends and I occasionally watched fishermen's boats with the day's catch. We would race to meet them, competing to grab whatever fell from their nets. They would quickly shuck tiny shellfish for us, and we would slurp the insides on the spot (yes, envision a less refined oyster dinner experience).

And of course, there were many trips to the fish market with my dad, where I learned a lot watching him make his selections: "The eyes should be shiny and bulgy, and the fish should feel firm and should look like it's about to jump up and swim away!"

You get the point: I am a fish kid. I ate fresh fish prepared every which way: grilled, baked, simmered in soups, or stuffed with colorful veggies and roasted with head and tail intact—like I do with snapper (see page 179).

Now, living nowhere near the Mediterranean waters, the idea of "fresh" fish is quite different, and I have had to adjust. Thankfully, freezing technology has vastly improved, and the quality and variety of wild-caught fish that are flash-frozen right on the boat are greater than ever. And with the right technique and some bold flavors, a good fish dinner is still achievable.

Give me a fish and I will show you. Shall we?

A SEAFOOD MANIFESTO

How to Buy a Fish

A little seafood 101 before we get to the recipes in this chapter . . .

The first rule of buying fresh fish, is to shop at a place you trust. A good fishmonger should be able to tell you all about the fish, like how long it has been on display or the best way to store it, and maybe even offer a few ideas for preparing it. And you can have the fishmonger clean and fillet or butterfly the fish, too, so it's ready to cook.

To me, one of the giveaways of fresh fish is how it smells. Fresh fish should smell mild and pleasant, like the salty sea or ocean, and not strong and off-putting. If the fish is whole, the eyes should look glossy and clear, rather than dehydrated or cloudy; and the fish scales should be shiny and tightly adhering. If you're buying frozen fish, make sure it's frozen solid (no trace of liquid in the package), and check the label for additives. For example, sodium tripolyphosphate is a chemical used to retain the moisture of the frozen fish. It also adds weight, essentially increasing your cost and decreasing your experience.

Lately, I've taken to buying bags of frozen already peeled and deveined wild-caught shrimp. There is so much you can do with frozen shrimp on a whim, from a deliciously garlicky appetizer like Spanish-Style Garlic Shrimp with Potatoes (page 81), to recipes in this chapter, including bites of fluffy Shrimp Kofta (page 198) or a big pot of Shrimp Vermicelli Soup (page 202)—you'll find some of my favorite dinner recipes in this section. And honestly, in much of the country, "fresh" shrimp is just thawed, previously frozen shrimp, so buying it frozen is actually . . . freshest!

How to Thaw Frozen Fish

For the best texture, thaw frozen fish fillets in the refrigerator the night before. If there are package directions, always read them first. And if you didn't think that far ahead? No problem! You can also thaw fish quickly, in 15 to 20 minutes. Here is how:

- First, be sure to leave the fish fillet in its vacuum packaging. If it is not in some sort of separate packaging, place it in a zippered plastic bag. (Do not place it in water "naked"—you don't want a waterlogged fish.)

- Arrange the vacuum-sealed fish fillet in a bowl and cover it with cold tap water. Do NOT use warm or hot water; this creates more risk for bacterial growth and will also affect the texture of the fish.

- Check after 15 to 20 minutes to see if the fish feels tender and thawed through. If it is hard in some parts, leave it in for a little bit longer.

- Never rush the process by microwaving—the texture will suffer.

How to Test for Doneness

Fish cooks quickly, whether it is grilled like Grilled Swordfish Skewers with Basil Vinaigrette (page 180), or crusted with dukkah and baked with veggies (see page 184), or simply fried in a pan or stewed with other goodies, such as in My Big Seafood Stew with Lobster and Clams (page 205). It's important to pull the fish off the heat or out of the oven at the right time so it does not overcook and become dry. That can be a bit tricky, since the cooking time can vary depending on how thick the fish is. If the fish is on the thin side, start checking a few minutes before the time the recipe calls for.

Stick a fork in the thickest part of the fish and gently twist it to see if it's done. It should flake easily and, if it's a white fish, the flesh should look opaque white rather than a grayish-translucent (which is what it looks like raw).

For meatier fish, such as swordfish, that don't necessarily flake when done, use an instant-read meat thermometer and stick it into the fish in its thickest part; I like to pull it off the heat once it reaches about 130°F, knowing that the temperature will continue to rise a bit before I'm ready to serve. The USDA recommends an internal temperature of 145°F for fish to make sure you've killed any possible pathogens.

alexandria-style grilled branzino with salata mashwiya

SERVES 2 TO 4

Alexandria is a three-hour drive west of Port Said, on the opposite side of the Nile Delta, and it was a frequent summer vacation spot for my family. This iconic Mediterranean city established by Alexander the Great is full of history, with a strong Greek presence that's been there for a millennium, and the city is both an economic hub and a popular tourist destination. We typically stayed in chalets or villas in one of the many resort areas, my favorite being Ma'amurah beach, a bustling spot that seemed to never sleep. I have vivid memories of eating samak mashwi—marinated whole fish grilled over a makeshift wood-fired steel griddle—by the water and, late at night, grilled corn on the cob, while we meandered through the crowds in the sticky, salty air.

Saba and I have managed to get pretty darn close to recreating the Alexandria samak mashwi experience on our back porch in Atlanta. A simple onion marinade and a cast-iron griddle over an outdoor gas grill did the trick. I threw on some tomatoes, onion wedges, and hot peppers to make the salata mashwiya (grilled salad). The whole fish and grilled vegetables are best served hot off the grill, with a generous drizzle of Lime-Tahini Sauce (page 290) and some tangy preserved lemons (see page 285 for homemade). If branzini are not available, try whole rainbow trout, mackerel, sea bass, or even red snapper. Ask your fishmonger to gut and scale the fish to save you time (but leave the head and tail on!).

Fish

2 large whole branzino fish, trout, mackerel, or snapper (about **2½ pounds** total), cleaned and scaled

Kosher salt and ground black pepper

1 teaspoon ground cumin

1 medium yellow onion, grated

Juice of **1** large lemon (about **¼ cup**), plus 1 whole lemon reserved for serving

Extra-virgin olive oil

Lime-Tahini Sauce (page 290), to serve

1. **Marinate the fish:** With a sharp knife, score each fish in 3 places on both sides. Rub each fish on all sides (especially in the cavity) with 1 teaspoon each salt and black pepper and the cumin.

2. In a large, shallow ceramic or glass baking dish, mix the grated onion with the lemon juice and ¼ cup of the olive oil. Add the fish and rub them with the marinade on all sides (including the cavity). Cover the dish and refrigerate for 1 to 2 hours, turning the fish over a couple of times during the marination.

3. **Make the Salata Mashwiya:** Heat a gas grill to 450°F and brush a flat cast-iron griddle or pan with some of the olive oil.

4. Toss the tomatoes, onion wedges, and hot peppers with 3 tablespoons of the olive oil, and season with salt and pepper and the cumin.

Recipe continues

Salata Mashwiya

2 vine-ripened medium
tomatoes, halved

1 large red onion, cut into thick
wedges

2 or more hot peppers, such as
jalapeño

Extra-virgin olive oil

Kosher salt and ground black
pepper

2 teaspoons ground cumin

5. Place the oiled griddle over the preheated grill. Once very hot, place the veggies on the griddle and cook, turning over once or twice, until tender and charred in some parts, 10 to 15 minutes. Transfer the veggies to a serving platter.

6. Grill the fish: If needed, brush the griddle with more olive oil. Brush the fish on both sides with some olive oil and set them on the hot griddle with the spines facing you (this makes it easier to flip the fish later). Grill the fish for 6 to 8 minutes, then using a spatula, flip (invert) the fish with the spine away from you (if they don't flip easily, give them an extra minute or so on the griddle). Cook on the other side until the skin crisps, another 6 to 8 minutes.

7. Serve the fish: Transfer the fish to a large serving platter and immediately squeeze the remaining whole lemon all over the hot fish. Serve the fish with the platter of grilled veggies and drizzle with the lime-tahini sauce. For instructions on boning the fish, see the tip below.

HOW TO BONE A COOKED FISH

You may wonder how two people will share a whole fish. There is a fillet on each side of the backbone. My best advice is to pull up your sleeves and embrace the mess to release the fillets from the bone. If completely cooked (see page 173 for checking for doneness), the meat should easily release. Pull away the skin and run a fork alongside the spine of the fish to separate the fillets on each side. Still, there will be some tiny bones to navigate, so don't be shy about running your hands along the fillets to pull out any remaining bones. It's worth it.

fish and freekeh casserole

SERVES 4 TO 5

My dad's family is from southern Egypt, where people are called *sa'ayda*, meaning "from Upper Egypt." It's also an expression used to describe people from the south: big-hearted, generous, and very good cooks. This comforting casserole is my take on sa'ayda food. As with sa'aydi-style cooking, it begins with a simmered tomato sauce, heady with warm spices and sautéed onion. Then nutty, smoky-flavored freekeh is added with a bit of water to cook for a few minutes, before a few pieces of seasoned fish are nestled in. Traditionally, one would use large fish steaks—bone in and all—to make this recipe, but I've simplified it a bit by using cod fillets (salmon fillets also work).

Spice Mixture

1¼ **teaspoon**s ground allspice

1¼ **teaspoon**s ground coriander

1 **teaspoon** ground black pepper

½ **teaspoon** ground cumin

½ **teaspoon** cayenne pepper, or
   to your liking

Casserole

2 **cups** cracked freekeh

1¼ **pounds** meaty white fish
   fillets, such as cod (thawed,
   if frozen)

Kosher salt

2 large garlic cloves, minced

Juice from 1 large lemon

¼ **cup** extra-virgin olive oil

1 large yellow onion, chopped

2 **cups** canned crushed tomatoes

¼ **cup** chopped fresh cilantro

¼ **cup** roughly chopped fresh dill

¼ **cup** chopped flat-leaf parsley

1 **cup** water

1 large green bell pepper, cored,
   seeded, and sliced into
   ¼-inch-thick rounds

1. **Prepare the spice mixture:** In a small bowl, combine the allspice, coriander, black pepper, cumin, and cayenne.

2. **Make the casserole.** Place the freekeh in a large bowl. Pick through and remove any stones. Rinse well, then add plenty of cold water to cover and let the freekeh soak for 30 minutes to 1 hour, until tender. Drain well.

3. Meanwhile, cut the fish fillets into large chunks and place them in a shallow dish. Season the fillets well with salt on both sides, then rub with 1¼ teaspoons of the spice mixture. Add the minced garlic and lemon juice and toss.

4. Position a rack in the center of the oven. Preheat the oven to 375°F.

5. In a large oven-safe skillet with a lid, heat the olive oil over medium-high heat until shimmering. Add the onion and cook, stirring frequently, until golden, tender, and fragrant but not browned, about 5 minutes.

6. Add the remaining spice mixture and toss with the onion. Add the tomatoes, cilantro, dill, parsley, and water. Season with salt (about ½ teaspoon). Bring to a boil, then add the freekeh. Cook on high heat for 5 minutes, then cover and cook on low for 10 minutes.

7. Uncover the skillet and add the fish, tucking it into the freekeh. Top with the bell pepper. Transfer the skillet to the oven and roast until the fish and freekeh are fully cooked (the fish should flake easily and the freekeh should be of a tender, chewy consistency), about 20 minutes.

8. Transfer the fish and freekeh to a serving platter. If you like, squeeze a bit more lemon juice over the fish, and serve.

oven-roasted stuffed snapper with multi-colored veggies, fresh dill, and lots of garlic

SERVES 4

Red snapper is a beautiful-looking fish: it has reddish skin, a long triangular face, large eyes, and enlarged canine-like teeth, which is why it's called a "snapper." To make a bit of a show, I love to cook this fish whole, stuffed with dill and colorful bell peppers. The key in flavoring a whole fish is to season it outside and in (yes, including the gut cavity).

15 large garlic cloves

Kosher salt

2 teaspoons ground coriander

2 teaspoons ground cumin

1 teaspoon sumac

¾ teaspoon ground black pepper

2 whole red snappers (about 4 to 5 pounds in total), scaled and cleaned (ask your fishmonger to do this for you), head and tail left on

½ cup chopped fresh dill fronds, with some tender stems

3 large bell peppers, different colors, cored, seeded, and thinly sliced into ¼-inch rounds

1 large slicing tomato, cut into ¼-inch rounds

1 medium red onion, sliced into ¼-inch rounds

Extra-virgin olive oil

2 lemons

1. Position a rack in the lower third of the oven. Preheat the oven to 425°F.

2. In a mortar, combine the garlic with about ¾ teaspoon salt and pound with the pestle until the garlic turns to a paste. (If you don't have a mortar and pestle, chop the garlic with the salt and mash with the side of a knife until it forms a paste.) In a small bowl, combine the coriander, cumin, sumac, and black pepper and mix well.

3. Pat the fish dry and, using a large knife, score the skin of each fish 2 or 3 times on each side. Fill the slits and cavity with the garlic, then rub the fish all over, including in the cavity, with about three-fourths of the spice mixture.

4. Open the cavities of the fish and stuff them with the dill and as much peppers, tomato, and onion as will fit.

5. Lightly brush a 13 × 18 × 1-inch sheet pan with some of the olive oil and place the stuffed fish in the pan. Arrange the remaining sliced vegetables around the fish. Sprinkle the vegetables with a small pinch of salt (about ¼ teaspoon) and the remaining spice mixture. Drizzle the fish and vegetables generously with some olive oil.

6. Roast the fish on the low rack until cooked through, 20 to 25 minutes. (See page 173 for information on testing for doneness.) At this point, if the tops of the fish need a little color, stick the pan under the broiler (about 6 inches from the heat source) for a minute or two, watching carefully.

7. Transfer the fish to a large serving platter and scatter around the roasted veggies. Squeeze 1 lemon all over the fish and vegetables. Using the slits you made earlier in each fish, cut through the whole fish and portion the servings. Cut the remaining lemon into wedges to serve alongside.

grilled swordfish skewers with basil vinaigrette

SERVES 6

Swordfish is like the steak of the ocean; it is sturdy enough to be poked with a skewer and flipped with big tongs without falling apart. Plus, it takes well to smoking and all kinds of bold seasonings and marinades. Here I cut it into chunks, soak the chunks for a few minutes in Basil Vinaigrette (page 281), then thread them on skewers with slices of summer squash and red onion (a very delicious low-carb meal on a stick!). Feel free to add a side of Blistered Plum Tomatoes with Burrata, Basil, and Pomegranate Molasses (page 152) or a big summer salad, like Mid-Summer Tomato and Peach Panzanella (page 50).

1 medium yellow squash or zucchini, ends trimmed and sliced into ½-inch rounds

1 medium red onion, halved and each half quartered into chunks

2 pounds swordfish steaks, cut into 1½-inch chunks

Kosher salt and ground black pepper

1 teaspoon dried oregano

¾ teaspoon ground coriander

½ teaspoon red pepper flakes

2 large garlic cloves, crushed

¼ cup extra-virgin olive oil

Basil Vinaigrette (page 281)

1 lime, cut into wedges

1. In a large bowl, combine the squash, red onion, and swordfish chunks. Season with ¾ teaspoon each salt and black pepper. Add the oregano, coriander, red pepper flakes, garlic, and olive oil. Pour in ¼ cup of the vinaigrette and toss to coat the fish pieces well. Cover the bowl with plastic wrap and refrigerate for 1 hour.

2. Meanwhile, soak 6 bamboo skewers in water. Preheat a gas grill to 400°F and oil the grates.

3. When ready to grill, thread a chunk each of squash, red onion, and swordfish onto each skewer. Continue threading the chunks in this order until the skewers are filled.

4. Arrange the skewers on the grill and shut the grill. Cook for 7 minutes on one side, then using a pair of tongs, turn the skewers over once, shut the cover again, and cook until the fish is cooked through, 5 to 7 minutes, for medium to medium-well or until the center registers 130°F on an instant-read thermometer. Let the skewers rest off the heat for a few minutes before serving; the swordfish will continue to "cook" to an internal temperature of 145°F.

5. Squeeze the lime all over the fish and serve the skewers with the remaining vinaigrette.

foil-baked salmon with cherry tomatoes, olives, and thyme

SERVES 4 TO 6

This smart and unfussy method of cooking *en papillote* (in paper) is the surest way I know to keep salmon from drying out. Instead of making individual pouches, I place one large fillet of salmon and a savory tomato and olive mixture together on a sheet pan lined with parchment and foil, then top with another piece of foil and crimp the edges tightly to seal for baking. The steam trapped inside infuses the salmon with flavor and the aromas from the other ingredients, while keeping it nice and moist as it cooks. I like to remove the salmon from the oven just before it's done, remove the top foil, and stick the pan under the broiler for a brief couple of minutes, just until the fish begins to flake and the tomatoes burst some, which is absolute magic. (Bonus…cleanup is a breeze!)

1½ **cups** halved cherry tomatoes

3 **ounces** pitted olives (about ½ **cup**), halved (a combo of kalamata and green olives is great)

1 medium shallot, finely chopped

4 large garlic cloves, minced

1 **tablespoon** fresh thyme leaves

2 **teaspoons** dried oregano

Kosher salt and ground black pepper

3 **tablespoons** extra-virgin olive oil

1 large (1½-**pound**) salmon fillet, skin removed (thawed, if frozen)

Juice of ½ large lemon (about 2 **tablespoons**)

1. Position one oven rack in the center of the oven and another 4 or 5 inches under the broiler. Preheat the oven to 375°F. Line a 13 × 18 × 1-inch sheet pan with enough aluminum foil to hang over the edges on all sides. Top the foil with parchment paper.

2. In a medium bowl, combine the tomatoes, olives, shallot, garlic, thyme, and oregano. Season with salt and pepper to taste. Drizzle with the olive oil, then toss to combine.

3. Season the salmon well on both sides with some salt and black pepper and place the salmon in the middle of the pan. Drizzle the lemon juice all over the salmon and spoon the tomato and olive mixture on top. Take another large piece of foil and tent it over the salmon. Go around the edges to fold them shut, making a parcel to enclose the salmon.

4. Bake the salmon on the middle rack until almost fully cooked, about 15 minutes.

5. Carefully remove the top piece of foil, then turn the oven on to broil. Return the salmon to the oven, this time placing it on the top rack directly under the broiler, for 2 to 3 minutes, watching for some color and for some of the tomatoes to burst.

6. Check the salmon for doneness. If it still looks undercooked, cover it with foil again and set aside for a couple of minutes (do not return it to the oven). Your salmon is ready when it reaches 145°F on an instant-read thermometer or flakes easily with a fork.

lemony dukkah-crusted sea bass with smashed peas

SERVES 4 TO 6

Here I mash up thawed frozen green peas a bit in a baking dish before mixing in minced shallots and a simple sauce of lemon juice, olive oil, and garlic. Then I nestle in some sea bass fillets, drizzle them with more of the sauce, and top them with Dukkah (page 282)—I'm a sucker for the nutty stuff and will sprinkle it on almost anything! The crunchy dukkah, creamy peas, and zippy sauce have just the right balance for the luxurious, meltingly tender texture of wild-caught Chilean sea bass.

5 large garlic cloves, minced

Juice of **2** large lemons (about **½ cup**)

⅓ cup extra-virgin olive oil

2 cups frozen peas, thawed

Kosher salt and ground black pepper

2 small shallots, minced

1½ pounds Chilean sea bass fillets, skin on (thawed, if frozen), or cod, halibut, or other meaty white fish

6 tablespoons Dukkah (page 282)

½ cup roughly chopped fresh flat-leaf parsley

Lemon wedges, for serving

1. Position a rack in the center of the oven. Preheat the oven to 400°F.

2. In a small bowl, whisk together the garlic, lemon juice, and olive oil.

3. In a 9 × 13 × 2-inch baking dish, place the peas and season with ½ teaspoon each salt and black pepper. Using the back of a fork, roughly mash the peas a little. Add the shallots and 4 tablespoons of the lemon-garlic sauce, then mix to combine and spread the mixture evenly over the bottom of the baking dish.

4. Nestle the fish, skin side down, in the pea mixture. Season the fish well with salt and black pepper. Pour the remaining sauce over the fish, then top with 5 tablespoons of the dukkah, pressing it down on the fish with the back of a spoon. Bake until the fish is cooked through and flakes easily, about 15 minutes (start checking earlier, as baking time depends on thickness of the fillets).

5. Garnish the fish with the parsley and remaining dukkah. Serve immediately from the baking dish, with the lemon wedges alongside.

sautéed trout
with cilantro-lime sauce

SERVES 4

A simple, pan-seared fish fillet doused in a light cilantro-lime sauce with capers is the perfect fancy meal in minutes. I went with rainbow trout fillets for this, but other thin fillets, such as dover sole or even cod, would also work well.

1 teaspoon Aleppo pepper flakes

1 teaspoon ground cumin

¾ **teaspoon** ground coriander

1¼ **pounds** rainbow trout fillets, or thin saltwater fish fillets (thawed, if frozen)

Kosher salt and ground black pepper

⅓ **cup** extra-virgin olive oil

5 large garlic cloves, minced

½ **cup** dry white wine

2 tablespoons drained capers

Juice of **2** limes (about ¼ **cup**)

1 cup low-sodium chicken broth

1½ **cups** roughly chopped fresh cilantro leaves

1. In a small bowl, mix the Aleppo pepper, cumin, and coriander. Pat the fish dry and season well on both sides with salt and pepper, then season with the spice mixture.

2. In a large skillet, heat the olive oil over medium-high until shimmering. Carefully add the fish and cook, flipping once, until it is cooked through and flakes easily, about 3 minutes. Transfer to a plate lined with paper towels.

3. Turn the heat down to medium, and in the same skillet, add the garlic and cook, stirring regularly, until golden but not brown, about 30 seconds. Add the wine and cook for about 30 seconds, then add the capers, lime juice, broth, and cilantro. Cook for 5 minutes over medium heat.

4. Return the fish to the skillet, making sure to spoon a good bit of the sauce over it. Cook for another minute, then transfer to a serving platter and serve immediately.

crispy chickpeas and scallops with garlic-harissa oil

SERVES 2 TO 3

I get why people may be skittish about cooking scallops at home. They're not a small investment, after all, and no one loves a tough, chewy scallop. The good news is that they are easier to cook than most people think. Follow the instructions for pan-searing here and you'll have perfectly caramelized and meltingly tender scallops (plus crisp-fried chickpeas) in about 20 minutes! The generous drizzle of garlicky harissa oil to finish this dish is a must, and thinly sliced preserved lemons (see page 285) take it up another notch.

12 ounces wild-caught sea scallops (thawed, if frozen), side muscles removed

Kosher salt and ground black pepper

Extra-virgin olive oil

1 (15-ounce) can chickpeas, drained and rinsed

2 scallions, trimmed, whites and greens separated and chopped

¾ **teaspoon** sumac

½ **teaspoon** ground cumin

2 medium garlic cloves, thinly sliced

3 to 4 tablespoons Homemade Harissa Paste (page 286) or quality store-bought harissa

1 large lemon, cut in half

1. Pat the scallops dry. Season well with salt and pepper.

2. In a large cast-iron skillet, heat 2 tablespoons of the olive oil over medium-high heat until shimmering. Arrange the scallops in the pan in a single layer (do not crowd the pan). The first scallop to go in the pan should sizzle immediately on contact; if that does not happen, wait a few seconds to add the rest.

3. Cook the scallops, using tongs to carefully flip them over only once, until golden brown, about 2 minutes on each side. If the scallop doesn't release easily from the skillet, give it a few more seconds until it does. Place the scallops on a plate.

4. Add another tablespoon of the olive oil to the skillet. Add the chickpeas and the white parts of the scallions. Season with the sumac, cumin, and a big pinch of salt and black pepper (about ½ teaspoon each). Cook over medium-high heat, tossing occasionally, until the chickpeas crisp and turn golden brown, about 5 minutes.

5. In a small skillet, heat ¼ cup olive oil over medium heat. Add the garlic and cook, stirring frequently, until it barely gains some color but hasn't browned. Remove the pan from the heat and stir in the harissa.

6. Place the scallops back in the large skillet and give them a few seconds to warm up with the chickpeas.

7. Transfer the scallops and chickpeas to a platter, squeeze the lemon all over, then add the scallion greens. Spoon the garlic and harissa oil over all, stir, and serve.

turmeric-tinged shrimp and arugula pitas

SERVES 4

During our teen years, my brother and I spent many summer nights roaming Port Said's boardwalk area near the Suez Canal with our friends, often until well past midnight. Clothing boutiques and knickknack shops bustled with locals and tourists, and street carts blasting loud Egyptian music sold snacks like roasted nuts and grilled corn on the cob. Nearby was a popular food truck where everyone lined up for a late-night sandwich. For the life of me, I cannot remember its name, but I'll never forget their tasty sandwiches stuffed with spicy, golden-tinged shrimp cooked to order on a flat grill, served with arugula and a generous pour of tahini sauce.

So, here's to you, food truck of my childhood—whatever your name was!

5 large garlic cloves

Kosher salt

Extra-virgin olive oil

Juice of **2** large limes (about **¼ cup**)

1 teaspoon ground coriander

½ to 1 teaspoon cayenne pepper

½ teaspoon ground cumin

½ teaspoon ground turmeric

1½ pounds wild-caught medium or small shrimp (thawed, if frozen), peeled and deveined

5 ounces baby arugula

1 medium onion, halved and thinly sliced crosswise

Pita pockets, for serving

Lime-Tahini Sauce (page 290)

Homemade Preserved Lemons (page 285), thinly sliced (optional)

1. Place the garlic and 1 teaspoon salt in a mortar. Pound using the pestle until the garlic is mashed. (If you don't have a mortar and pestle, chop the garlic with the salt and mash with the side of a knife until it forms a paste.) Place in a small bowl. Add ¼ cup of the olive oil, the juice of 1 lime (2 tablespoons), the coriander, cayenne, cumin, and turmeric. Stir to combine.

2. Pat the shrimp dry and place in a medium bowl. Pour the garlic and lime juice mixture all over the shrimp and toss to coat. Set aside for 10 minutes.

3. Meanwhile, put the arugula in a medium bowl. Add 1 to 2 tablespoons of the olive oil, the juice of the remaining lime (2 tablespoons), and a big pinch of salt (about ½ teaspoon). Toss to coat well.

4. In a large skillet, heat 2 tablespoons of the olive oil over medium-high heat until shimmering. Add the onion and cook, stirring, until softened and golden brown, 5 to 7 minutes. With a slotted spoon, add the shrimp (without the liquid) and cook, tossing, until pink, 3 to 4 minutes.

5. Serve the shrimp piled into pita pockets and top with the arugula, a drizzle of the tahini sauce, and the preserved lemon (if using).

herby rice-stuffed squid

SERVES 4 AS MAIN COURSE, 8 AS AN APPETIZER

Everyone knows about fried calamari, but if you want a little show, turn the squid tubes into vessels for an herby rice filling. This is not as hard as you think, and after you've filled the first couple of tubes, you'll feel like a pro!

Unless you have access to a stellar fish counter, the freezer section is likely your best bet for wild-caught, cleaned squid tubes (also called calamari) for a relatively affordable price. You can skip the tentacles in the recipe if you can't find them. It is best to thaw frozen squid in the fridge overnight, but in a pinch you can run it under cold running water for about 10 minutes to thaw (the squid should separate easily when no longer frozen and rigid). I love serving this sizzling stuffed squid with a side of Tzatziki (page 296).

Be sure to allow time for the squid to soak in the salted milk bath—a good 30 minutes to 1 hour in the fridge. This soak will help flavor and tenderize the squid, while taming any strong odors.

1 cup whole milk

Kosher salt and ground black pepper

1 pound cleaned squid (thawed, if frozen), tentacles and tubes separated

1 cup basmati rice

Extra-virgin olive oil

1 large shallot, finely chopped

2 large garlic cloves, minced

2 tablespoons tomato paste

¼ cup plus 2 tablespoons roughly chopped fresh dill fronds

¼ cup plus 2 tablespoons roughly chopped fresh mint leaves

½ teaspoon ground cumin

1¼ cups water

Juice of **1** large lemon (about **¼ cup**)

1 small fresh hot pepper, such as jalapeño or serrano, chopped (remove seeds for less heat; optional)

1. In a medium bowl, combine the milk with 1 teaspoon salt. Add the squid and refrigerate for 30 minutes to 1 hour. Drain well and discard the milk.

2. Place the rice in a sieve and rinse under cold running water until the water runs clear. Drain.

3. If using tentacles, remove them from the fridge and chop them into bite-sized pieces to use for the filling, while keeping the squid tubes refrigerated until you're ready to stuff them.

4. In a medium saucepan, heat ¼ cup of the olive oil over medium-high heat until shimmering. Add the shallot and half the garlic, and season with a small pinch of salt. Cook, stirring regularly, until softened, adjusting the heat as needed to make sure the garlic does not burn, about 5 minutes.

5. Add the chopped tentacles (if using), the tomato paste, and ¼ cup each of the dill and mint. Add the cumin, ½ teaspoon black pepper, and the rice. Toss to combine. Add the water, bring to a boil, then cover the rice and turn the heat to low. Cook over low heat until the rice is tender, 15 to 20 minutes. Let cool briefly.

6. Remove the tubes from the refrigerator and pat dry. Turn them inside out. (This is optional, but because the outside skin tends to curl outward, it will hold the stuffing better if inside out.) Fill the tubes with the rice mixture

(a small spoon kept at the opening will help weigh it down, keeping it open for easier stuffing). Stuff the tubes full, but do not over-stuff them to the point of breaking. Leave about ½ inch at the top. Thread a wet toothpick through the top of each tube to seal the opening shut.

7. In a small bowl, combine the remaining garlic, remaining 2 tablespoons each dill and mint, the lemon juice, hot pepper (if using), and 2 tablespoons of the olive oil.

8. In a large cast-iron skillet, heat 3 tablespoons of the olive oil over medium-high heat until shimmering. Carefully add the stuffed squid tubes and cook on one side for 2 minutes, then turn over and cook on the other side for another 2 minutes, until the squid is nicely browned on both sides. (For safety, it helps to use a splatter screen to catch any bouncing oil droplets.)

9. Transfer the squid to a serving platter. Immediately top with the finishing sauce and any remaining rice.

date-night crab spaghetti

SERVES 2 TO 3

When Saba and I have an evening to ourselves, I often reach for some sort of seafood and a bag of spaghetti so as to make a quick yet fancy, restaurant-style meal like this one, with jumbo lump crab meat. Tossed in a delicate wine and lemon sauce that's punctuated with briny capers, chunks of fresh tomato, and plenty of parsley, it's an easy and elegant way to enjoy a little fresh crab taste.

Jumbo lump crab meat, which comes from the center of the blue crab, is an undeniable splurge, but I think it's worth every penny. It's sweeter and more succulent than the less expensive claw meat, whose taste I find overpowering for pasta. But you can also make this pasta with ¾ pound peeled and deveined large shrimp instead. Cook them up in a bit of olive oil for about 3 minutes or until just pink, then toss them in the already dressed pasta just before serving.

Kosher salt and ground black pepper

½ **pound** thin spaghetti

Extra-virgin olive oil

½ large red onion, finely chopped

5 large garlic cloves, minced

2 **teaspoons** dried oregano

1 **teaspoon** Aleppo pepper flakes, or ½ **teaspoon** red pepper flakes, plus more as desired

1 (8-ounce) container wild-caught jumbo lump crab meat

2 **tablespoons** drained capers

1 **cup** dry white wine, such as Pinot Grigio

1 large lemon, zested and juiced (about ¼ **cup** juice)

1 **cup** roughly chopped fresh flat-leaf parsley

3 vine-ripened medium tomatoes, roughly chopped (about 2½ **cups**)

½ **cup** grated Parmesan cheese, plus more as desired

1. In a large pot of boiling salted (about 2 tablespoons) water, cook the pasta until al dente, according to package instructions, about 9 minutes. Reserve 1 cup of the pasta cooking water, then drain the pasta well.

2. Meanwhile, in a large skillet, heat ¼ cup of the olive oil over medium heat until shimmering. Add the onion, garlic, oregano, and Aleppo or red pepper flakes. Cook, stirring constantly, adjusting the heat as needed to make sure the garlic softens but doesn't burn. Add the crab meat and stir briefly to coat.

3. Add the capers and wine to the skillet and cook until reduced a bit, about 1 minute, then add the lemon zest and juice, parsley, and tomatoes. Season with salt and stir for about 30 seconds.

4. Add pasta to the skillet, then add a little of the reserved pasta cooking water and a generous drizzle of olive oil. Toss to make sure the pasta is well coated. Top with a sprinkle of Parmesan cheese and toss gently.

5. Immediately transfer the pasta to serving bowls. Add another drizzle of olive oil and a sprinkle more of lemon zest, Parmesan cheese, and Aleppo pepper, as needed.

sheet-pan baked halibut with green beans in lemon-dill sauce

SERVES 4 TO 5

I feel like the sheet-pan queen, given how much I use mine. But really—what's better than having an entire meal cooked in one single pan? (I'm not complaining about fewer dishes to clean!) Any firm, mild-tasting white fish benefits from a coating of this simple, citrusy sauce, which infuses the fillets with flavor while keeping them moist and tender as they bake. This fish dinner cooks quickly, so watch it closely—no checking email while it's in the oven!

2 large lemons, zested and juiced (about ½ **cup** juice)

¾ **cup** extra-virgin olive oil

5 large garlic cloves, minced

2 teaspoons dried dill

1 teaspoon dried oregano

¾ **teaspoon** ground coriander

Kosher salt and ground black pepper

1 pound (15 to 20) cherry tomatoes

1 pound fresh green beans, ends trimmed

1 large yellow onion, sliced into thin half-moons

1½ **pounds** halibut fillet (thawed, if frozen), sliced into 1½-inch-wide strips

1. Position one rack in the center of the oven and another one 4 or 5 inches under the broiler. Preheat the oven to 425°F.

2. In a large bowl, whisk together the lemon zest and juice, olive oil, garlic, dillweed, oregano, coriander, and salt and black pepper (about ¾ teaspoon each). Add the cherry tomatoes, green beans, and onion and toss to coat all with the sauce.

3. With a large slotted spoon, transfer the vegetables to a large sheet pan and push them to occupy half the space, making sure they are spread out in a single layer in that half.

4. Add the halibut strips to the remaining sauce in the bowl, tossing to coat well. Transfer the fish to the other half of the sheet pan and pour any remaining sauce on top.

5. Bake the fish and vegetables on the middle rack of the oven for 15 minutes, then move the sheet pan to the top rack and broil until the cherry tomatoes begin to pop a bit and the fish turns white and flakes easily, another 2 to 3 minutes, watching carefully.

6. Transfer the fish and vegetables to a serving platter and add a sprinkle more salt, if desired. Serve immediately.

shrimp kofta

SERVES 4 AS A MAIN COURSE, 8 AS AN APPETIZER

The Port Saidi way of making use of less prestigious small shrimp was to grind them in a tantalizing mixture of fresh herbs and spices and to fry them quickly, turning them into fluffy morsels of shrimp kofta. I made these recently for a dinner with friends, but the kofta never made it to the table, as we finished them on the spot while standing around the kitchen island! My friend Molly took one bite and declared them even fluffier than hush puppies (a *very* strong sentiment from a Southerner!) I like these kofta with a good splash of lemon juice and a drizzle of Lime-Tahini Sauce (page 290), although Tzatziki (page 296) is excellent, too.

1 small yellow onion, quartered

1 cup fresh flat-leaf parsley leaves and tender stems

¼ cup fresh dill fronds

4 large garlic cloves

1 pound wild-caught small shrimp (thawed, if frozen), peeled and deveined

Kosher salt and ground black pepper

1 teaspoon ground coriander

½ teaspoon Aleppo pepper flakes

½ teaspoon ground cumin

½ teaspoon sweet paprika

1 tablespoon chickpea flour

1 large egg

1 cup grapeseed or other neutral-tasting oil

Lemon wedges

Lime-Tahini Sauce (page 290) or Tzatziki (page 296), to serve

1. In the bowl of a large food processor fitted with the multipurpose blade, combine the onion, parsley, dill, and garlic. Pulse a few times until the onion is finely chopped. Add the shrimp and about ¾ teaspoon each salt and black pepper, along with the coriander, Aleppo pepper, cumin, and paprika. Place the lid on the processor and pulse again, until the mixture is well combined and the shrimp is the texture of wet meatball mixture.

2. Transfer the shrimp mixture to a medium bowl. Add the chickpea flour and the egg and mix with a wooden spoon until well incorporated.

3. Line a large plate with paper towels.

4. In a large skillet, heat the oil over medium-high heat until shimmering. Carefully spoon portions of the shrimp mixture (about 2 tablespoons each) into the oil. Do not crowd the pan; do this in batches, if you need to. You should have about 16 koftas. Fry the kofta on one side until golden brown, then turn over to cook until the other side is also golden brown, 3 to 4 minutes total. Transfer the kofta to the paper towel–lined plate as they finish cooking.

5. Place the kofta on a serving platter and serve hot or warm with lemon wedges and your choice of sauce for drizzling or dipping.

seafood shakshuka

SERVES 4 TO 6

Most people familiar with shakshuka think of eggs as the common denominator, but here I pay tribute to shakshuka made in the style of Egypt's Mediterranean cities, where seafood and local fish stand in for the eggs. While I do take liberties with the spices I use in this recipe, the method of braising the fish on the stovetop in a chunky tomato and pepper sauce is in the spirit of classic shakshuka. Serve it over couscous or Middle Eastern Rice Pilaf (page 161).

2 teaspoons ground coriander

2 teaspoons sumac

1½ teaspoons ground cumin

1 teaspoon dried dillweed

½ teaspoon ground turmeric

Extra-virgin olive oil

1 large yellow onion, chopped

1 large green bell pepper, cored, seeded, and chopped

8 large garlic cloves, minced

5 vine-ripened medium tomatoes, diced (**3½ cups**), or **1 (28-ounce)** can diced tomatoes

3 tablespoons tomato paste

Juice of ½ large lemon (about **2 tablespoons**)

1 cup water

Kosher salt and freshly ground black pepper

1¼ pounds firm white fish fillet, such as halibut or cod, or a combination (thawed, if frozen), cut into large pieces

8 ounces large wild-caught shrimp (thawed, if frozen), peeled and deveined

1. In a small bowl, mix the coriander, sumac, cumin, dillweed, and turmeric.

2. In a large pot with a lid, heat 6 tablespoons of the olive oil over medium heat until shimmering. Add the onion, bell pepper, and garlic and cook, stirring frequently, until very tender and fragrant, 10 to 12 minutes, adjusting the heat as needed to make sure the garlic does not burn.

3. Add the tomatoes, tomato paste, lemon juice, and water. Season with about ½ teaspoon each salt and black pepper. Stir in half the spice mixture. Bring the chunky sauce to a boil, then turn the heat to medium-low, cover, and simmer until the tomatoes are very soft and melded with the other vegetables, 15 to 20 minutes.

4. Pat the fish dry and season well on both sides with salt and black pepper. Apply all of the remaining spice mixture except ½ teaspoon to the fish, patting it on both sides. Nestle the seasoned fish pieces in the bubbling shakshuka sauce. Cover and cook over medium-low heat until the fish turns white and flakes easily, and is cooked through, 10 to 15 minutes.

5. Meanwhile, pat the shrimp dry and toss with a big pinch of salt and black pepper (about ½ teaspoon each) and the remaining ½ teaspoon spice mixture. Nestle the shrimp in the shakshuka, cover, and continue to cook over medium-low heat, turning the shrimp as needed so that they turn pink all over, about 3 minutes more. (Remember that the shrimp will continue to cook in the hot sauce even after you remove the pan from the heat, so be careful not to overcook it.)

6. Spoon the seafood shakshuka into bowls and serve immediately.

shrimp vermicelli soup

SERVES 6

This will likely be the easiest "fancy seafood soup" you'll ever make—but no one needs to know that! The main thing to remember here is that, once you drop your shrimp in, give it no more than a minute before you remove the pot from the stovetop. By the time you grab the serving bowls, your beautiful large shrimp will turn pink but remain nice and juicy. And do not skip the final finishing touches. The fresh lemon juice and herbs really do make all the difference.

¼ **cup** extra-virgin olive oil

1 large green bell pepper, cored, seeded, and roughly chopped

1 large red bell pepper, cored, seeded, and roughly chopped

1 medium red onion, chopped

5 large garlic cloves, minced

Kosher salt and black pepper

3 vine-ripened medium tomatoes, diced (**2 cups**)

3 **tablespoons** tomato paste

2 **teaspoons** dried oregano

1 **teaspoon** sweet paprika

5 **cups** vegetable stock or low-sodium chicken broth

1 **cup** broken vermicelli or orzo pasta

1½ **pounds** large shrimp (thawed, if frozen), peeled and deveined

1 large lemon, zested and juiced (about ¼ **cup** juice)

1 **cup** chopped flat-leaf parsley

⅓ **cup** roughly chopped fresh dill fronds

1 scallion, trimmed, white and green parts chopped

1. In a Dutch oven, heat the olive oil over medium-high heat until shimmering. Add the green and red peppers, red onion, and garlic. Season with about ¾ teaspoon each salt and black pepper. Cook, stirring frequently, until the veggies soften a bit, 5 to 7 minutes.

2. Add the tomatoes, tomato paste, oregano, and paprika. Stir to combine. Cook until the tomatoes soften a bit, about another 4 minutes. Add the stock and bring to a boil, then reduce the heat to low and simmer for 10 minutes.

3. Add the vermicelli or orzo and cook until the pasta is tender (vermicelli will cook more quickly than orzo), about 6 minutes.

4. Add the shrimp and cook for 1 minute, then immediately turn the heat off (the shrimp will continue to cook in the hot stock). Add the lemon zest, lemon juice, parsley, dill fronds, and green onions and stir. Ladle into serving bowls and serve immediately.

my big seafood stew with lobster and clams

SERVES 6

My favorite restaurant when I was growing up was a modest, hyperlocal seafood place called El Borg, which used to be just a few feet from the water in Port Said. It was a big hall that smelled of sea, spice, and smoke from the massive grills billowing in the back. Eating there was never a hurried experience; we would typically arrive around three p.m. and leisurely hang out until seven or so. You selected what you wanted to eat from bins of just-caught seafood on display next to the kitchen, and you told the staff how you wanted it prepared: grilled, fried, seared, simmered in a saucy tagine, stuffed with herbs, baked with pasta and veggies—anything you liked. Everything was made to order, and while we waited, they brought out trays of fresh salads, mezze, sauces, and pickles for us to nosh on.

What I remember most was their famous seafood stew: clay bowls filled to the brim with chunks of the freshest fish and other catches of the day, swimming in garlicky, vinegar-spiked broth. It never tasted the same twice. Baba always ordered a bowl for each of us before the main dishes came, but for me this was all I wanted. I've tried to re-create the idea of El Borg's "big stew," using whatever seafood I could get. It's a great way to stretch out a couple of lobster tails, fresh or frozen, for a special occasion. But if you're not feeling that fancy, feel free to improvise!

2 lobster tails (1 pound total)

Kosher salt and ground black pepper

¼ **cup** extra-virgin olive oil

1 large red onion, roughly chopped

4 large garlic cloves, minced

1 yellow bell pepper, cored, seeded, and roughly chopped

2 vine-ripened medium tomatoes, chopped **(1 cup)**

2 **tablespoons** tomato paste

1 **teaspoon** ground coriander

½ **teaspoon** Aleppo pepper flakes

½ **teaspoon** ground cumin

½ **teaspoon** smoked paprika

1 **cup** dry white wine

1 **cup** low-sodium chicken broth

15 littleneck clams, cleaned

1 **pound** haddock fillet, or other white fish (thawed, if frozen), cut into 2-inch chunks

12 large wild-caught shrimp (thawed, if frozen), peeled and deveined

2 to 3 **tablespoons** white wine vinegar

½ **cup** roughly chopped fresh cilantro leaves

½ **cup** roughly chopped fresh flat-leaf parsley leaves

Recipe continues

1. In a large pot, bring 4 to 5 cups of water to a boil (the water needs to be enough to cover the lobster tails) and add salt. Carefully add the lobster tails and cook until the meat is firm and turns a translucent pinkish white and the shells are just red, about 13 minutes (the lobster will go back in the water later, so don't overcook it). Reserve 1 cup of the lobster cooking water, then drain the lobster. Allow the lobster to cool briefly, then use a pair of kitchen shears to cut down the length of the tail. Remove the shells and discard. Cut the lobster meat into 1-inch pieces.

2. In the same large pot, heat the olive oil over medium-high heat until shimmering. Add the red onion, garlic, and bell pepper. Season with a big pinch of salt and black pepper. about ½ teaspoon each). Cook, stirring regularly, until the vegetables soften, 5 to 7 minutes.

3. Add the tomatoes, tomato paste, coriander, Aleppo pepper, cumin, and paprika. Pour in the white wine, chicken broth, and reserved cup of lobster cooking liquid. Bring to a gentle boil and cook until the tomatoes soften a bit, about 5 minutes.

4. Turn the heat down to medium and add the clams. Cover with a lid and cook for 5 minutes. Add the fish pieces, cover again, and cook for another 4 minutes. The clams should be fully open by now (the majority of them, at least). At this point, stir in the shrimp and the lobster pieces. Watch the shrimp carefully, and as soon as it turns pink, turn the heat off, in 1 to 2 minutes. (Remember that the seafood will continue to cook after you turn the heat off, and the fish should turn opaque white and flake easily with a fork.)

5. Stir in the vinegar, cilantro, and parsley. Taste for seasoning and remove any unopened clams before ladling the stew into individual serving bowls.

saucy tomato baked cod with garlic, capers, and raisins

SERVES 4 TO 6

Tangy, savory, and just a tiny bit sweet, this oven-to-table fish dinner is all about the sauce. Not one person who's tried this dish at my house has immediately detected the raisins (inspiration came from a Sicilian stew I have made). Their presence is subtle, but they provide balance for the salty, briny capers, abundant garlic, and warm spices.

⅓ **cup** extra-virgin olive oil

1 small red onion, finely chopped

5 or 6 Roma (plum) tomatoes, diced (about **3 cups**)

10 large garlic cloves, chopped

⅓ **cup** golden raisins

2 **tablespoons** drained capers

1½ **teaspoons** ground coriander

1 **teaspoon** ground cumin

1 **teaspoon** sweet paprika

½ **teaspoon** cayenne pepper (optional)

Kosher salt and ground black pepper

1½ **pounds** cod fillets, or other white fish fillets (thawed, if frozen), cut into 4-ounce pieces

2 large lemons, 1 zested and juiced (about ¼ **cup** juice), 1 thinly sliced crosswise

¼ **cup** roughly chopped fresh flat-leaf parsley leaves

1. In a medium saucepan, heat the olive oil over medium-high heat until shimmering but not smoking. Add the red onion and cook, stirring regularly, until it begins to turn deep golden but not brown, 5 to 7 minutes.

2. Add the tomatoes, garlic, raisins, capers, coriander, cumin, paprika, cayenne (if using), and ½ teaspoon each salt and black pepper. Bring to a boil, then turn the heat down to medium-low and let the sauce simmer for 20 minutes, stirring occasionally.

3. Position a rack in the center of the oven. Preheat the oven to 400°F.

4. Pat the fish dry and season with ½ to ¾ teaspoon each salt and black pepper. Pour half the tomato sauce into the bottom of a 9 × 13-inch baking dish with 2-inch sides. Arrange the fish on top. Sprinkle with the lemon zest and drizzle with the lemon juice, then top with the remaining tomato sauce. Arrange the lemon slices over the top. Bake until the fish is cooked through and flakes easily, about 15 minutes.

5. Garnish the fish with the parsley and serve immediately.

meaty things

THE BIG TABLE

When I was young, whenever we had friends over for an azooma (feast), Mama moved the meal to The Big Table. It was the long, heavy, solid-wood kind with filigree carvings of intricate detail, hand-made by carpenters in Damietta, which was one hour west of Port Said. (Damietta is also known for its sweets and dairy, and scoring a special treat after a trip to the furniture shop was always reason enough to join a trip there.) The Big Table was made to fit eight people, but somehow Mama was able to stretch it endlessly by adding makeshift extensions on either side, depending on the size of the azooma and the number of guests—both young and old—joining.

"If you have much, give of your wealth; if you have little, give of your heart."
—Arabic proverb.

For every Egyptian azooma she threw, and there were many, Mama seemed to fill every inch of that table with platters of food, from salads and starters to her famous mahshi (see page 230)—rice-stuffed vegetables—to lamb or baked chicken (or both), fish trays, and salads and vegetables galore, such as Egyptian Moussaka (page 139) and Fasolia (Braised Green Beans; page 142). homemade fruit salad, baklava (see page 262), or buttery Ghorayebah (page 273) followed, along with a pot of shai (see page 250).

The thing about The Big Table and our azoomas was this: the adults and the little ones were never separated. We did not have a smaller kids' table set up in the kitchen. Every meal was a multigenerational affair with *tetas* (grandmothers), aunts (everyone is your aunt, even if not a blood relative), men, women, and children of all ages—everyone together in the same space.

The adults made room for us kids in an intentional way. "Come here by me, *habibiti*" (darling), one of the tetas would call, motioning for little eight-year-old me to take the cushioned seat next to her. I would sit and eat while listening to stories and jokes, and taking in life lessons from all corners of The Big Table.

More than the gift of food, to me The Big Table is the gift of hearts.

tuesday night skillet chicken cutlets with artichokes and mushrooms

SERVES 4

This skillet situation happens a lot at my house because it is so darn quick and is loaded with bright flavors. I could eat the artichokes and mushrooms, swimming in the white wine sauce, straight from the skillet! Instead of spending extra for prepped chicken cutlets, I do it myself by butterflying boneless breasts so they are thinner for quick and even cooking. It's easy!

1½ **pounds** boneless, skinless chicken breast halves (4 large half-breasts)

Kosher salt and ground black pepper

2 **teaspoons** dried oregano

⅓ **cup** all-purpose flour (or flour of your choice)

¼ **cup** extra virgin olive oil, plus more as needed

8 **ounces** baby bella mushrooms, sliced (about **3 cups**)

2 **cups** grape tomatoes, halved

4 large garlic cloves, minced

1 (**15-ounce**) can artichoke hearts, drained, rinsed, and quartered

½ **cup** dry white wine

½ **cup** low-sodium chicken broth

Juice of **1** large lemon (about ¼ **cup**)

¼ **cup** fresh basil leaves, torn

Your favorite plain grains, cooked according to package directions, for serving

1. Pat the chicken dry. Place a chicken breast half on a cutting board and put one hand flat on top of it. Using a sharp knife, carefully slice horizontally through the breast starting at the thicker end and finishing at the thin point where the breast should remain attached (do not fully split the breast). Open the chicken breast so that it resembles a butterfly. Repeat with the rest of the chicken breasts.

2. Season both sides of the chicken breasts well with salt and black pepper and 1 teaspoon of the oregano. Put the flour on a wide plate and coat the chicken cutlets with the flour on both sides, dusting off excess.

3. In a 12-inch cast-iron skillet, heat the olive oil over medium-high heat until shimmering. Add the chicken and cook, flipping once, until each side is golden brown, 2 to 3 minutes per side. Transfer the chicken to a large plate.

4. In the same skillet, add more olive oil if the skillet is dry and add the mushrooms. Cook until tender, about 2 minutes. Add the tomatoes and garlic and season with about ½ teaspoon each salt and black pepper and the remaining teaspoon oregano. Cook, stirring regularly, until the tomatoes begin to release some of their juices, about another 3 minutes. Add the artichoke hearts and wine, and cook until the liquid reduces by half, 1 to 2 minutes, then add the chicken broth and lemon juice. Bring to a boil.

5. Return the chicken to the skillet and turn the heat to medium-low. Cover the skillet and simmer until the chicken is fully cooked, another 5 to 6 minutes.

6. Transfer the chicken and tomatoes to serving plates, top with the fresh basil, and serve with a side of grains.

cheater's hawawshi pitas

SERVES 6 TO 12

Whenever I need to explain this popular Egyptian street food to my Atlanta friends, I find myself resorting to this lazy answer: Hawawshi (pronounced ha-wow-shi) is basically Egypt's answer to a hamburger—but it is so much more! Here ground beef is transformed to a patty with a mix of exciting spices, onions, garlic, hot peppers, and fresh herbs, typically enveloped in a made-from-scratch dough. In this homemade version, I kept true to the seasoning but ditched the fresh dough for pita pockets; no one is ever mad about a shortcut.

Hawawshi Seasoning

1 teaspoon ground allspice

1 teaspoon ground black pepper

1 teaspoon ground coriander

1 teaspoon sweet paprika

¾ teaspoon ground cardamom

½ teaspoon ground cumin

¼ teaspoon ground cinnamon

Meat Filling

1 large yellow onion, quartered

2 large garlic cloves

1 large green bell pepper, cored, seeded, and cut into chunks

1 fresh jalapeño pepper, halved (remove seeds for less heat)

1 cup roughly chopped fresh flat-leaf parsley

2 pounds extra-lean ground beef (90% lean)

2 tablespoons tomato paste

Kosher salt

Extra-virgin olive oil

6 thick pocket-style pitas, cut in half crosswise

1. Position a rack in the center of the oven. Preheat the oven to 400°F.

2. **Make the seasoning:** In a small bowl, mix the allspice, black pepper, coriander, paprika, cardamom, cumin, and cinnamon.

3. **Make the meat filling:** In the bowl of a food processor fitted with the multipurpose blade, combine the onion, garlic, bell pepper, jalapeño, and parsley. Pulse a few times until all the ingredients are finely chopped. Transfer the mixture to a sieve and push down on the mixture with the back of a spoon to drain excess liquid.

4. Transfer the onion mixture to a large bowl. Add the ground beef and tomato paste. Mix to combine. Add the hawawshi seasoning and about 1 teaspoon of salt. Mix again until well combined and the spices are incorporated into the meat.

5. Lightly brush a 13 × 18 × 1-inch sheet pan with olive oil.

6. **Make the pita pockets:** Stuff each pita pocket with ⅓ cup of the meat mixture. Using the back of a spoon, spread the meat mixture on the insides of the pita pockets. Arrange the pitas on the sheet pan. Brush the tops of the pita pockets very lightly with olive oil, then bake for 15 minutes. Carefully turn the pitas over and bake on the other side until the meat is fully cooked and the pitas are a little crispy on both sides (the meat will release some juices into the pan, so it is important to turn the pita over so it will crisp on both sides), another 5 to 10 minutes. Serve immediately!

charred chicken thighs
with dill greek yogurt sauce

SERVES 4

This chicken number made me some good friends when we first moved to Atlanta. We lived in an extended-stay hotel for a few months, and because there wasn't a proper kitchen, we used the community grill often. One night, I invited some new acquaintances, a group of welders from Chattanooga, Tennessee, to try our style of BBQ. They were somewhat skeptical digging in the oddly seasoned chicken and the yogurt sauce (in place of their usual sweet sauce). By the end of the evening, Wayne, the leader of the pack, gave it a thumbs-up: "Well, Miss Suzy, I reckon I'm okay with Mediterranean barbecue."

Chicken Thighs

10 large garlic cloves, minced

1 teaspoon ground allspice

½ teaspoon ground cardamom

½ teaspoon ground nutmeg

½ teaspoon sweet paprika

Extra-virgin olive oil

8 boneless, skinless chicken thighs

Kosher salt and ground pepper

1 medium red onion, halved and thinly sliced crosswise

Juice of **2** medium lemons (about **6 tablespoons**)

Dill Greek Yogurt Sauce

1 medium garlic clove, minced

1¼ cups plain full-fat Greek yogurt

1 cup roughly chopped fresh dill

1 tablespoon extra-virgin olive oil

Juice of **½** large lemon

¼ teaspoon cayenne pepper (optional)

Kosher salt

1. **Marinate the chicken:** In a small bowl, mix the garlic, allspice, cardamom, nutmeg, paprika, and 3 tablespoons of the olive oil. Pat the chicken thighs dry and season well with salt and black pepper on both sides, then rub with the garlic and spice mixture.

2. Put the red onion in a large rimmed dish. Arrange the chicken on top of the onion and pour the lemon juice and 2 tablespoons of the olive oil all over. Cover and refrigerate for 2 to 4 hours.

3. **Make the sauce:** In the bowl of a food processor fitted with the multipurpose blade, combine the garlic, yogurt, dill, olive oil, lemon juice, and cayenne (if using). Run the food processor briefly (or pulse several times) until all the ingredients are well blended and a smooth, thick sauce develops. Taste and add salt to your liking. Transfer the sauce to a small bowl or container. Cover and refrigerate until ready to serve. (I like to let the sauce sit in the fridge for 30 minutes or so before serving to allow it to thicken a bit and develop flavor.)

4. **Grill the chicken:** Heat a gas grill to medium-high and lightly oil the grates. Remove the chicken thighs from the marinade (discard the onion) and place on the hot grates. Cover the grill and cook for 5 to 6 minutes, then turn the chicken over, cover again, and grill until the chicken is fully cooked through, about another 5 minutes.

5. Transfer the chicken thighs to serving plates and serve with the yogurt sauce.

sumac-rubbed
drumsticks with marinated onions

SERVES 6

During the olive oil season, my Palestinian friends prepare a celebratory chicken dish called musakhan, whereby chicken pieces, generously seasoned with sumac and spices, are slow-roasted until tender, then served with silky, caramelized onions atop a bed of olive oil–drenched flatbread. It is as comforting and bold as it sounds.

These rosy-hued drumsticks are sort of an abbreviated barbecue version of this dish. The marinated onions are essential, so don't skip them. Macerating the onion in vinegar tames its sharpness and softens it a bit, while holding on to just enough of its pleasant crunch.

Allow the chicken to marinate in the fridge for several hours to turn up the flavor volume even more, but if you're short on time, even 30 minutes will be sufficient. I serve the bread on the side.

1 medium red onion, quartered

4 or 5 large garlic cloves

2 teaspoons sumac

1½ teaspoons Aleppo pepper flakes

1½ teaspoons ground allspice

1 teaspoon ground coriander

½ teaspoon ground black pepper

½ teaspoon cayenne pepper

½ teaspoon ground cinnamon

½ teaspoon ground turmeric

⅓ cup extra-virgin olive oil

Juice of 1 large lemon (about ¼ cup)

3 pounds chicken drumsticks

Kosher salt

Sumac and Vinegar-Marinated Onions (page 295), to serve

1. In the bowl of a small food processor fitted with the multipurpose blade, combine the red onion, garlic, sumac, Aleppo pepper, allspice, coriander, black pepper, cayenne, cinnamon, and turmeric. Add the olive oil and lemon juice. Blend until everything is well combined and in a thick marinade.

2. Pat the chicken dry and season well with salt all over, making sure to season under the chicken's skin. Put the chicken in a large zippered plastic bag and pour in the marinade and then seal the bag. Massage the bag to make sure the marinade is well distributed, and all the chicken is covered in marinade. Place the sealed bag on a plate and refrigerate anywhere from 1 to 4 hours, turning the bag midway through the marinating time.

3. When ready, preheat a gas grill for two-zone grilling, with the direct heat set at 400°F.

4. Arrange the chicken over the indirect heat on the grill (the chicken should not be in direct contact with the flame). Close the grill and cook, turning every 7 to 8 minutes, until the chicken is fully cooked through, 25 to 30 minutes total. Remove from the heat and let the chicken rest for 5 minutes or so.

5. When ready to serve, arrange half the marinated onions on a platter. Arrange the chicken drumsticks on top, then finish with the remaining marinated onions.

chicken shawarma bowls

SERVES 4 TO 6

Shawarma is one of my absolute favorite Middle Eastern street foods: heavily marinated meat—beef or lamb—or chicken, layered on a vertical spit and slow-roasted until perfectly tender and the very outer layer is well charred. Street vendors use a sharp knife to thinly shave the charred layer of meat off the spit and then stuff it into a pillowy pita with chopped veggies, pickles, and a good drizzle of tahini. My humble homemade version calls for boneless chicken thighs and a sheet pan—no rotisserie required! The secret is in the bold shawarma seasoning, which hits all the notes of the street food of my childhood. And word-to-the-wise: If you have just a few minutes, allow the chicken to marinate before cooking so it can soak up as much flavor as possible.

For shawarma night at my house, Saba and I like to let everyone make their own shawarma bowls with our go-to Everyday Tomato and Cucumber Salad (page 36) or tabbouleh, and hummus, tzatziki, or even labneh for dip options, plus whatever olives or pickles we have on hand—cucumber refrigerator pickles or marinated onions are my personal favorites with shawarma.

Shawarma Seasoning

2¼ **teaspoons** ground coriander

2¼ **teaspoons** ground cumin

2¼ **teaspoons** garlic powder

2¼ **teaspoons** sweet paprika

2¼ **teaspoons** ground turmeric

1½ **teaspoons** ground cloves

½ **teaspoon** cayenne pepper, or more to your liking

Chicken

8 boneless, skinless chicken thighs

Kosher salt

1 large onion, thinly sliced

Juice of 1 large lemon (about ¼ **cup**)

⅓ **cup** extra-virgin olive oil, plus more for pan

1. In a small bowl, mix the coriander, cumin, garlic powder, paprika, turmeric, cloves, and cayenne.

2. Pat the chicken thighs dry and thinly slice into bite-sized pieces. In a large bowl, add the chicken, the shawarma seasoning, and about 1 teaspoon salt. Toss to coat. Add the onion, lemon juice, and ⅓ cup olive oil. Toss again. Cover and refrigerate for 2 hours or overnight. (If you don't have time, let the chicken marinate at room temperature for up to 30 minutes.)

3. Position one rack in the center of the oven and another one 4 or 5 inches under the broiler. Preheat the oven to 425°F. Brush a 13 × 18 × 1-inch sheet pan with olive oil.

4. Spread the chicken and onion in a single layer on the sheet pan. Roast on the middle rack until the thickest piece is cooked through, 20 to 30 minutes. For a more browned, crispier chicken, move the pan to the top rack and broil a minute or two, watching very carefully to avoid burning.

To Serve

Everyday Tomato and Cucumber
Salad with Dad's Salad
"Whisky" (page 36)

The Smoothest, Fluffiest
Hummus (page 60)

Lime-Tahini Sauce (page 290)

Herbed Labneh (page 293)

Crunchy Cucumber Refrigerator
Pickles (page 292), sliced

Sumac and Vinegar-Marinated
Onions (page 295)

Warm pita (optional)

5. Prepare to serve: While the chicken is roasting, set out the salads, hummus, or herbed labneh, and anything else you're using in your shawarma bowls.

6. When ready to serve, divide the cooked chicken shawarma among 4 to 6 dinner bowls. Add the salad, dip, and pickles. Serve immediately.

butterflied za'atar chicken with caramelized red onions and toasted almonds

SERVES 4 TO 6

Nothing is as special as a whole roast chicken, except when lovingly coated in loads of garlic, lemon juice, and za'atar, which I became obsessed with via my mother-in-law, Dina. She possesses jars upon jars of the magical wild thyme and toasted sesame seed blend; it travels to her Michigan kitchen from "al blad," referring to her home in Jordan. This recipe is inspired by an older one from Sami Tamimi and Yotam Ottolenghi, two of my culinary crushes, and I tell you this as a friend: if you don't know what a flavor bomb za'atar is over chicken, it is time to find out!

Marinade

Extra-virgin olive oil

Juice of **2** large lemons (about **½ cup**)

10 large garlic cloves, minced

1½ tablespoons za'atar

1 tablespoon ground allspice

2 teaspoons sumac

1 teaspoon ground cinnamon

Chicken

1 medium roasting chicken **(about 4 pounds)**, butterflied by a butcher, or according to the method on page 227

Kosher salt

Extra-virgin olive oil

1 large red onion, sliced into wedges

1 tablespoon za'atar

½ cup blanched almonds, toasted

⅓ cup roughly chopped fresh flat-leaf parsley

1. **Make the marinade:** In a large bowl, mix ½ cup olive oil with the lemon juice, garlic, za'atar, allspice, sumac, and cinnamon.

2. **Prepare the chicken:** Pat the chicken dry and place it, breast side up, on a large cutting board. Season with about 3 teaspoons salt, making sure to get it under the skin and under the breasts (this is very important for flavor).

3. Massage the chicken with the marinade, making sure to lift the skin up and apply some of the marinade underneath. Leave the chicken in the bowl for 30 minutes at room temperature (or cover and refrigerate for 2 hours).

4. Position a rack in the center of the oven and preheat the oven to 425°F. Brush a 12-inch cast-iron skillet with olive oil.

5. Arrange the red onion wedges in the skillet, place the chicken on top of the onion, and pour any remaining marinade over. Slide the skillet all the way to the back of the oven, with the handle of the pan pointing left. Roast the chicken for 20 minutes. Then, using oven mitts, carefully turn the skillet 180 degrees around so that the handle is now pointing right. Roast until the chicken is golden brown all over and its juices run clear, another 30 to 40 minutes, until an instant-read thermometer reads 157°F when inserted in the thickest part. Remove the chicken from the oven, loosely tent with some aluminum foil, and let sit for 10 to 15 minutes.

6. When ready to serve, transfer the chicken to a serving platter, sprinkle the remaining za'atar all over and garnish with the toasted almonds and parsley. Slice and serve.

sheet-pan smoky chicken, chickpeas, and carrots

SERVES 6

One late Sunday afternoon, I called our neighbors, the Kardel family, over for dinner. It was an impromptu invite, and the extension of it came even before I had any idea of what to make. Not too long later, as we stood over the stove mopping up the juice of my big sheet-pan chicken with some crusty bread, I knew this recipe was a winner!

What takes this chicken dinner to next-level deliciousness is the saucy, smoky tomato rub! The base of the rub is tomato paste with olive oil and a good splash of lemon juice. But the warmth and smokiness come from smoked paprika, assisted by an appropriately ample amount of minced garlic (you can never use enough garlic) and a couple dashes of cumin and Aleppo pepper.

Tomato Rub

½ **cup** extra-virgin olive oil

Juice of **2** large lemons (about ½ **cup**)

5 tablespoons tomato paste

5 large garlic cloves, minced

1½ **teaspoons** ground cumin

1½ **teaspoons** smoked paprika

1 teaspoon Aleppo pepper flakes

Chicken and Vegetables

Extra-virgin olive oil

6 carrots (9 to 10 ounces total), peeled, halved lengthwise, and cut into 2-inch pieces

2 medium onions, halved and cut into ½-inch slices

1 (15-ounce) can chickpeas, drained

Kosher salt and ground black pepper

10 boneless, skinless chicken thighs

1. Position one rack in the center of the oven and another one 4 or 5 inches under the broiler. Preheat the oven to 425°F.

2. **Prepare the tomato rub:** In a small bowl, combine the olive oil, lemon juice, tomato paste, garlic, cumin, paprika, and Aleppo pepper. Whisk well to combine.

3. **Prepare the chicken and vegetables:** Lightly brush a large sheet pan with some of the olive oil. In a large bowl, combine the carrots, onions, and chickpeas. Season well with salt and black pepper (about ½ teaspoon each). Add 4 tablespoons of the tomato rub and a small drizzle of olive oil (about 1 teaspoon), and mix well to coat. Transfer the mixture to the sheet pan.

4. Pat the chicken dry and season with salt and black pepper on both sides. Place the chicken in the bowl and add the remaining tomato mixture, tossing until the chicken is well coated.

5. Transfer the chicken to the sheet pan along with the chickpeas and vegetables. Roast on the center rack until the chicken is cooked through, 25 to 30 minutes. Then move the sheet pan up to the top rack directly under the heat and broil until the chicken gains some color, 3 to 4 minutes, watching carefully. The onions and carrots may also gain some char.

6. Serve with your favorite rustic bread.

adam's split chicken with garlic-harissa rub

SERVES 4 TO 5

Our good friend Adam Courtney knows his way around two things: guitars and grills. He plays several instruments and leads worship at our church, while my husband Saba occasionally plays the bass guitar with him. I do not actually know whether either of them is good because, well, I am pretty much tone deaf. But I do feel qualified to vouch for Adam's juicy barbecued chicken!

This recipe is a bit of a collab between us. I supplied the garlic-harissa rub (you'll be making this rub on the regular once you try it) and Adam did his magic with the grill. See the sidebar on the opposite page for Adam's grilling tips.

It takes about 45 minutes to an hour on the grill, but that is the perfect excuse for a little mezze while the grill is working.

Garlic-Harissa Rub

2 large shallots, quartered

10 large garlic cloves

6 tablespoons Homemade Harissa Paste (page 286)

1 teaspoon ground black pepper

¾ teaspoon ground nutmeg

½ to 1 teaspoon cayenne pepper (optional)

Juice of **2** large lemons (about **½ cup**)

¼ cup extra-virgin olive oil

1 teaspoon kosher salt

Chicken

1 3½- to 4-pound chicken, halved with backbone removed (the butcher can do this for you, or see opposite)

Kosher salt

1. **Make the rub:** In the bowl of a small food processor fitted with the multipurpose blade, combine the shallots and garlic and pulse a few times until finely chopped. Add the harissa paste, black pepper, nutmeg, cayenne (if using), lemon juice, olive oil, and salt. Run the processor until everything is well combined and has formed a thick paste.

2. **Prepare the chicken:** Pat the chicken dry and season with about 3 teaspoons salt, making sure to lift the skin and apply some salt underneath. Apply the garlic-harissa rub generously all over the chicken, especially underneath the skin. Refrigerate, uncovered, for 2 hours (or, if you do not have the time, set the chicken aside for 30 minutes while the grill heats).

3. When ready to grill, preheat only the outer burners over medium-high heat (to 400°F). When hot, lightly oil the grates.

4. Place the chicken, skin side up, directly over the burners that are turned off (this is what is meant by indirect heat). Cover the unit and grill until the chicken is cooked through, 45 minutes to 1 hour. Check every few minutes, and if the chicken gains some color on one side, rotate as needed. (For the juiciest chicken, remove it from the heat when the internal temperature of the thickest part reaches 157°F on an instant-read thermometer.)

5. Remove the chicken from the grill and set aside to rest for 10 to 15 minutes, before slicing and serving.

A FEW TIPS ON CHICKEN

HOW TO SPLIT THE CHICKEN: Place the whole chicken on a cutting board with the backbone facing you. Using a pair of sturdy kitchen shears, cut along both sides of the backbone. Remove the backbone and discard it. Push down on the breasts to flatten the chicken. Flip the chicken over and remove the wing tips, if you like. Split the chicken into 2 halves so that the bird can easily lay flat on the grill. (Hint: You can always ask your butcher to do this for you, and you'll have the chicken split and ready for cooking.)

HOW TO SEASON THE CHICKEN: For best flavor, salt the chicken well first, then spread the garlic-harissa rub all over and especially underneath the skin. I like to allow the chicken to marinate in the fridge for about 2 hours, but if you don't have the time, even 30 minutes will help. For extra heat, make my Homemade Harissa Paste (page 286) as per the recipe, adding a a teaspoon or more cayenne to kick it up a notch.

HOW TO GRILL THE CHICKEN: For grilling this split chicken, indirect heat is what you need. Fire up the gas grill over medium-high heat, but leave the burner(s) directly below the chicken turned off (or bank the coals of a charcoal grill to one side, so one side is low heat and the other is medium-high). This is a slow-cook situation; the grilling will take somewhere between 45 minutes and 1 hour, but the resulting succulent, extra juicy bites are so worth it!

For the juiciest chicken, and to make sure the chicken doesn't overcook, Adam advises that you pull the chicken off the heat when the internal temperature taken at the thickest part reaches 157°F on an instant-read thermometer. Then, loosely tent the chicken with foil and let rest for 10 to 15 minutes to allow the juices to redistribute. In the process, the chicken's internal temperature should rise to 165°F (the recommended safe temperature) before slicing and serving.

braised chicken, mushrooms, and poblano peppers with pomegranate molasses

SERVES 4 TO 8

Sometime early in my married life I discovered the thrill of playing with pomegranate molasses—that sticky, sweet-tart reduction of pomegranate juice. And it is the sneaky ingredient in this cozy chicken and mushroom situation that I concocted to bring to a friend's house for a potluck dinner. Between the fragrant spices and the brightness and subtle tang of the syrup, no one could guess what was in it. But they had fun trying.

2 teaspoons dried rosemary

1 teaspoon ground coriander

1 teaspoon sweet paprika

¾ teaspoon ground allspice

½ teaspoon ground black pepper

½ teaspoon ground nutmeg

8 skinless, bone-in chicken thighs

Kosher salt

Extra-virgin olive oil

8 medium shallots, halved

10 large garlic cloves, minced

2 poblano chiles, seeded and roughly chopped

2 cups low-sodium chicken broth

3 tablespoons tomato paste

¼ cup pomegranate molasses

2 dried bay leaves

1 pound baby bella mushrooms, trimmed and halved

Juice of **1** large lemon (about **¼ cup**)

½ cup roughly chopped fresh flat-leaf parsley

1. Position a rack in the center of the oven and preheat the oven to 375°F.

2. In a small bowl, combine 1 teaspoon of the rosemary, the coriander, paprika, allspice, pepper, and nutmeg.

3. Pat the chicken dry and season well on both sides with about 1½ teaspoons salt. Rub the spice mixture all over it.

4. In a braising pan or large, heavy ovenproof pan with a lid, heat ¼ cup of the olive oil over medium-high heat until shimmering. Add the shallots, garlic, and poblanos. Season with salt (about ½ teaspoon). Cook, stirring frequently, until the veggies are tender, about 5 minutes. Adjust the heat as needed to keep the garlic from burning.

5. Add the broth and stir in the tomato paste, 3 tablespoons of the pomegranate molasses, the bay leaves, and the remaining teaspoon rosemary. Bring to a boil, then nestle the chicken in the liquid and continue to cook for 5 minutes. Then transfer the pan to the middle rack of the oven and cook, uncovered, for 25 to 30 minutes, until the chicken is cooked through and its juices run clear.

6. In a medium skillet, heat 2 tablespoons olive oil. Add the mushrooms and about ½ teaspoon salt. Cook and stir over medium-high heat until the mushrooms lose their liquid and gain some color, 7 to 10 minutes.

7. Add the mushrooms to the pan and continue cooking another 5 more minutes or so. Remove the bay leaves and discard. Drizzle the chicken with the lemon juice and the remaining tablespoon pomegranate molasses. Garnish with the parsley and serve immediately.

mahshi (stuffed vegetables)

SERVES 4 AS A MAIN COURSE, 8 AS A SIDE DISH

I used to sit at Mama's round kitchen table while she cored and hollowed out all sorts of vegetables—bell peppers, tomatoes, zucchini, small eggplants, and potatoes—making room for her herby rice and meat filling. We call it *mahshi*, which means "stuffed" in Arabic. It is an institution and a bit of a sport among Egyptian women, who lovingly compete to throw the best mahshi dinner in the neighborhood. For this recipe, I selected bell peppers and tomatoes because, frankly, they are the easiest to work with and make for a colorful presentation.

4 large bell peppers, in different colors

5 large, somewhat firm round tomatoes

¾ **cup** basmati rice, rinsed well until the water runs clear and drained

½ **pound** lean ground beef (or lamb)

1 small yellow onion, grated

2 large garlic cloves, minced

1 **cup** chopped fresh parsley leaves and tender stems

½ **cup** chopped fresh dill fronds

1 **tablespoon** dried mint

1 **teaspoon** ground allspice

½ **teaspoon** ground cumin

½ **teaspoon** red pepper flakes (optional)

Kosher salt and ground black pepper

Extra-virgin olive oil

2 **tablespoons** tomato paste

½ **cup** water

1 medium yellow onion, sliced into ¼-inch rounds

1 (14.5-**ounce**) can tomato sauce

¾ **cup** low-sodium chicken broth

1. Cut the tops off the peppers and set them aside (you will use the tops to cover the stuffed peppers). Remove the seeds and cores to hollow out the peppers and make room for the filling.

2. Set 1 tomato aside for later. Cut about ½ inch from the top of the remaining tomatoes (you will use the tops to cover the stuffed tomatoes). Using a small paring knife, carefully work your way around the inside edge of the tomatoes to loosen and separate the flesh from the skin. Then using a spoon, carefully scoop out the tomato flesh onto a cutting board. Chop the tomato flesh into small pieces and put them in a large bowl.

3. Add the rice, ground beef, onion, garlic, parsley, dill, mint, allspice, cumin, and red pepper flakes (if using). Season the mixture with about ¾ teaspoon each salt and black pepper. Drizzle with 2 tablespoons of the olive oil. In a small bowl, combine the tomato paste with the water and stir until the paste dissolves, then add it to the filling mixture. With a wooden spoon, mix until the ingredients are well combined.

4. Use about 2 tablespoons of the olive oil to coat the bottom of a large braising pan or large, heavy oven-proof pan with a lid. Cut the remaining tomato into ¼-inch slices and arrange them and the sliced onion on the bottom of the pan, covering the surface.

5. Gently stuff the hollowed-out peppers and tomatoes about three-fourths full with the rice mixture and arrange the stuffed peppers and tomatoes, open side up, in the pan. Crown the peppers and tomatoes with their tops and drizzle about 2 tablespoons olive oil over them. Pour the

tomato sauce and the stock into the pan alongside the stuffed vegetables.

6. Position a rack in the center of the oven. Preheat the oven to 375°F.

7. Bring the liquid in the pan to a rolling boil over medium-high heat, then cover the pan and transfer it to the oven and bake for 45 to 50 minutes, until the vegetables are tender and the rice has swelled and cooked thoroughly (you can check occasionally to see if a little liquid may be needed on the bottom of the pan).

8. Let the stuffed peppers and tomatoes rest for 10 minutes before serving.

maglooba

SERVES 8

Maglooba (or maqlubeh) is a celebratory rice dish. Mama Dina served her Jordanian version to my parents when our two families first met. In Arabic it literally means "upside down" or "turned over," referring to the way the pot is turned over and lifted to reveal a cake-shaped tower with layers of rice, chicken or lamb, cauliflower, eggplant, and sometimes potatoes. It's a generous dish that is truly a labor of love. And because my girls adore it, I had to find my own maglooba mojo with Mama Dina's help. I make a couple of shortcuts by using boneless chicken thighs and by roasting the vegetables rather frying them—not traditional, but still delicious. And I will say, maglooba is something you will want to try on a leisurely Sunday afternoon.

2 cups basmati rice

Kosher salt and ground black pepper

1 medium globe eggplant, trimmed and cut into ¾-inch rounds

Extra-virgin olive oil

1 large head of cauliflower (2½ **pounds**), trimmed, cored, and cut into florets

3 pounds boneless, skinless chicken thighs, or a mix of thighs and breasts

2 teaspoons ground allspice

1½ teaspoons ground cinnamon

1 medium yellow onion

3 large garlic cloves, sliced

2 dried bay leaves

3 cardamom pods, lightly crushed

5 cups water

1 or 2 vine-ripened medium tomatoes, sliced into ½-inch rounds

¼ teaspoon ground turmeric

½ cup whole blanched almonds

1. Rinse the rice until the water runs clear, then put in a medium bowl and cover with water by at least 1 inch; add 1 teaspoon salt and let sit for 10 minutes or so. Drain well.

2. Season the eggplant slices on both sides with about 1 teaspoon salt and arrange them on a clean work surface or large tray. Let sit for 20 to 30 minutes to "sweat" any bitterness. With a paper towel, wipe the eggplant dry, removing the excess salt.

3. Position a rack in the center of the oven and another one below it. Preheat the oven to 425°F. Lightly brush two 13 × 18 × 1-inch sheet pans with some of the olive oil.

4. In a large bowl, season the cauliflower florets with 1½ teaspoons salt. Add ¼ cup of the olive oil and toss to coat well. Transfer the cauliflower to one of the sheet pans and spread the florets in a single layer, making sure every floret is touching the pan. Arrange the eggplant slices on the other sheet pan in a single layer.

5. Roast the cauliflower and eggplant until the eggplant is soft, 15 to 20 minutes, then remove the eggplant from the oven. Keep the cauliflower in the oven and raise the heat to 450°F. Roast the cauliflower until soft and charred in some parts, about another 30 to 40 minutes. Remove from the oven.

Recipe continues

6. While the vegetables are roasting, place the chicken pieces in a large bowl and season with a scant teaspoon each salt and black pepper. Add 1 teaspoon of the allspice and ½ teaspoon of cinnamon. Toss to coat well.

7. In a nonstick 8-quart pot with a lid that is about 6 inches deep (or similar vessel of at least that depth), heat 3 tablespoons of olive oil. Add the chicken and onion, and cook over medium-high heat, tossing around, until the chicken is browned on both sides and the onion is tender and lightly caramelized, 8 to 10 minutes total.

8. Add the garlic, bay leaves, cardamom, and water to the pot with the chicken. Season with a big pinch of salt (about ½ to ¾ teaspoon), and bring to a boil, then reduce the heat to medium-low and cover the pot. Let the chicken simmer for 20 minutes. Then remove the chicken from the pot and set it on a large plate. Strain the cooking liquid and discard the bay leaves, onion, and cardamom pods. Reserve the liquid.

9. Wipe the bottom of the pot clean. Add 2 tablespoons of the olive oil and arrange the tomato slices on the bottom of the pot, followed by the eggplant slices, the cauliflower, and the chicken. Pour in the rice on top (it will fill in the spaces between the chicken and vegetables), then sprinkle on the turmeric, the remaining teaspoon allspice, and the remaining teaspoon cinnamon.

10. Measure 2 cups of the saved cooking liquid and pour over the rice. Push the rice and chicken down gently in the pot; you should be able to see the liquid rise up to the level of the rice, barely covering parts of it. If needed, add a little bit more cooking liquid (about ¼ cup).

Bring to a simmer over medium-high heat and cook for about 10 minutes. Turn the heat to low, cover the pot, and cook until the rice has absorbed all the liquid and is tender, about 30 minutes When the rice is done, turn off the heat, leave the lid on the pot, and let rest for 15 to 20 minutes.

11. In a small skillet, heat 1 tablespoon olive oil over medium-high heat. Add the almonds and cook, tossing gently, until golden, 3 to 4 minutes. Using a spoon, transfer them to a plate lined with a paper towel.

12. When ready to serve, carefully remove the lid of the pot and place a large, round serving platter on top of the pot (the platter needs to be larger in diameter than the pot). Using both hands, quickly invert the pot so that the platter is now on the bottom (call for help if you need it here; the pot may be heavy). Gently tap the bottom of the pot to help coax the rice and veggies to release. Carefully remove the pot to reveal the maglooba! Top with the toasted almonds and serve.

TIP

For fluffier rice, place a thin, clean kitchen towel over the pot, set the lid on top of the towel, and then tie the ends of the towel over the lid, above the handle—this is important so the towel doesn't catch fire! The towel helps absorb extra steam to keep the rice from getting mushy. Be careful doing this and keep the heat setting on low.

VARIATION

Sans the chicken, maglooba makes a great vegetarian meal. My editor, Raquel Pelzel, also adds 1 cup of cooked brown lentils to the rice for a little more protein—brilliant!

bulgur chicken and vegetable stew

SERVES 6

I'm what you might call a "souper." Left to my own devices, I will choose to eat something soupy all day, every day, no matter the season. So, given my expertise, I can tell you that my Dutch oven and I have come up with a new take on chicken stew that prompted someone who tried the recipe on my site to comment: "My taste buds are having a party right now, this is so dang GOOD!!" This one is even heaftier with the addition of bulgur wheat.

½ **cup** coarse bulgur wheat #3 (do not use finer bulgur)

1½ **pounds** boneless, skinless chicken thighs

Kosher salt and black pepper

2 **tablespoons** extra-virgin olive oil

1 medium yellow onion, chopped

2 large garlic cloves, minced

2 medium carrots, peeled and roughly chopped

1 red bell pepper, cored, seeded, and roughly chopped

1 small zucchini, diced small

1 medium Yukon Gold or yellow potato, peeled and diced

1 **teaspoon** ground coriander

1 **teaspoon** dried oregano

1 **teaspoon** sweet paprika

1 **(28-ounce)** can whole San Marzano tomatoes, or other canned whole tomatoes

3 **cups** low-sodium chicken broth

2 sprigs of fresh thyme

2 **tablespoons** white wine vinegar

1 **cup** chopped flat-leaf parsley

1. Place the bulgur in a small bowl and cover with water. Soak the bulgur for 15 minutes. Drain well.

2. Pat the chicken dry and season on both sides well with 1 teaspoon each of salt and black pepper.

3. In a Dutch oven or large pot, heat the olive oil over medium-high heat until shimmering. Add the chicken and brown on both sides, about 8 minutes total. Set the chicken on a plate.

4. Add the onion, garlic, carrots, bell pepper, zucchini, and potato to the Dutch oven. Season with ½ teaspoon each salt and black pepper. Add the coriander, oregano, and paprika. Toss to combine and cook over medium-high heat for 7 to 8 minutes, stirring occasionally, until the veggies have softened somewhat. (I like to let them gain a little char, too.)

5. Add the tomatoes and break them up with a wooden spoon. Add the chicken stock and thyme. Raise the heat to high and bring to a boil. Add the chicken and the bulgur, and cook for 5 minutes. Then lower the heat to medium-low and cover the Dutch oven partway, leaving just a bit of an opening at the top for steam. Simmer the stew until the chicken is fully cooked and the bulgur is tender (the bulgur will absorb a lot of the liquid), 25 to 30 minutes.

6. Remove and discard the thyme sprigs. Stir in the vinegar and parsley, and serve.

lamb lollipops with pomegranate, mint, and pistachio sauce

SERVES 6

I once heard someone say that the rack is to lamb what prime rib is to beef. I couldn't agree more—and like prime rib, rack of lamb has a hefty price tag, making it a special-occasion meal, for sure.

The good news is that it's thankfully hard to mess it up. And it can stand up to bold flavors. Here I coat it first in a peppery seasoning, which also gives it a nicely caramelized crust, then bathe it in a bright, minty sauce to balance the richness, and garnish with a sprinkling of pistachios and pomegranate seeds for color and crunch. A platter of Cara Cara Orange, Cucumber, and Avocado Salad with Pomegranate Seeds (page 40) would look great on the table next to this elegant little number!

Lamb Rub

1 teaspoon Aleppo pepper flakes

1 teaspoon sumac

½ teaspoon ground nutmeg

Kosher salt and black pepper

Pomegranate, Mint, and Pistachio Sauce

2 large garlic cloves

2 cups (packed) fresh mint leaves

½ cup extra-virgin olive oil

Juice of **1** large lemon (about **¼ cup**)

¼ cup pomegranate molasses

Kosher salt and ground black pepper

Lamb and Garnish

2 racks of lamb (8 chops per rack, about **3 pounds** total), frenched

¼ cup lightly crushed shelled pistachios

½ cup pomegranate seeds (arils)

1. **Make the rub:** In a small bowl, combine the Aleppo pepper, sumac, nutmeg, and about ¾ teaspoon each salt and black pepper.

2. **Make the sauce:** In a small food processor, combine the garlic, mint, olive oil, lemon juice, and pomegranate molasses. Add a big pinch of salt and pepper (about ½ teaspoon each). Blend until everything is well combined as a thick sauce. Transfer 6 tablespoons of the sauce to a small bowl and reserve the rest in another bowl for serving.

3. **Prepare the lamb:** Place the racks of lamb in a shallow tray or rectangular baking dish and use paper towels to pat the meat dry on both sides. Massage the rub all over the meat and then spread with the reserved sauce. Let the lamb rest at room temperature for 20 to 30 minutes (or, for even deeper flavor, refrigerate for 2 to 4 hours).

4. Position a rack in the top third of the oven and preheat the oven to 450°F.

5. Place the lamb fat side up in a 13 × 18 × 1-inch sheet pan, side by side, and roast for 15 minutes. Carefully remove the sheet pan from the oven and turn the racks over. Return to the oven and roast for another 5 to 10 minutes, depending on how you like your lamb cooked: An instant-read thermometer inserted in the lamb's thickest part should register 120°F for rare and 150°F for well-done. I prefer mine at about 130°F, or medium-rare. (Remember that the meat's temperature will continue to rise by about 5 degrees after

it comes out of the oven, so err on the lower side.) Loosely tent the racks in the sheet pan with aluminum foil and allow the lamb to rest for 7 to 10 minutes before serving.

6. Uncover and transfer the racks to a cutting board. Using a sharp knife, cut the racks into chops by slicing between the bones. Arrange the chops on a platter. Stir the remaining sauce and then drizzle it all over the lamb chops. Sprinkle the crushed pistachios and pomegranate arils on top and serve.

A FEW TIPS ABOUT LAMB CHOPS

Loin lamb chops can be small—I plan on 2 or 3 per person. Each rack yields about 8 chops.

You can usually buy racks of lamb that have already been frenched, which means the cartilage and fat between the rib bones has been cut away so that the tops of the rib bones are exposed, making for a more dramatic presentation. If not already done, it's not hard to do this yourself with a small, sharp knife.

To avoid overcooking the lamb, roast to 5 degrees below the final temperature you are looking for. Remember that the meat will continue to cook as it rests.

saucy baked kofta and potatoes

SERVES 4

For me, this hearty dish carries with it a bit of a thrill. It begins with boldly seasoned lamb patties that are nestled between slices of yellow potatoes and onion, and then baked in a chunky tomato sauce. This is the kind of meat-and-potato dinner I make on a leisurely Sunday. While we play some board games (or take naps), the kofta casserole is bubbling happily in the oven, filling the air with all sorts of delicious aromas. Even though Saba and the girls have had several versions of this dish over the years, there is always a bit of a "voilà!" moment when I pull the pan out of the oven. I use whole wheat bread that's been soaked in water and drained to bind the kofta mixture while giving it a sweet-nutty flavor.

Tomato Sauce

2 tablespoons extra-virgin olive oil

1 small yellow onion, roughly chopped

2 large garlic cloves, minced

2 (15-ounce) cans diced tomatoes, no salt added, with juices

¾ **teaspoon** ground allspice

Kosher salt and ground black pepper

Kofta and Potatoes

1 slice whole wheat sandwich bread

1 pound ground lamb

1 large egg, lightly beaten

1 medium yellow onion, grated on the largest holes of a box grater

3 large garlic cloves, crushed

1 cup finely chopped fresh flat-leaf parsley

1 teaspoon ground allspice

½ **teaspoon** ground cardamom

1. Make the sauce: In a large saucepan with a lid, heat the olive oil over medium heat until shimmering. Add the onion and garlic and cook, stirring occasionally, until fragrant and tender, 5 to 7 minutes, adjusting the heat as needed so that the garlic doesn't burn. Add the tomatoes and the juices. Stir in the allspice and ½ teaspoon each salt and black pepper. Bring to a boil, then lower the heat to medium-low and partly cover with the lid. Let simmer for about 15 minutes, until slightly thickened. Taste and adjust the seasoning.

2. Prepare the meat mixture: Soak the bread slice in a bowl of warm water for a minute or two, just until the bread is softened. Squeeze the bread dry (it will crumble, which is what you want). Discard the soaking water and add the crumbled bread to a large bowl.

3. Add the lamb, egg, onion, garlic, parsley, allspice, cardamom, cinnamon, red pepper flakes, and ¾ teaspoons each salt and pepper. Using clean hands, knead the meat mixture until the ingredients are well blended.

4. Take about 2 heaping tablespoons of the kofta mixture and form into a ball, then very lightly pat the ball between your hands to form a small, thick patty (don't flatten it too much). Set the patty on a large plate or pan. Repeat until the meat mixture is finished; you should have 12 to 15 patties. Cover the pan with plastic wrap and refrigerate for about 30 minutes to firm up slightly.

5. Position a rack in the center of the oven and preheat the oven to 425°F. Lightly oil the sides and bottom of a 10-inch round baking dish or a well-seasoned cast-iron skillet.

½ **teaspoon** ground cinnamon

½ **teaspoon** red pepper flakes

Kosher salt and ground black pepper

4 large Yukon Gold or other yellow potatoes, peeled and sliced into ¼-inch-thick rounds

1 large red onion, halved and cut into ½-inch-thick slices

6. Spread about 1 cup of the tomato sauce in the dish. Place 1 kofta patty upright along the edge of the dish, followed by 3 slices of potatoes and a slice of onion. Repeat this pattern around the perimeter of the dish. Assemble the remaining kofta patties, potato slices, and onion slices in the middle of the dish. Ladle the rest of the tomato sauce evenly over the kofta and potatoes in the dish.

7. Place the baking dish on top of a 13 × 18 × 1-inch sheet pan to catch any spill over. Cover the baking dish with parchment paper, then with aluminum foil. Bake for 50 minutes. Then carefully uncover the baking dish and continue baking for another 20 to 30 minutes, until the kofta gains color and the potatoes are cooked through.

8. Serve immediately, or allow to cool and then cover and refrigerate for up to 2 days; when ready to serve, reheat in a warm oven.

middle eastern
triple-layer shepherd's pie

SERVES 6

I was describing this simple three-layer mashed potato casserole to my friend Lisa, who was in my kitchen one day to help with some recipe testing. "You mean sort of like a Middle Eastern shepherd's pie?" she asked. Brilliant! Except this Middle Eastern version has a layer of mashed potatoes on the top and the bottom, and in between, an allspice-scented meat mixture that's flecked with herbs and studded with toasted pine nuts. Sure, given the ratio of potato to meat, you can serve it as a side dish, but I often serve it as the main with a little plate of Pan-Grilled Zucchini with Dukkah and Fresh Herbs (page 78) or a colorful salad like Rainbow Baby Bell Pepper Salad (page 39). Also, see the vegetarian variation that follows.

3 pounds Yukon Gold or other yellow potatoes, peeled and diced

Kosher salt and ground black pepper

Extra-virgin olive oil

1 small yellow onion, roughly chopped

1 large garlic clove, minced

1 pound ground beef

1½ teaspoons ground allspice

½ teaspoon ground nutmeg

¼ teaspoon red pepper flakes

½ cup toasted pine nuts

½ cup roughly chopped fresh flat-leaf parsley

¼ cup milk or non-dairy alternative

2 large eggs

¼ teaspoon distilled white vinegar

1 tablespoon water

2 tablespoons bread crumbs

1. In a large pot, place the potatoes and cover with cold water by about 2 inches. Add 2 teaspoons of salt, bring to a boil over medium-high heat and cook until the potatoes are very tender, 15 to 20 minutes.

2. While the potatoes are cooking, make the meat mixture. In a large skillet, heat 1 tablespoon of the olive oil. Add the onion and garlic and cook over medium-high heat, stirring regularly, until soft and fragrant, 3 to 5 minutes. Reduce the heat to medium and add the ground beef, breaking it up with a wooden spoon. Add the allspice, nutmeg, red pepper flakes, and about ¾ teaspoon each salt and black pepper. Stir to combine, and cook until the meat is fully browned and cooked through, about 10 minutes total. Stir in the pine nuts and parsley, then remove from the heat.

3. Position a rack in the center of the oven and another one 4 or 5 inches under the broiler. Preheat the oven to 375°F.

4. In a large bowl, smash the potatoes with a potato masher or a fork and taste, adding salt to your liking. Add the milk, 1 egg, and 2 tablespoons olive oil, then mix until well combined.

5. Lightly brush a 2-quart baking dish with 1 tablespoon of the olive oil. Spread half the potato mixture in the dish. Spread the meat mixture on top, then add the remaining potatoes for the top layer and spread well with the back of a spoon.

6. In a small bowl, whisk the second egg with the vinegar and water. Use this egg wash to brush the top layer of the casserole, then sprinkle the top with the bread crumbs.

7. Bake the casserole on the middle rack of the oven for 20 minutes. Turn the heat to broil, move the casserole to the top rack, and broil for 2 to 3 minutes, until the top turns a beautiful golden brown.

VARIATION

Vegetarian Option

For a vegetarian version, omit the meat and replace it with a mixture of roughly chopped bell peppers, mushrooms, and carrots. Sauté the veggies until very tender, using the same spice combination as for the meat, and adjust to your taste. Layer with mashed potatoes as instructed, and garnish as desired.

kickin' kofta kebabs with allspice and cardamom

SERVES 4 TO 5

This recipe is my best rendition of my favorite kebab served at the iconic Abdou Kofta restaurant on El Shaheed Atef El-Sadat Street, a quick stroll from Port Said's boardwalk. It's a mixture of ground beef and lamb (though you could totally use one or the other), blended with onions, garlic, parsley, and several Middle Eastern spices, including allspice and cardamom. Flavor heaven! The biggest secret to the juiciness of these kebabs is a small piece of toasted bread that's been soaked in water, squeezed dry, and crumbled into the meat mixture before molding it around the skewers. (Yes, I'm a big fan of the toasted bread trick.) The Lime-Tahini Sauce (page 290) is a must to drizzle on top. From there, add any number of your favorite salads or small plates from the Mezze chapter to complete this meal.

8 to 10 wooden or bamboo skewers

1 small slice of toasted sandwich bread, crust removed

1 medium yellow onion, quartered

2 large garlic cloves

2 cups (packed) fresh parsley leaves and tender stems

1 pound lean ground beef

8 ounces ground lamb

1½ teaspoons ground allspice

¾ teaspoon ground cardamom

¾ teaspoon ground nutmeg

½ teaspoon ground black pepper

½ teaspoon cayenne pepper, or more as desired

½ teaspoon sweet paprika

½ teaspoon sumac

Kosher salt

Lime-Tahini Sauce (page 290)

Pita bread, homemade (see page 99) or store-bought

1. Soak the skewers in water for 1 hour before grilling.

2. Place the bread slice in a small bowl and cover with water. Soak until the bread is very soft, about 10 minutes. Discard the water and squeeze the bread dry.

3. Lightly oil the grates of a gas grill and preheat the grill to 450°F.

4. In the bowl of a large food processor fitted with the multipurpose blade, combine the onion, garlic, and parsley. Pulse until finely chopped. Transfer to a large bowl and add the beef, lamb, the soaked bread, the allspice, cardamom, nutmeg, black pepper, cayenne, paprika, sumac, and about 1 teaspoon salt. Mix until well blended.

5. Take a fistful of the meat mixture and mold it onto a wooden skewer. Repeat the process until you have used all the meat mixture. For best results, make sure each kofta kebab is about 1 inch thick. You should have 8 to 10 skewers.

6. Place the kofta skewers on the grill over direct heat. Cook for 4 minutes on one side, then turn them over and cook until the kofta are cooked through, another 3 to 4 minutes.

7. Serve immediately with the tahini sauce, pita bread, and any sides of your choice.

wine-braised lamb shanks
with cinnamon and rosemary

SERVES 6

For my family, leg of lamb is hands-down the roast of choice for the holidays, or whenever a showstopper is needed for a large gathering. But here's a little secret: A cheaper and less intimidating cut that's equally impressive is lamb shanks. The shank is a cut that comes from the well-exercised lower section of the lamb leg, and it practically begs to be slowly braised until meltingly tender and full of flavor. This was my dad's favorite dish that I ever made for him, and I think of him every time I make it.

2¼ teaspoons garlic powder

1 teaspoon sweet paprika

1 teaspoon kosher salt

1 teaspoon ground black pepper

¾ teaspoon ground nutmeg

6 lamb shanks (about **1 pound** each)

Extra-virgin olive oil

1 medium yellow onion, chopped

2 celery stalks, chopped

3 large carrots, peeled and cut into large pieces

1 pound baby potatoes, scrubbed

2 cups Merlot or other dry red wine

3 cups low-sodium beef broth

1 (28-ounce) can whole tomatoes, with juices

2 cinnamon sticks

4 sprigs fresh thyme

2 sprigs fresh rosemary

Crusty bread or Middle Eastern Rice Pilaf with Toasted Vermicelli and Pine Nuts (page 161)

1. Position a rack in the center of the oven. Remove the top rack, if necessary, to allow enough space for the Dutch oven to fit comfortably. Preheat the oven to 425°F.

2. In a small bowl, mix the garlic powder, paprika, salt, pepper, and nutmeg. Pat the lamb shanks dry and sprinkle on all sides with the seasoning.

3. In a large Dutch oven or oven-safe pot, heat 2 tablespoons olive oil over medium-high heat until shimmering. Working in batches, brown the lamb shanks on all sides, 8 to 10 minutes per batch. Transfer the shanks to a large platter or tray. Carefully pour off all but about 2 tablespoons of the fat from the pot into a heat-safe bowl.

4. Return the pot to the stovetop and add the onion, celery, carrots, and potatoes. Cook for 7 to 10 minutes over medium-high, stirring occasionally. Add the wine and, with a wooden spoon, work to scrape up any brown bits from the bottom of the pot. Cook for a couple of minutes more.

5. Add the stock, tomatoes, cinnamon sticks, thyme, and rosemary. Season with salt and pepper, then return the lamb to the pot and press down to submerge them.

6. Bring the pot to a boil and boil for 10 minutes, then partly cover with the lid and transfer the pot to the oven. Cook for 2½ hours, checking periodically to add more liquid if needed. The meat should be falling off the bone and the liquid will have reduced to about one-third of what it was when you started.

7. Serve the lamb shanks with your favorite crusty bread or over a bed of rice pilaf.

after dinner
and in between

TEA BETWEEN FRIENDS

Throughout the Middle East and parts of the eastern Mediterranean, hot mint tea is a tonic, a comfort, a social drink, and a means of getting to know one another. Shai (hot tea) is an integral part of hospitality. Back in Egypt, if you stop by someone's home or office, even if just for a few minutes, you will be offered a seat and a cup of shai. Most business deals, conversations, heck, even marriage proposals, may begin with a fragrant, warm cup enhanced with any number of add-ins—fresh mint leaves, sage, cinnamon sticks, lightly crushed green cardamom pods—and served with a bite of something sweet.

It would not be too odd for a stranger, out of the blue, to offer you a cup of tea. I experienced this first-hand on a tour in Jordan. While our group climbed the rugged mountains of the magnificent stone-carved city of Petra, we took several breaks with local Bedouins who insisted we sit under their canopies to rest. To sustain us for the long hike, they served black tea, brewed over an open flame, along with dates. (Dates, too, have been a symbol of hospitality for thousands of years in that part of the world.) The tea and their kind hospitality were equally sweet and nourishing in the best way.

To close the book on this sweet note, I walk you through how to make my favorite after-dinner-and-in-between-drink: mint tea, or Shai Bil Na'ana'a (page 250). Plus, cold drinks and sweet bites—some traditional desserts like Umm Ali (page 266), Egypt's version of a bread pudding, and modern favorites like No-Churn Tahini and Hazelnut Ice Cream (page 261) and Charred Honeyed Apricots with Pistachios (page 258).

shai bil na'ana'a

MAKES 6 CUPS

If you visit me at home, you can expect a pot of hot mint tea, or shai bil na'ana'a, made in a well-used heirloom pot that was passed down over the years. (I'm convinced it tastes far better poured out of this old pot than out of fancy china.) As we catch up on life, we'll likely drink it out of small, clear cups to show off its color, and we'll end up refilling them over and over until the pot is finished. To me, shai is a heart-binding ritual. The very act of sharing it with another invites intimacy and joy.

6 cups water

2 teaspoons loose-leaf black tea, or more if you like your tea strong

A large handful of fresh mint leaves

Sugar or sweetener (optional)

1. Bring the water to a rolling boil in a tea kettle or medium saucepan. Stir in the tea and allow it to boil for 1 minute to help "agitate" the tea leaves.

2. Turn off the heat and immediately add the fresh mint leaves. Cover and allow the tea to steep for 5 minutes. Ideally, your tea should be an amber red (a deep red indicates that the tea may have over-steeped).

3. Divide the tea among cups (preferably clear teacups), pouring through a small mesh strainer to strain the leaves. Serve with sugar on the side so guests may add as much as they like.

NOTE
It is more traditional to sweeten the water in the pot ahead of time, but I like to allow everyone to add sugar to their taste.

frothy mint limonada

MAKES 6 CUPS

They say if you want to see and *hear* Egypt, all you need to do is hang out at an ahwa. Ahwas are small coffeehouses that are open to the busy streets and are filled with tiny round tables for two. They're loud with the sound of the traffic outside, with older men talking politics, and with young people competing in domino tournaments and waiters shouting drink orders that range from Arabic coffee to black tea, and limonada, or mint limeade.

Limonada is typically made in the blender with lime juice, crushed ice, and fresh mint. I like to use both lemons and limes, and I leave the skin on some of the citrus, which intensifies the flavor and produces froth. You can adjust this recipe to suit your taste: for a frothier drink, leave more of the citrus fruit skin on. You can also adjust the sugar to your liking.

2 cups crushed ice

4 cups cold filtered water

1 large organic lemon, washed, cut into wedges, and seeded (leave the skin on)

Juice of **3** large limes (about **6 tablespoons**)

1 cup fresh mint leaves, plus more for garnish

½ to ¾ cup sugar, or more to your liking

1. In a high-powered blender, combine the ice, water, lemon wedges, lime juice, mint, and ½ cup of the sugar. Cover and blend on high speed (usually, "liquefy") until everything is well blended and a frothy layer floats to the top.

2. Taste and add more sugar or mint leaves, if you like, and blend again.

3. Pour the limonada into a glass pitcher, cover, and refrigerate until ready to serve. If you prefer your limonada without the foamy top, pour it through a fine-mesh strainer and into glasses. Garnish with fresh mint leaves and serve.

hibiscus iced tea

MAKES 6 CUPS

Here in "Hotlanta," Georgia, a tall glass of iced sweet tea is *the* traditional drink of choice in summertime—and for that matter, anytime! But my version is called karkade (kar-ka-deh), which is made from sweet-tart dried hibiscus flower petals. I got my first taste of it when I was very small, while visiting Old Cairo one sweltering summer with my family. I can still picture the "karkade man" in his turban and white garb, roaming the narrow streets yelling "Karkade!" and offering people cold glasses of the deep-red, extra-sweet elixir poured from the large carafe strapped to his waist.

Said to have been the thirst-quencher of pharaohs thousands of years ago, karkade has long been prized not only for its refreshing cranberry-like taste but also for its high level of vitamin C and reputed medicinal properties, such as improving heart health and regulating blood pressure.

Many love their karkade with lots of sugar, but this recipe gives you room to use a sweetener of your choice and to adjust it to your liking. I also like mine with a splash of lime juice and a sprig of fresh mint. And for my friends who are thirsty for something a little stronger, it's totally okay to add a shot of tequila to the serving glasses for an Egyptian-style margarita. Now, we're talking, eh?!

6 cups filtered water

¾ cup dried hibiscus flowers

¼ to ½ cup sugar, agave nectar, or honey

2 large limes, 1 juiced, the other cut into thin wheels

Fresh mint sprigs, for serving

1. In a medium saucepan, bring the water to a boil and add the hibiscus petals and sweetener (I usually add ¼ to ½ cup of sugar). Boil for 3 minutes over high heat, until the sugar or sweetener is completely incorporated, then turn the heat off, cover the pan, and let the hibiscus steep for 20 to 30 minutes.

2. Position a fine-mesh strainer over a heat-safe glass pitcher or bowl. Pour the steeped hibiscus tea through the strainer, being careful to not spill any on your countertops or any porous surface because it stains easily. Discard the hibiscus flowers and stir in the lime juice.

3. Set aside to cool completely, then taste. If it is too concentrated or bitter, you can dilute it by adding a little more filtered water and more sweetener of your choice. Remember not to dilute it too much, especially if you plan to serve it over ice. Transfer to the fridge and chill for a few hours.

4. To serve, pour the hibiscus iced tea into glasses (with ice, if you like). Serve with a lime slice and a sprig of fresh mint in each glass.

cherry and berry fruit salad with lime and honey syrup

SERVES 6

There is not a summer without bags of cherries in my kitchen, and I love combining them with other berries to create an appropriately "red fruit salad." And if you really want those pom seeds and can't find them fresh, use the already-prepared cups from your supermarket's refrigerator section (just give them a quick sniff or taste one before adding them to your salad; sometimes they're too tart or they may smell a bit funky). Fruit salad with fresh herbs and a sprinkle of crushed nuts is next-level delicious!

Syrup

Juice of **3** large limes (about **6 tablespoons**)

3 tablespoons honey

½ teaspoon rosewater or orange blossom water (optional)

Fruit Salad

1 cup pitted fresh cherries, halved

2 cups hulled and thinly sliced fresh strawberries

1 cup fresh blackberries

½ cup fresh raspberries

¼ cup fresh pomegranate seeds (arils; optional; see Headnote)

⅓ cup roughly chopped walnuts, toasted if desired

2 tablespoons roughly chopped fresh mint leaves

1. **Make the syrup:** In a small saucepan, combine the lime juice and honey, and stir over medium heat until just warmed through and the honey is incorporated. Remove from the heat and stir in the rosewater (if using). Set aside to cool.

2. **Prepare the salad:** In a large bowl, combine the fruit and pomegranate seeds (if using). Add the syrup and give the fruit a gentle toss to combine.

3. Add the walnuts and mint, and gently toss. Transfer the salad to a platter or individual bowls and serve.

charred honeyed apricots with pistachios

SERVES 6

I'm not going to call this a dessert because this little number is something I can eat any time of the day when my sweet tooth begs for a treat. But these soft, charred, well-honeyed apricots also make a simple yet superlative way to end a summer feast without having to work too hard. A dollop of whipped cream or a spoonful of a creamy, tangy labneh (page 101) makes for a perfect finish. And if you're not a fan of apricots, ripe peaches or nectarines are good options, too.

3 tablespoons dark brown sugar

Juice of **1** large lemon (about **¼ cup**)

6 ripe fresh apricots, halved and pitted

¼ cup honey

1 tablespoon extra-virgin olive oil

¼ cup roughly chopped, roasted pistachios

Whipped cream or Labneh (page 101), for serving

1. Position an oven rack about 6 inches from the heat source and turn on the broiler to high.

2. In a medium bowl, whisk together the brown sugar and lemon juice. Add the apricots and toss to coat, making sure the flesh side of the apricots is well coated with the mixture.

3. Arrange the apricots, cut side up, in a sheet pan or cast-iron skillet large enough to hold them. Pour in about ⅓ cup water along the side of the pan and place the pan under the broiler for the apricots to soften and the flesh to char nicely in some parts, 5 to 7 minutes. Watch carefully to make sure the apricots do not burn.

4. In a small saucepan, warm the honey briefly until thinned out, then stir in the olive oil. Remove from the heat.

5. Using a pair of tongs, carefully transfer the apricots to a serving platter. Pour the honey and olive oil mixture all over them and finish with a sprinkle of the pistachios. Serve warm, topped with whipped cream or labneh (if using).

no-churn tahini and hazelnut ice cream

MAKES 2 QUARTS

Some of the tastiest treats happen almost by accident! Saba and I had a few friends over for dinner one night to taste a bunch of the recipes I made for this book. I had completely forgotten all about dessert. Like a champ, I quickly arranged a make-your-own-sundae bar with a bucket of store-bought vanilla ice cream, some roughly chopped hazelnuts, warmed honey, and a jar of tahini. The tahini was the magic surprise element! It added a nutty, rich flavor that balanced the sweetness of the ice cream. My friend Marsha, who also works with us, couldn't stop raving about it; within days, she had re-created the sundae for her book club and other dinner guests.

So, in Marsha's honor, I decided to turn this idea into homemade ice cream. And it turned out even better—plus no ice cream maker needed! The ice cream does need to sit in the freezer for six hours or so to harden, so be sure to work that into your day's plan.

2 cups heavy (whipping) cream

1 (14-ounce) can sweetened condensed milk

1 teaspoon vanilla extract

½ cup quality tahini, plus more for serving

¾ cup hazelnuts, roasted and roughly chopped

Warm honey, for serving

1. Place the cream in a large bowl (if using a hand mixer) or in the bowl of a stand mixer and beat on medium-high speed until stiff peaks form, taking care not to overwhip the cream.

2. In a medium bowl, whisk together the condensed milk, vanilla, and tahini until well combined.

3. Carefully and slowly fold the tahini mixture into the whipped cream using a rubber spatula. Fold in half the hazelnuts.

4. Pour the mixture into a 9 × 5-inch loaf pan and smooth the top with your spatula. Top with the remaining hazelnuts. Cover the surface flush with plastic wrap and freeze until the mixture is hard, about 6 hours.

5. To serve, remove the pan from the freezer and let sit on the counter for about 10 minutes to soften enough to scoop. Serve scoops of the ice cream in bowls and top with a drizzle of more tahini and warm honey.

triple nutty baklava

MAKES 24 PIECES, SERVING 12

Iconic baklava (or baklawa) needs no big introduction. But when you grow up eating it at nearly every special gathering, you become a bit of a baklava snob, accepting nothing less than the best homemade stuff made with layers of appropriately honeyed, crisp phyllo sheets and just the right amount of nuts tucked in between.

Traditionalists make baklava with either walnuts or pistachios, but I love mine extra nutty with a trio of nuts and a generous hint of cinnamon. Baklava is not hard to make, and if you know how to assemble a lasagna, you'll find the soothing process of layering is pretty similar. I know it's a bit of a labor of love, but I think it's worth it. Plus, it's the kind of dessert that's even better the next day—great for making ahead of time for parties and holidays.

Honey Syrup

¾ **cup** sugar

1 **cup** cold water

1 **cup** honey

1 **tablespoon** orange extract

5 whole cloves

Juice of 1 large lemon

Baklava

6 **ounces** shelled pistachios, roasted and chopped (about 1¼ **cups**), plus extra for garnish

6 **ounces** walnuts, roasted and chopped (about 1¼ **cups**)

6 **ounces** hazelnuts, roasted and chopped (about 1¼ **cups**)

¼ **cup** sugar

1 **tablespoon** ground cinnamon

¼ **teaspoon** ground cloves

1 (1-**pound**) package phyllo dough, thawed if frozen

2 sticks (1 **cup**, 16 **tablespoons**) unsalted butter, melted

1. **Make the honey syrup:** Place the sugar and water in a medium saucepan set over medium-high heat and simmer until the sugar dissolves, about 1 minute, stirring occasionally. Stir in the honey, orange extract, and whole cloves, then bring to a boil, turn the heat to medium-low, and simmer about 25 minutes. Remove the saucepan from the heat and let the syrup cool, then stir in the lemon juice (the syrup should be sticky and not too runny).

2. Position a rack in the center of the oven. Preheat the oven to 350°F.

3. **Make the baklava:** In the bowl of a food processor fitted with the multipurpose blade, combine the pistachios, walnuts, and hazelnuts. Pulse a few times to finely chop. Transfer to a large bowl and add the sugar, cinnamon (start with less if you're not sure), and ground cloves. Mix well to combine.

4. Unroll the phyllo pastry and place the sheets on a clean kitchen towel, then cover the stack with a second clean kitchen towel.

5. Brush a 9 × 13 × 2-inch baking pan with some of the melted butter. Take 1 sheet of phyllo and place it in the pan (if the phyllo sheets are larger than your pan, feel free to fold them to fit or use kitchen shears to trim). Brush the top of the phyllo with more melted butter. Repeat this process a few more times, until you have used about one-

Recipe continues

third of the phyllo dough. Now, sprinkle half the nut mixture evenly over the top layer of phyllo. Continue adding sheets of phyllo and brushing each with melted butter until you have used about half of the remaining phyllo sheets. Distribute the remaining nut mixture evenly over the top of that second layer of phyllo. Finish with the remaining batch of phyllo, following the same process, and after adding the last sheet, brushing the top with melted butter.

6. Use a thin sharp or a serrated knife to cut the baklava in a gentle sawing motion on the diagonal in both directions so you have 24 to 36 diamond-shaped pieces.

7. Bake the baklava for 30 to 45 minutes, until the top turns a light golden brown and a skewer inserted in the center comes out clean. (Note: Because ovens vary, be sure to check your baklava halfway through baking.)

8. As soon as you remove the baklava from the oven, pour the cooled syrup all over it (it will make a sizzling sound). Set aside at room temperature for at least 1 hour before serving to make sure the syrup has been absorbed. Cut through the earlier marked pieces and serve with a garnish of chopped pistachios, if you like.

9. Store the baklava in the pan, covered with plastic wrap, at room temperature for the first night or two. To store leftovers for a longer period, transfer the baklava to airtight containers and leave in the fridge for a few days, or freeze for up to 3 months. Thaw the frozen baked baklava in the fridge overnight or at room temperature for a few hours before serving.

A FEW TIPS ON MAKING BAKLAVA

Thaw the phyllo pastry in the fridge overnight and take it out of the fridge 1 hour before using.

Set the phyllo dough on a clean kitchen towel and cover with a second towel to keep the sheets pliable, so they do not break as you're working.

Prepare the syrup ahead and let it cool so that when the baklava comes out of the oven, the syrup is ready to be poured over it. You want to hear that fun sizzling sound when you pour the syrup over the hot baklava; it means the crisp sheets of pastry are lovingly receiving the syrup.

Resist serving the baklava immediately. Give it at least 1 hour to set up, or preferably several hours if you can stand it, so the pastry cools completely and the syrup is fully absorbed.

cashew-stuffed chocolate date bonbons

MAKES 20 BONBONS

Medjool dates are plump and sweet, so they are great on their own, but you can also turn them into something even more dessert-y by stuffing them with a mixture of raw cashews and shredded coconut, and then dipping them in melted chocolate (yes, strawberries aren't the only fruit that like a little chocolate bath). One hour in the freezer, and your delicious bonbons are ready. Do remember to leave them at room temperature for 15 minutes before serving!

½ **cup** raw cashews

½ **cup** finely shredded unsweetened coconut

20 large Medjool dates

1½ **cups** semisweet chocolate chips

1 tablespoon sunflower oil or other neutral-tasting oil

1. In a small bowl, mix the cashews and coconut.

2. Cut a slit in each date and remove the pit. Fill the cavities with a bit of the cashew and coconut mixture. Close the dates and press to completely cover the mixture.

3. In a heat-safe medium glass bowl, combine the chocolate chips and oil. Place in the microwave and heat until the chocolate is fully melted, stopping the microwave to stir every 20 seconds. Carefully remove the bowl from the microwave (the bowl may be hot).

4. Line a sheet pan or freezer-safe tray large enough to hold the dates in a single layer with parchment paper.

5. Drop a few of the stuffed dates into the melted chocolate and gently toss with a fork until the dates are fully coated with chocolate. Transfer them to the sheet pan, arranging them in a single layer and making sure they don't touch one another.

6. Place the pan with the dates in the freezer until the chocolate hardens, about 1 hour. Take them out of the freezer and leave at room temperature for 15 to 30 minutes before serving. (If you have any left over, they will keep in the refrigerator in an airtight container for up to 1 week.)

umm ali
(egyptian bread pudding)

SERVES 8 TO 12

Umm Ali, which translates to "mother of Ali," is Egypt's idea of a bread pudding, and it is somewhat of a national treasure that, they say, dates back to the twelfth century. Ask an Egyptian about the woman for whom the dish is named, and you may get any number of stories: She was the wife of an Ayyubid ruler who saved the day with her sweet dessert, or she was a humble peasant who made the best dessert from scraps of dough and some milk to please the Sultan . . . and so on. Regardless of its origins, this dessert is a popular one, found in many of Egypt's restaurants and cafés. My favorite was from Pizza Pino, a popular pizzeria near the Suez Canal at the corner of El Gomhoria Street in Port Said. Many years ago, I remember them serving individual-sized umm Ali right out of their domed pizza oven—warm, sweet, and indulgent in every way.

At home, I use store-bought puff pastry, a perfect shortcut, plus shredded coconut and any nuts I have on hand. The topping of whipped cream is optional, but if you're going to make umm Ali, why hold back? You can serve it warm or cold in bowls to hold the milk.

1 (1-pound) package puff pastry, thawed if frozen

½ cup roughly chopped hazelnuts

½ cup sliced almonds

½ cup roughly chopped pistachios

¼ cup shredded coconut

¼ cup dark or golden raisins

2 cups whole milk or plant-based alternative

½ cup granulated sugar

1 teaspoon vanilla extract

1 cup heavy (whipping) cream

1 tablespoon dark brown sugar

1. Position a rack in the center of the oven. Preheat the oven to 400°F. Line a 13 × 18 × 1-inch sheet pan with parchment paper.

2. Lay the puff pastry in the pan on top of the parchment. Bake for 10 to 12 minutes, until the pastry puffs up and turns a light golden brown. Set aside briefly to cool. Keep the oven on, but switch to the broil setting.

3. Tear the puff pastry into pieces and lay about three-fourths of them in the bottom of a 9 × 13 × 2-inch baking dish. Sprinkle the hazelnuts, almonds, pistachios, coconut, and raisins on top in an even layer.

4. In a medium saucepan, combine the milk, granulated sugar, and vanilla and bring to a boil over medium-high heat, stirring until the sugar has dissolved, about 3 minutes. Pour the hot milk over the pastry and nuts, then arrange the remaining pastry pieces on top and push down on them with the back of a spoon.

5. In a medium bowl, and using an electric hand mixer set to medium, beat the cream until it thickens and stiff peaks form, 5 to 7 minutes. Spread the whipped cream on top of the pastry and sprinkle the brown sugar over it.

6. Place the baking dish on the center rack of the oven and broil for 3 to 6 minutes, watching carefully for the top to turn a nice golden brown.

7. Remove the baking dish from the oven and let the pudding sit for a few minutes. Serve in bowls (there will be some liquid). (Store leftover pudding covered in fridge for up to 3 days.)

orange-cardamom–olive oil cake

SERVES 8

Even die-hard butter fans agree that high-quality, fruity olive oil makes an exceptional alternative to butter in a cake and adds wonderful richness and nuance. And because, at room temperature, olive oil is liquid, it adds superior moisture over time, even with leftovers. And it doesn't hurt that this cake is laced with flavors of bright orange and fragrant ground cardamom.

1 cup high-quality extra-virgin olive oil (fruity, more neutral-tasting), plus extra for the pan

2 cups all-purpose flour, plus more for the pan

1 teaspoon kosher salt

1 teaspoon baking powder

¼ teaspoon baking soda

1½ cups plus **2 tablespoons** granulated sugar

¾ to 1 teaspoon ground cardamom

3 large eggs

Grated zest of **2** oranges, plus **2 tablespoons** fresh orange juice

1¼ cups whole milk or plant-based alternative

2 tablespoons sifted confectioners' sugar, for garnish

1. Position a rack in the center of the oven and preheat the oven to 350°F.

2. Brush the bottom and sides of a 9-inch round cake pan with a little olive oil. Line the bottom of the pan with a round of parchment paper and dust with a bit of the flour, shaking out the excess.

3. In a medium bowl, whisk together the 2 cups flour, the salt, baking powder, and baking soda.

4. In a large bowl, combine the 1½ cups granulated sugar, the cardamom, and eggs. Using an electric hand mixer set on high, beat the mixture until thick and fluffy, about 5 minutes. (Or, use a stand mixer on high speed.) While the mixer is running, slowly drizzle in the olive oil and beat until incorporated. Reduce the speed to low and add half the orange zest, the orange juice, and milk. Beat until smooth. Slowly add the dry ingredients and beat until just combined.

5. Pour the cake batter into the pan and sprinkle the top with the remaining 2 tablespoons granulated sugar. Bake the cake for 40 to 45 minutes, or until the center is set and a skewer inserted into the middle comes out clean (ovens do vary, so check your cake at 30 minutes and go from there).

6. Allow the cake to cool for 30 minutes in the pan, then run a small knife around the edge, invert the cake onto a large plate, then invert again onto a rack to cool completely.

7. Before serving, sprinkle the cake with the remaining orange zest and dust with the confectioners' sugar.

laura's gluten-free lemon cheesecake with pistachio-walnut crust

SERVES 12

My friend Laura King is a chef, culinary instructor, and the best cake baker I know. Before she moved to the Atlanta area, she ran a popular bakery called Lil' Somethin' Sweet in Athens, Tennessee, which specialized in exquisitely crafted wedding cakes and more. When I started this cookbook project, I reached out and asked if she would contribute a familiar American dessert, giving it a bit of a Mediterranean twist. A few days later, she showed up at my house with this cheesecake, which my family devoured within the hour! For the batter, Greek yogurt shares the spotlight with cream cheese. And in place of the typical graham cracker crust, Laura used a mixture of pistachios and walnuts with almond flour.

Crust

4 tablespoons unsalted butter, melted, plus **2 tablespoons** softened, for the pan

1 cup almond flour

½ cup toasted chopped pistachios

½ cup toasted chopped walnuts

3 tablespoons sugar

Filling

3 cups (3 8-ounce packages) cream cheese, at room temperature

1 cup sugar

2 tablespoons cornstarch

1 tablespoon vanilla extract

1 cup plain whole-milk Greek yogurt

3 large eggs, at room temperature

Topping

1 cup quality lemon curd

Sugared lemon rinds (optional)

1. **Make the crust:** Position an oven rack in the center of the oven and preheat the oven to 350°F. Grease an 8-inch springform pan with the 2 tablespoons butter.

2. In a large bowl, mix the flour, nuts, and sugar with a wooden spoon until well combined. Add the 4 tablespoons melted butter and mix until smooth but somewhat crumbly.

3. Transfer the mixture to the springform pan, and with your clean hand, press into the pan's bottom. Bake for 5 minutes, until the crust is slightly golden brown. Allow the crust to cool. Leave the oven on. Heat several cups of water in a kettle to use in the water bath.

4. **Prepare the cheesecake filling:** In the bowl of an electric mixer fitted with the paddle attachment, beat the cream cheese for 2 minutes on medium-high speed. Scrape down the sides and bottom of the bowl as needed. Add the sugar and beat for another 2 minutes, scraping down the sides of the bowl again. Reduce the speed to medium-low and add the cornstarch, vanilla, and yogurt. Continue to mix, adding the eggs and mixing until just combined and you don't see any lumps, stopping to scrape down the sides and bottom of the bowl as needed. (You need to mix the batter well enough to remove the lumps, but do not overmix or the cake may crack when baked.)

5. Pour the batter into the crust and give the pan a gentle shake to even out the filling. Set the springform pan in a larger roasting pan and add enough of the hot

water to reach halfway up the sides of the springform pan.

6. Carefully place the roasting pan on the oven rack and bake the cheesecake for 60 to 75 minutes, until the middle of the cheesecake slightly jiggles. (Note: if you notice the cheesecake browning too quickly on top, tent it with foil halfway through baking.)

7. Turn the oven off and let the cheesecake sit in the oven in the water bath to gradually cool for 1 hour. Remove the baking pan from the oven and remove the springform pan from the water bath. Let the cake fully cool in the pan on the counter for 45 minutes to 1 hour, then cover with plastic wrap and chill in the fridge for at least 6 hours or overnight.

8. Take the cheesecake out of the fridge and use an offset spatula to gently loosen the crust from the sides of the pan, releasing it with the springform hinge. Set the cake, still on the springform bottom, on a platter or cake plate.

9. **Add the topping:** Use an offset spatula to gently spread the lemon curd in an even layer over the top of the cake. Top with lemon rinds, if desired.

10. To serve, place a pitcher of warm water next to the cake, along with a few paper towels. Using a clean, sharp knife, cut the cake into 12 slices for serving, dipping the knife into the warm water and wiping it clean between slices.

banana-walnut bread
with dates

MAKES 1 LOAF

Here in the American South, banana desserts are a *thing*. Every family seems to have a secret recipe for banana pudding, bananas foster, banana cream pie, banana—fill in the blank. My favorite, though, is banana bread, which shows up more often for breakfast or brunch, but I also like it as a not-too-sweet way to end a meal in place of sweet cake. No surprise, mine is a little different. Enriched (again) with olive oil instead of butter, and naturally sweetened with honey and chunks of Medjool dates, this loaf is, as a reader named Elsa who made this recipe attested, "incredibly moist and deliciously satisfying" and "now MY Saturday morning start to the weekend."

⅓ **cup** extra-virgin olive oil, plus some for the pan

½ **cup** honey (top quality, if possible)

2 large eggs

3 ripe bananas, peeled and mashed

2 **tablespoons** plain whole-milk yogurt

¼ **cup** whole milk or plant-based alternative

1 **teaspoon** baking soda

1 **teaspoon** vanilla extract

¾ **teaspoon** ground cinnamon

½ **teaspoon** ground nutmeg

1⅓ **cups** all-purpose flour

6 Medjool dates, pitted and chopped (about ½ **cup**)

⅓ **cup** chopped walnuts, toasted

1. Set an oven rack in the middle position and preheat the oven to 325°F. Use a little olive oil to lightly coat a 9 × 5-inch nonstick loaf pan.

2. In a large bowl, whisk together the ⅓ cup olive oil and the honey. Whisk in the eggs, followed by the bananas, yogurt, milk, baking soda, vanilla, cinnamon, and nutmeg.

3. Using a rubber spatula, fold in the flour, then add the dates and walnuts. Stir the batter until everything is well combined and no dry patches of flour remain.

4. Pour the batter into the loaf pan and shake the pan very gently so the batter evens out. Bake for 50 to 60 minutes, until a toothpick inserted into a few places comes out with only a couple of moist crumbs attached. If the loaf needs a little more time, continue to bake, checking every 5 minutes.

5. Set the loaf aside to cool for 10 minutes in the pan. Run a knife around the edges of the pan and invert the loaf onto a cooling rack for another 20 to 30 minutes. When ready, slice and serve. (If you have leftovers, wrap the loaf, or individual slices, in foil and place in a zippered plastic bag. Banana bread will keep for up to 4 months in the freezer.)

ghorayebah

MAKES 30 BITE-SIZED COOKIES

Some may compare Ghorayebah (gho-ra-ye-bah) to shortbread. Maybe. But these cookies have a less dense, crumbly, and far softer texture—almost like velvet, if the word *velvet* could ever be used to describe a cookie. Point is, pop one of these little cookies in your mouth, and it will melt on your tongue like a giant snowflake.

1 cup ghee (clarified butter; see Note)

½ cup sifted confectioners' sugar, plus more for dusting

Scant **⅛ teaspoon** baking powder

2 cups all-purpose flour, sifted again

Handful of slivered unsalted almonds (optional)

NOTE

Ghoryebah owes its extraordinarily smooth texture both to the confectioners' sugar and to the ghee. If you're wondering whether regular unsalted butter will work in place of ghee, the answer is no. Don't do it! If you're not familiar with it, ghee is a wonderfully aromatic, highly clarified butter with a subtle nutty flavor that forms by slowly simmering regular butter until the water evaporates and the liquid fats separate from the milk solids. The solids are then removed, leaving behind only pure buttery goodness. If you use butter instead, you will end up with crispy butter cookies because of the greater water content—not bad, perhaps, but frankly, completely different cookies from ghorayebah.

1. Place the ghee in a large bowl. Using a hand-held electric mixer set on the lowest speed, mix until the ghee is whipped, 2 to 3 minutes.

2. Add the ½ cup confectioners' sugar and continue to mix, first on low speed until combined and then on medium until the ghee and sugar mixture is smooth and fluffy.

3. Add the baking powder, then add 1 cup flour. Using your hands, mix and knead to work the flour in (if using a stand mixer, remove the bowl from the stand), then add the remaining cup flour. Knead again until the flour is well incorporated, forming a very soft dough.

4. Cover the dough with plastic wrap and refrigerate for 20 to 30 minutes; this helps the dough firm up.

5. Position a rack in the center of the oven and preheat the oven to 350°F. Line a baking sheet with parchment paper.

6. Remove the dough from fridge and unwrap. Take small portions of the chilled dough (about a heaping ½ tablespoon) and roll into walnut-sized balls. Ever so lightly, press the tops of the balls (do not flatten). Arrange the cookies on the baking sheet, pressed side up, making sure to space them 2 to 3 inches apart. Lightly press a slivered almond (if using), into each one or just some of the cookies. Bake the cookies for 12 to 15 minutes, until they firm up and gain a bit of color on the bottom but remain pretty light on top.

7. Remove the cookies from the oven. Do NOT touch the cookies until they are fully cooled (they will fall apart, otherwise). Once cooled, sprinkle them with the confectioners' sugar. (Store the cookies in a tightly covered tin or container, where they will keep for a couple of weeks.)

simple anise biscotti

MAKES 24 BISCOTTI

Italian biscotti are a centuries-old classic that made its way to different parts of the Mediterranean. Anise biscotti are the ones I grew up with, and are also Saba's favorite thing to have with his morning coffee, so I make them often. There's no claim that these are authentic Italian biscotti because, as with all popular things, there are tons of variations and family recipes.

2 cups all-purpose flour

1½ teaspoons baking powder

⅛ teaspoon kosher salt

3 teaspoons anise seeds

3 large eggs

¼ teaspoon distilled white vinegar (optional)

¾ cup sugar

⅓ cup grapeseed oil or mild-tasting extra-virgin olive oil

1 teaspoon vanilla extract

1. Position a rack in the center of the oven. Preheat to 350°F. Line a large baking sheet with parchment paper.

2. In a medium bowl, sift together the flour, baking powder, and salt. Stir in the anise seeds.

3. In the bowl of a stand mixer fitted with the whisk, combine the eggs and vinegar, beating at medium speed until frothy, about 3 minutes. Gradually add the sugar and beat for another minute, then add the oil and vanilla. Whisk for a minute longer. Slowly add the dry ingredients and whisk until just combined. (If you don't have a stand mixer, use a blender for this step.)

4. Turn the biscotti dough out onto the baking sheet and, using your hands, form the dough into a somewhat oval-shaped log about 1 inch thick and 8 inches long. Bake for 25 to 30 minutes, until lightly browned, rotating the baking sheet halfway through for even browning. Remove from the oven; keep the oven turned on.

5. Allow the log to cool for about 20 minutes. (If you cool the log too long, it will be hard to cut the slices; if you cut while it is still hot, you'll have a crumbly mess on your hands.) Using a serrated knife (important for clean cutting), cut the log into ½-inch-thick slices, using a gentle sawing motion to reduce crumbling.

6. With the biscotti slices placed on their side on the baking sheet, return them to the oven to bake for another 15 minutes, until golden, turning them over halfway through.

7. Transfer the biscotti to a cooling rack and allow to cool completely. (Be sure the biscotti are completely cooled before storing in a container. They should keep for a good week, or you can stick them in the freezer to pull out later.)

sauces,
pickles, and
extras to jazz
up the meal

DON'T SKIP THE EXTRAS!

Don't glaze over this section on "extras" so quickly. Even though it appears at the end of the book, it's one of the most important sections. Sauces and condiments are powerful components of Mediterranean cooking that add depth and complexity, turning the humblest of dishes into a "flavor party," as I like to say. You'll see these condiments paired and used with many of the recipes in this book, but I'll bet that once you try them, you'll find new ways to use them to jazz up your own cooking.

basil vinaigrette

MAKES ¾ TO 1 CUP

I love this versatile vinaigrette tossed in all sorts of salads, particularly grain salads, which can easily absorb big flavors. It's also a great way to dress up grilled meats or even fish. One of the frustrating things we run into when making a pesto or dressing like this, though, is how fast the fresh basil oxidizes and blackens. Quickly blanching the basil in boiling water for 5 to 10 seconds, then transferring it to a ice-cold water bath to stop cooking, helps preserve its beautiful bright green color by killing off the decomposing enzymes that are responsible for turning those leaves brown. It's an optional step, but one that I think is worth the time.

2 cups (packed) fresh basil leaves (about **1⅛ ounces**)

1 medium shallot, roughly chopped

1 large garlic clove

Juice of **1** lime (about **2 tablespoons**)

2 tablespoons white wine vinegar

½ **cup** extra-virgin olive oil

½ **teaspoon** red pepper flakes

Kosher salt

1. Fill a medium bowl with ice cubes and water and set it next to the stove.

2. Fill a small saucepan about three-fourths full of water. Bring the water to a boil over medium-high heat. Add the basil and cook for 10 seconds. Using a slotted spoon, immediately transfer the basil to the bowl of ice water and let cool for 5 minutes. Using the slotted spoon, remove the basil from the ice water, wrap the wilted basil in a paper towel, and squeeze to wring out as much water as possible.

3. Place the blanched basil, the shallot, garlic, lime juice, vinegar, olive oil, and red pepper flakes in the bowl of a small food processor fitted with the multipurpose blade. Blend until well combined and smooth. Season to taste with salt and refrigerate in a tightly closed mason jar for up to 4 days.

dukkah

MAKES 1 HEAPING CUP

Egypt's famous blend of nuts, seeds, and warm spices is the heady seasoning you never knew you needed! Make this quick, nutty mixture and store it in your pantry (or freezer, even) to have on hand as a snack with bread and olive oil, as a crust for fish or meats, or as a topping to add texture and flavor to anything from soups and salads, or roasted vegetables. I like to use a combination of three nuts here—hazelnuts, almonds, and pistachios—but you can use just one type if you like.

½ **cup** raw hazelnuts

3 tablespoons raw almonds

¼ **cup** white sesame seeds

3 tablespoons shelled pistachios

1 tablespoon fennel seeds

1 teaspoon ground coriander

1 teaspoon ground cumin

½ **teaspoon** cayenne pepper

Kosher salt

1. Put the hazelnuts and almonds in an ungreased cast-iron skillet. Toast briefly over medium heat, tossing regularly, until the nuts turn a nice golden brown. Transfer to a dish.

2. Place the sesame seeds in the same skillet. Toast over medium heat, stirring regularly, until the sesame seeds turn golden brown (this will happen fairly quickly so watch carefully).

3. Add the toasted nuts and sesame seeds to the bowl of a small food processor fitted with the multipurpose blade. Add the pistachios, fennel seeds, coriander, cumin, cayenne, and salt to taste. Pulse for about 10 seconds, or until the nuts are broken into a coarse mixture. (Do not over-process the dukkah; the mixture should not be too fine.) Taste and adjust the seasoning.

4. Serve immediately or transfer to an airtight jar and store in a tight-lidded mason jar in your pantry for up to 2 weeks or freeze for up to 3 months.

easy preserved lemons

MAKES 8 PRESERVED LEMONS

Although most people associate them with North African and Moroccan cuisine, salt-preserved lemons have long been a part of Mediterranean and Middle Eastern cooking. They add brightness and flavor to stews and soups or a simple sandwich, as well as to roasted vegetables, any meat from the grill, Chicken Shawarma Bowls (page 220)—the possibilities are endless! While you can find jars of preserved lemons in some specialty grocery stores (usually near the pickles and marinated artichoke hearts), they're super-easy and far cheaper to make at home. Take 20 minutes to pack them with the salt and spices into jars, and after a few weeks in the fridge (the hardest part of this recipe is the waiting!) the lemons will gently deflate and soften, their strong tartness mellowing. Since you'll be eating the entire fruit, I recommend buying organic lemons, which have not been sprayed or treated with chemicals. Select ones that are heavy for their size, with thin, fine-textured peels and deep yellow color. Meyer lemons are also a great option, since their thin skins are not very bitter.

8 organic large lemons, washed and dried

½ cup kosher salt

2 tablespoons sugar

2 tablespoons black peppercorns

4 dried bay leaves

2 cups fresh lemon juice (from **7 or 8** large lemons)

1. Cut about ¼ inch off the tops and bottoms of the lemons. Cut each lemon into quarters partway through so they remain attached at the bottom.

2. Transfer the lemons to a large bowl and toss well with the salt and sugar. Open up the lemons and stuff them with the salt and sugar mixture. Cover the bowl with plastic wrap and refrigerate overnight, and up to 24 hours. During this time, the lemons will release some juice.

3. The next day, transfer the lemons and their juices to a large clean mason jar. Press them down firmly to fit them snugly in the jar. Add the peppercorns and bay leaves. Fill the jar to the top with the fresh lemon juice so that the lemons are submerged in the juice.

4. Cover the jar tightly with the lid and store in the fridge for at least 4 weeks before using. Once the lemons have softened, they are ready to enjoy, sliced or chopped. (The lemons will keep in the fridge in the tightly closed jar, and fully submerged in the lemon juice, for up to 6 months.)

homemade harissa paste

MAKES 1 ½ CUPS

I've heard people describe harissa as the ketchup of North Africa and the Middle East. But comparing these two popular crimson condiments does not do harissa justice, as harissa is much more complex in flavor. This Tunisian sauce or paste is typically made with dried red chiles, garlic, citrus, olive oil, and several toasty spices like caraway seeds and ground cumin. I much prefer my homemade version to anything sold in jars or tins at the grocery store. It's relatively mild with just enough kick, sweetness, smokiness, and tang. Keep it in the fridge to dress up meats, chicken, fish, or even veggies. Or stir a bit of harissa into your soups and stews, or add a little to give a punch to your shakshuka or hummus!

7 dried New Mexico or guajillo chiles

1 (6-ounce) jar roasted red peppers (¾ **cup**), drained

2 **tablespoons** tomato paste

4 large garlic cloves

1 **teaspoon** caraway seeds, toasted and ground

2 **teaspoons** ground coriander

2 **teaspoons** ground cumin

1 **teaspoon** smoked paprika

½ **teaspoon** cayenne pepper (optional)

Kosher salt

Juice of **1** large lemon (about ¼ **cup**)

2 **tablespoons** extra-virgin olive oil, plus more for storing the harissa

1. Place the chiles in a heat-safe bowl and cover with hot water. Soak until the chiles are tender and rehydrated, about 30 minutes. Drain the chiles and remove the stems and seeds.

2. Transfer the chiles to the bowl of a large food processor fitted with the multipurpose blade. Add the roasted red peppers, tomato paste, garlic, ground caraway seeds, coriander, cumin, smoked paprika, cayenne (if using), and a large pinch of salt (about ½ teaspoon). Add the lemon juice.

3. With the food processor running, drizzle in the olive oil through the top opening. Stop the processor to scrape down the sides and continue processing until the harissa has a chunky, paste-like texture. Taste and adjust the seasonings to your liking (remember that harissa paste will deepen in flavor as it sits in the fridge over the next day or two).

4. Transfer the harissa paste to a clean mason jar. Cover with a very thin layer of olive oil, then cover the jar tightly with the lid and refrigerate. The harissa will keep up to 3 weeks if properly stored; that is, after every time you use a bit of it—even if you just take away a little—be sure to add enough extra-virgin olive oil to cover the top before returning the jar to the fridge. You can also freeze harissa paste in small portions (silicone ice cube trays work well for this) for individual use for up to 1 month or so.

spicy walnut-cilantro chili sauce

MAKES 1 CUP

This herby, garlicky, and somewhat spicy sauce has a bit of texture to it, thanks to a handful of walnuts. If you like it extra spicy, use habanero chiles instead of the serrano. I like this sauce with my roasted potatoes or drizzled over fish.

3 or 4 fresh serrano chiles (or similarly spicy chiles), finely chopped (seeds removed for less heat)

3 large garlic cloves, minced

1 cup roughly chopped fresh cilantro

Juice of **1** large lemon (about ¼ **cup**)

2 tablespoons white wine vinegar

¼ **cup** finely chopped walnuts

Kosher salt

¾ **cup** extra-virgin olive oil

1. In a small bowl, combine the chiles, garlic, cilantro, lemon juice, vinegar, and walnuts. Add a large pinch of salt (about ½ teaspoon) and the olive oil and mix well. Taste and adjust the seasoning.

2. Store any unused sauce tightly closed in a mason jar in the fridge for up to 3 days. The chiles will mellow a bit as they rest.

busy mama's spaghetti sauce

MAKES 2 TO 3 CUPS

I am all for from-scratch tomato sauce made from perfectly ripened tomatoes that have been simmered for hours until thick and properly concentrated. But thank goodness for the perfect shortcut that is canned crushed tomatoes, a lifesaver on busy weeknights and whenever tomatoes are not in season. I always use it in Summer Squash Roll-ups with Herbed Ricotta and Walnut Stuffing (page 140). I might add a couple tablespoons of tomato paste for a little extra umami, and if I'm making this sauce for pasta night, I thicken it quickly and add a little bit of sweetness with two grated carrots. The sauce is easy and unfussy enough to make any night of the week, and once you try this semi-homemade version, I bet you'll ditch that store-bought pasta sauce for good!

¼ **cup** extra-virgin olive oil

1 medium yellow onion, grated

3 garlic cloves, minced

2 medium carrots, peeled and finely grated (use a food processor or a grater)

1 (**28-ounce**) can crushed tomatoes

½ **cup** water, or more as needed

Kosher salt and ground black pepper

1 **tablespoon** dried oregano

1 **teaspoon** sweet paprika

Pinch of red pepper flakes (optional)

About ½ **cup** torn fresh basil leaves, or more as desired

About ½ **cup** roughly chopped fresh parsley

1. In a large stainless-steel skillet, heat the olive oil over medium heat until just shimmering. Add the onion, garlic, and carrots. Cook, stirring regularly, until softened, 5 to 7 minutes.

2. Add the crushed tomatoes and water. Add a large pinch of both salt and pepper (about ½ teaspoon each). Add the oregano, paprika, and red pepper flakes (if using), and stir. Finally, stir in the basil and parsley.

3. Bring the sauce to a boil, then turn the heat down to low. Cover the skillet and simmer the sauce until slightly thickened, 15 to 20 minutes. Check partway through, and if you feel the sauce is getting too thick, add a bit more water (ideally, use reserved pasta cooking water, if that's what you're making with this sauce). When the sauce is ready, add more fresh basil, if you like.

4. Let the sauce cool, then refrigerate in an airtight container for up to 4 days. If you want to freeze the sauce, let it cool completely and then transfer to a freezer-safe container or freezer bag, allowing some room for the sauce to expand as it freezes. Cover tightly or seal and add the date; the sauce can be frozen for up to 3 months. When ready to use, thaw it in the fridge overnight.

Meat Sauce

If you want to add meat to the sauce, heat a little bit of extra-virgin olive oil in a Dutch oven or heavy pot, then brown 1 pound of your choice of ground beef, turkey, sausage, or other ground meat over medium heat. Cook, stirring regularly, until the meat is fully browned. Season with a large pinch of salt (about ½ teaspoon) or to your taste. Drain, and transfer the meat to a plate. In the same pot, add a little more olive oil, then add the onion, garlic, and carrots, and cook for about 5 minutes, or until softened. Return the cooked ground meat to the pot and stir to combine. Proceed with the recipe as directed.

lime-tahini sauce

MAKES 1 ½ CUPS

I use this tangy tahini sauce in more ways than I can count: as part of a mezze spread; to jazz up falafel-stuffed pita or chicken shawarma; or to drizzle over grilled fish, meaty kebabs, or roasted vegetables. I often add a large handful of chopped fresh parsley to make a popular Egyptian version of this sauce called *tahini bil bakdounis*, or tahini with parsley.

Generally, tahini sauce should have a creamy, runny salad dressing–like consistency. But if you prefer to use tahini more as a dip, simply use less water. And if you're serving a large number of people, double the recipe—I promise it will go fast!

1 or 2 large garlic cloves, minced

¾ cup tahini

Juice of **3** large limes (about **6 tablespoons**)

Kosher salt

1 cup roughly chopped fresh parsley leaves (optional)

1. In the bowl of a food processor fitted with the multipurpose blade, place the garlic, tahini paste, lime juice, and about ¼ teaspoon salt. Blend until the sauce thickens as it emulsifies.

2. Add 1 to 2 teaspoons of water at a time as needed, blending after each addition, until the mixture is creamy yet runny (like a creamy salad dressing). Taste and adjust the seasoning to your liking.

3. Transfer the sauce to a serving bowl and stir in the parsley (if using). Cover and refrigerate in an airtight container for up to 3 days.

crunchy cucumber refrigerator pickles

MAKES 1 LARGE JAR (ABOUT ½ GALLON)

I never had the patience to make my own pickles until I learned how to bypass the canning process and have a jarful of tangy cukes ready to enjoy the very next day! Super-crunchy, briny, and just-enough spicy, these refrigerator pickles are now a regular in my house—for family meals or as part of any mezze spread.

1¼ **pounds** Persian or English (hothouse) cucumbers, sliced into ½-inch-thick rounds

3 **cups** distilled white vinegar or white wine vinegar

2¼ **cups** cold water

2½ **tablespoons** kosher salt

3 **tablespoons** coriander seeds

3 **tablespoons** mustard seeds

3 **tablespoons** black peppercorns

2 dried bay leaves

4 scallions, trimmed, both white and green parts chopped

3 fresh jalapeño peppers, sliced into rounds (seeds removed for less heat)

6 large garlic cloves, minced

Few sprigs of fresh dill, to your liking

1. Place the cucumber slices and some ice cubes in a colander set in the sink and let chill for 30 minutes or so. Drain completely and pat dry. (The ice cubes create extra-crunchy pickles!)

2. In a large saucepan, combine the vinegar, water, salt, coriander seeds, mustard seeds, peppercorns, and bay leaves. Bring to a boil over high heat, then lower the heat and simmer for 10 minutes. Remove from the heat and let cool.

3. Pack the cucumber slices, then the scallions, jalapeños, garlic, and a few sprigs of dill tightly in a large jar.

4. Ladle the brine into the jar to cover the cucumbers (use the back of a spoon to push the cucumbers down to submerge). Give the jar a couple of taps on the counter to release any air bubbles.

5. Cover the jar tightly with its lid and refrigerate. For best results, allow the pickles a full night in the fridge before using, but you can enjoy them earlier, if you like. (The pickles can be refrigerated up to 2 months.)

CUSTOMIZE YOUR PICKLES!

The great thing about this versatile recipe is that you can easily pickle other vegetables as well. For example, green beans, asparagus, sliced carrots, and cauliflower florets (quickly blanched first) all work well with this brine.

I like my pickles extra tangy, so I use a higher ratio of vinegar to water in the brine. But if you prefer, use the standard 1:1 ratio of vinegar to water instead. If you like your pickles on the sweet side, add ¼ cup granulated sugar to the brine (or more or less, to your liking). You can also adjust the spices as you desire. For instance, some Middle Eastern pickle recipes use fresh ginger or red pepper flakes, or add ground turmeric for a gold-tinted color.

herbed labneh

MAKES 1 ½ CUPS

When I'm feeling a bit indulgent, I make this glorious herbed labneh as a dip or to dollop on roasted root vegetables (see page 155). But really, you can make it just to slather it on some warmed toast. Heaven!

1 cup labneh, store-bought or homemade (see page 101)

1 or 2 large garlic cloves, minced

¼ cup roughly chopped fresh flat-leaf parsley

1 tablespoon roughly chopped fresh oregano leaves

1 teaspoon roughly chopped fresh tarragon

1 teaspoon Aleppo pepper flakes

Kosher salt and ground black pepper

Juice of **1** large lemon (about **¼ cup**)

2 tablespoons extra-virgin olive oil

1. In a small bowl, combine the labneh, garlic, parsley, oregano, tarragon, Aleppo pepper, and about ½ teaspoon each salt and black pepper. Add the lemon juice and olive oil, and mix to combine.

2. Taste and adjust the seasoning, or add more fresh herbs to your liking. Cover and refrigerate in an airtight container for 3 to 4 days.

sumac and vinegar-marinated onions

MAKES ABOUT 1 CUP

Dunk the slices of a large red onion in a bath of vinegar, sumac, salt, and fresh herbs for 30 minutes. The result? Macerated onion slices that are mellow, slightly tangy, and perfectly crisp. And the possibilities are endless for this bright, jewel-toned condiment: tuck the slices into your sandwiches, add them to a salad, or serve them alongside grilled meat or chicken as in Sumac-Rubbed Drumsticks with Marinated Onions (page 219)—or anything else you can think of! If you have any marinated onions left, store them in the fridge, covered with a bit more vinegar, in a tightly closed jar (though the slices will lose some of their bite and crunch as they sit in the fridge).

1 large red onion, halved and thinly sliced

½ **cup** red wine vinegar

3 **tablespoons** sumac

1 **tablespoon** kosher salt

2 **tablespoons** finely chopped fresh parsley

2 **tablespoons** finely chopped fresh mint

1. In a medium bowl, combine the onion slices with the vinegar, sumac, salt, parsley, and mint.

2. Using your hands, toss the onion and massage the slices well with the vinegar and sumac mixture.

3. Cover and refrigerate for 30 minutes to 1 hour, to marinate and soften the slices. Use or store in the fridge in a tightly covered jar for up to 1 week.

tzatziki

MAKES 2 CUPS

There are a bazillion recipes out there for this classic Greek creamy yogurt and cucumber dip, but this one, adapted from one served in a restaurant called Rafeletti, on the Greek island of Paros, is about as authentic as they come. It's heavy on the garlic—just the way I like it (you may want to start with a smaller amount and keep adding to taste). I credit my friend Cheryl Sternman Rule for scoring the original recipe, which is featured in her gorgeous book *Yogurt Culture*. To change things a bit, feel free to stir in a tablespoon or so of chopped fresh mint or dill. Besides serving as a dip, tzatziki makes a perfect topping for baked potatoes, served as a condiment or sauce for pan-seared trout, lamb chops, or souvlaki.

1 English (hothouse) cucumber, partially peeled (in stripes)

Kosher salt

4 or 5 large garlic cloves, finely grated or minced, or less if desired

1 tablespoon extra-virgin olive oil, plus more for serving

1 teaspoon distilled white vinegar

2 cups plain Greek yogurt

¼ teaspoon ground white pepper

1 to 2 tablespoons finely chopped fresh dill (optional)

Warm pita bread and sliced vegetables, for serving

1. Using a box grater, grate the cucumber. Toss the grated cucumber with ½ teaspoon salt. Transfer to a fine-mesh strainer set over a deep bowl to drain for 5 to 10 minutes. Spoon the grated cucumber into a square of cheesecloth or into a double-thickness napkin and squeeze dry. Set aside.

2. In a large bowl, combine the garlic, olive oil, and vinegar. Add another ½ teaspoon salt and mix to blend well.

3. Add the grated cucumber to the bowl, then add the yogurt and white pepper. Stir thoroughly, then cover tightly and refrigerate for a couple of hours.

4. When ready to serve, stir the tzatziki and transfer it to a serving bowl. Stir in the dill (if using) and drizzle with a bit more olive oil. Serve with warm pita bread and your favorite vegetables, if you like. Store any leftovers in a tightly covered container in the fridge for up to 4 days.

ACKNOWLEDGMENTS

To my late Baba, I have known no heart more generous than yours. Your words continue to echo in my ears compelling me to do my best to "put a smile on someone's face." There is no greater honor than to be called my father's daughter.

My husband, Saba, my steady rock, my love. As with everything I have done since we met more than twenty-one years ago, this project would not have been possible without you, habibi.

Dara and Hannah, the two halves of my heart. I never thought that a recipe website I started for your sake—so you will know the sunshine and flavors of my beloved Mediterranean—would lead us here. My biggest critics and cheerleaders, thank you for inspiring me to be the mama I am.

My Mama, a teacher with the kindest of souls and the greatest cook I know. Thank you for your love and for your nafas for cooking and always sharing with joy. I hope to pass just a bit of your hospitality on. I love you deeply.

And my mother-in-law, Mama Dina, who has influenced the second half of my life in many delicious ways. Who knew a plate of tabbouleh from your Michigan restaurant's kitchen would change the course of my life?!

My brother, Maged, my favorite cup-half-full guy whose entrepreneurial spirit is simply contagious. Thank you for your unwavering love and support through the years, habibi.

Liz Hazlem and Lauren Allen, you believed in this cookbook before anyone else. Thank you for planting the seed and for gently pushing me to pursue it.

Janis Donnaud, my agent and a force of nature in the best way. You held my hand through a lot! For everything you have done to bring my debut book to light, I am beyond grateful.

Susan Puckett, my collaborator, for asking the questions and encouraging me to share my voice in a way I had not before.

My editor, Raquel Pelzel; it took but three minutes of a Zoom call for me to know you were the person to guide this book. That a friendship began in the process is a huge bonus for me. I am grateful to work with everyone at Clarkson Potter, including Francis Lam, Bianca Cruz, and publisher Aaron Wehner; creative director Marysarah Quinn and designer Robert Diaz; the production team, Mark McCauslin and Jessica Heim; and publicity and marketing's Erica Gelbard, Kate Tyler, Allison Renzulli, and Windy Dorresteyn. How did I get so lucky?!

Caitlin Bensel, Christine Keely, and M. M. McLean, not only did you produce beautiful, drool-worthy photos, but you've captured the very soul of this book—bright and joyful throughout.

My friends who are family: Lisa McCullar, who stood long hours with me in the kitchen, and Kate Kardel, Molly and Charlie Darwin, Matt and Marsha Janofsky, Rosanne Patton, and Alex Curtis, who tirelessly tested each recipe for months on end. You are my heroes.

Last but never least, the dear readers and followers of *The Mediterranean Dish* (the site and the book). Here is to each person who asked me, "when will you publish a cookbook?" I am so humbled by your love and encouragement throughout the years. It is first because of you that I penned these pages. And I know I can count on you to bring this book to life through cooking and sharing the recipes with your loved ones. To your joy and your health!

INDEX

Library of Congress Cataloging-in-Publication Data
Names: Karadsheh, Suzy, author. | Bensel, Caitlin,
    photographer.
Title: The Mediterranean dish: 120 bold and healthy
    recipes you'll make on repeat
Description: New York City: Clarkson Potter [2022]
Identifiers: LCCN 2021051906 | ISBN 9780593234273
    (hardcover) | ISBN 9780593234280 (ebook)
Subjects: LCSH: Cooking, Mediterranean. |
    LCGFT: Cookbooks.
Classification: LCC TX725.M35 K37 2022 |
    DDC 641.59/1822—dc23/eng/20211028
LC record available at lccn.loc.gov/2021051906

ISBN 978-0-593-23427-3
Ebook ISBN 978-0-593-23428-0

Printed in China

Photographer: Caitlin Bensel
Food stylist: M. M. McLean
Prop stylist: Christine Keely

Editor: Raquel Pelzel
Editorial assistant: Bianca Cruz
Designer: Robert Diaz
Production editor: Mark McCauslin
Production manager: Jessica Heim
Compositor: Merri Ann Morrell
Copy editor: Carole Berglie
Indexer: Elizabeth T. Parson
Marketer: Allison Renzulli
Publicists: Erica Gelbard, Windy Dorresteyn

10 9

First Edition